D1173868

THE MOST ILLUSTRIOUS ORDER
OF ST PATRICK
1783-1983

Saint Patrick's Hall, Dublin Castle.

The Most Illustrious Order
of
ST. PATRICK

1783~1983

Peter Galloway

PHILLIMORE

1983
Published by
PHILLIMORE & CO. LTD.
Shopwyke Hall, Chichester, Sussex

© Peter Galloway, 1983

ISBN 0 85033 508 6

Printed and bound in Great Britain by
THE CAMELOT PRESS LTD
Southampton, England

CONTENTS

LIST OF COLOUR PLATES

(between pages 18 and 19)

LIST OF BLACK AND WHITE PLATES

(between pages 50 and 51)

LIST OF TEXT FIGURES

FOREWORD

by *James Risk*, C.V.O., F.S.A.

Useful enterprises often can be traced to what may seem to have been very small beginnings. The origins of this graceful history of the Order of St Patrick can be traced to a schoolboy's early enthusiasm. It is fitting that the publication also marks a considerable personal achievement in another sphere, for in 1983 the author was ordained by the Bishop of London in St Paul's.

Peter Galloway has followed the not always clear trail left by The Most Illustrious Order from its foundation in the spring of 1783 down to our own times. There were enough obstacles to offer a challenge the young man could not resist. It was just over a decade ago that his search first led him to The Central Chancery of the Orders of Knighthood, then presided over by Major General Peter Gillett, C.B., O.B.E. (now Sir Peter, K.C.V.O.). Sir Peter's initial courtesy and subsequent help and encouragement had a great deal to do with the successful outcome of the author's efforts.

The histories of many of Britain's more recent Orders of Chivalry remain embalmed within the stilted phraseology of State documents. It can be argued that the need to create another means of rewarding services to the Crown in a specifically limited situation, as in the case of the Star of India for example, leaves little additional to be said. The Order of St Patrick, on the other hand, has much more to offer. Not the least interesting aspect of this book is Peter Galloway's ability to show how the Order reflected Irish events that began in 1782 and reached a certain climax in 1922. His final observations covering the last 60 years present much new material of great interest. The balanced and gently expressed conclusions can hardly be faulted.

The author writes with sympathy and understanding, not only about Ireland's historic Order and its attractive insignia, but about many facets of Ireland's story during the last two centuries. I take great pleasure in recommending this book to all those who are drawn to that story.

New York
1983

JAMES RISK

ACKNOWLEDGEMENTS

I have tried to be exhaustive in acknowledging the help I have received during the past 12 years but inevitably names will be overlooked and I can only ask pardon of those who feel themselves to have been excluded.

I must begin by expressing my gratitude to the following relatives and descendants of the Grand Masters, Knights and Officers of the Most Illustrious Order of Saint Patrick who have helped me in various ways: The Duke of Abercorn; The Marquess of Aberdeen and Temair; The Lord Annaly; The Earl of Bessborough; The Earl of Cavan; The late Earl of Donoughmore; The Marquess of Dufferin and Ava; The Earl of Eglinton and Winton; Ursula, Countess of Eglinton and Winton; The Marquess and Marchioness of Ely; The Earl of Enniskillen M.B.E.; The Lord Farnham; Brigadier Denis Fitzgerald, D.S.O., O.B.E.; The Viscount Gough; Lady Hyacinth Gough; The Earl of Granard, A.F.C.; The Honourable Mrs. Hastings; The Earl of Iveagh; Mr. Richard Needham, M.P. (The Earl of Kilmorey); Lady Patricia Kingsbury; The Earl Kitchener of Khartoum, T.D.; Sir Oliver Lambart, Bt.; Sir Hercules Langrishe, Bt.; The Duke of Leinster; The Earl of Limerick; The Earl of Listowel, P.C., G.C.M.G.; The Marquess of Londonderry; The Earl of Longford, K.G.; Lady Elizabeth Longman; The Lord Lurgan; The Viscount Massereene and Ferrard; The Earl of Meath; The Viscount Midleton; The Lord Monteagle of Brandon; The Lord O'Neill of the Maine, P.C.(N.I.); The Lord Oranmore and Browne; The Marquess of Ormonde, M.B.E.; The Earl of Portarlington; The Earl of Roden; The Baroness de Ros; The Earl of Rosse; The Earl of Shaftesbury; The Earl of Shrewsbury and Waterford; Lady Joanna Stourton; The Marquess of Waterford; and The Countess of Wicklow.

I am especially indebted to Mrs. Charles Byrte for kindly agreeing to talk about the life and work of her late husband Mr. Thomas Ulick Sadleir, Deputy Ulster King of Arms, and also to their son Mr. Randal Sadleir.

I am grateful to Lord Rosse for kindly allowing me to reproduce material from his history of Birr Castle relating to his two astronomer predecessors, the 3rd and 4th Earls. My warm thanks are also due to Mrs. P. B. Phair who generously allowed me to use her article on the Royal Installation of 1821 which she had intended for publication. Acknowledgement is also made to Colin Smythe Ltd. for permission to quote from Dr. Edward Maclysaght's book *Changing Times— Ireland since 1898.*

I would also record my thanks to the following: Mr. Timothy Wilson of the Department of Medieval and Later Antiquities of the British Museum; Mr. John Trew of the Belfast News Letter; Mr. Michael Kelly, M.V.O., of the Central Chancery of the Orders of Knighthood; Mr. John Brooke-Little, M.V.O., F.S.A., Norroy and Ulster King of Arms, and Mr. Richard Yorke, Archivist, both of the College of Arms; Mr. Donal Begley, Chief Herald of Ireland; Mr. D. G. Neville of De Tillens; Major R. Bullock-Webster of the Irish Guards R.H.Q. and Records Office; Miss Diana Condell of the Department of Exhibits and Firearms of the Imperial War Museum; Dr. Michael Wynn of the National Gallery of Ireland; Mr. Alf MacLochlainn of the National Library of Ireland; Miss Mairead Reynolds of the National Museum of Ireland; the Very Revd. Dr. Victor Griffin, Dean of Saint Patrick's Cathedral, Dublin, and Mr. Victor Jackson, the Cathedral Archivist; Mrs. Muriel McCarthy of Marsh's Library; Mr. Stephen Wood, Keeper of the Scottish United Services Museum, formerly of the National Army Museum; Mr. Peter Noble of Christopher and Co. Ltd.; Mr. A. Harrison of the Public Record Office of Northern Ireland; Sir Robin Mackworth-Young, K.C.V.O., F.S.A., Assistant Keeper of the Royal Archives; Miss Anne Neary of the Irish State Paper Office; Mr. Michael Naxton of Sotheby's; Mr. Robert Heslip of the Ulster Museum; and to the staff of the Public Record Office.

The items in Plates 4, 6, 7, 10, 11, 12, 14, 15, 20, 21, 34, 35 and 37 are reproduced by gracious permission of Her Majesty the Queen. I am also obliged to Her Majesty for allowing me to quote relevant passages from documents in the Royal Archives at Windsor. The other illustrations have been provided by the following people and institutions: The Controller of Her Majesty's Stationery Office, Plate 18; The Trustees of the British Museum, Plate 19; Christie's, Plate 37; The Imperial War Museum, Plate 2; The National Gallery of Ireland, Plate 24; The Regimental Lieutenant-Colonel of the Irish Guards, Plate 26; Jarrold and Sons Ltd, Plate 42; Sotheby's, Plates 3, 9, 13, 40 and 41; The National Army Museum, Plates 5, 23, 27, 28, 29 and 32; Spink and Son Ltd., Plates 2, 3, 4 and 5 (col.); The portrait of Lord Fitzalan in Plate 39 is by Oswald Birley and is reproduced by kind permission of His Grace the Duke of Norfolk. The Irish Board of Works kindly provided the photograph of St Patrick's Hall on the dust jacket. All the other items illustrated are from private collections and to their owners I extend my sincere thanks. Many of the items were photographed by Mr. Godfrey New and latterly by my friend The Revd. John Young, to both of whom I am grateful.

A special note of thanks must be reserved for Major-General Sir Peter Gillett, K.C.V.O., C.B., O.B.E., Secretary of the Central Chancery of the Orders of Knighthood from 1968 to 1979. By his patience and courtesy he did much to stimulate and encourage my interest in the Order and its history. My thanks are also due to Major J. M. A. Tamplin, T.D., of the Orders and Medals Research Society who gave freely and cheerfully of his time to encourage my flagging efforts. I would also record my warm thanks to Miss Dorothy Hahn of Sayreville, New Jersey, who generously contributed to the publication of this book in memory of her late brother-in-law, Joseph Bernard Doyle; and also to Dr. Christopher Rawll for all his help and advice.

The preparation of the manuscript was undertaken by Miss Kate Burling whose considerable technical skill resulted in the production of an immaculate typescript. The laborious task of reading the typescript was undertaken by my friend and colleague The Revd. William Burman, whose perception and counsel I value.

By asking him to write the Foreword to this book, I have only partially repaid the debt I owe to Mr. James Risk, C.V.O., F.S.A., for all his help and advice in writing the two chapters on the robes and insignias of the Order. His encyclopaedic knowledge of the technical minutiae in such areas, formed over many years, has been invaluable.

Language is at best an imperfect means of communication and no words are really adequate to express the debt I owe to my friends and research assistants Mr. Cedric Stephens and Mr. Alan Reynolds. There is no doubt in my mind that but for their friendship, support and encouragement over the last three years, this book would never have been written.

St. John's House,   PETER GALLOWAY
St. John's Wood,
London
September 1983

DEDICATION

To my Parents

PREFACE

On 5 May 1788, a certain Mr. J. C. Walker wrote to James Caulfield, 1st Earl of Charlemont and a Founder Knight of the Order of Saint Patrick, as follows:

'I hope your Lordship will pardon the liberty I have taken in giving to the public my essay on the Irish dress, in its original epistolary form, and honour with a place in your Lordship's library the copy which accompanies this.* Having made two feeble attempts to elucidate the antiquities of my country, I am now about to abandon the subject. Indeed, I doubt if I shall ever resume it again, unless it be for the purpose of doing what the herald of the Order of St Patrick (if there be such an officer) ought to do, that is, to collect materials for an historical memoir on knighthood in Ireland, chiefly with a view of preserving from oblivion the several circumstances attending the institution of that Order.'

A diligent search has failed to reveal any trace of Mr. Walker's proposed memoir on Irish knighthood so we must conclude that he did indeed abandon his attempts to 'elucidate the antiquities' of his country. Had he succeeded in doing so, his memoir might well have been of considerable assistance in the writing of the first chapter of this book since, writing only five years after the foundation of the Order, he would have had the valuable source of personal memory to aid his endeavour, quite apart from any documentary material which has not survived the passage of time. Though I know nothing of Mr. Walker apart from his name and his expressed intention, I must, nevertheless, record my gratitude to him for his silent yet continuous encouragement of my efforts at research these several years past. I discovered his letter to Lord Charlemont some time ago at a time when my interest in the Order of Saint Patrick was passing through a transitional phase from acquisitive curiosity to serious research. It has been constantly in my mind and on my desk ever since and it gives me great pleasure to hope that I have succeeded in fulfilling his view of 'preserving from oblivion' not only the circumstances surrounding the institution of the Order of Saint Patrick but also its fascinating history as the national honour of Ireland for nearly 140 years.

The 'Company of sixteen noble and worthy Knights' founded by George III 'for the dignity and honour of Our Realm of Ireland' has now been rendered obsolete by that honoured trinity of 'time, circumstance and parliamentary enactment' and its name will not be immediately familiar to many. But in its day it was the third of the three great national Orders of the United Kingdom, ranking

---

* *An Historical Essay on the Dress of the ancient and modern Irish . . . To which is subjoined a memoir on the Armour and Weapons of the Irish*, Joseph Cooper Walker, Dublin 1788.

after the Order of the Garter (of England) and the Order of the Thistle (of Scotland), and the post-nominal letters 'K.P.' attached to the name of some distinguished Irish peer meant as much to those in Ireland who understood and appreciated such things as the letters 'K.G.' do in England. As an elite group of 16 (later 22) Knights drawn exclusively from the ranks of the Irish nobility it did not achieve that level of public recognition gained, for example, by the three lower classes of the Order of the British Empire, but it was highly esteemed by those to whom it was given, and the majority of individuals who declined the honour generally did so from a sense of unworthiness.

Since the Order of Saint Patrick has now finished its useful life, it seems appropriate in this the bicentenary year of its foundation to record its interesting and unusual contribution to the history of Ireland during the past two hundred years.

Chapter One

ORIGIN AND FOUNDATION

'Pray let me have my Order of Knighthood as it is necessary for our House of Peers'

Lord Temple, November 1782

ON THE 5th February 1783, Letters Patent passed the Great Seal of Ireland, creating a new Order of Knighthood for that kingdom, the third of the three great national Orders, after the Garter of England, and the Thistle of Scotland. It was the first Order to be founded in the United Kingdom since the Order of the Bath more than half a century earlier. George III made his purpose for doing so quite clear: 'Whereas Our loving Subjects of Our Kingdom of Ireland have approved themselves steadily attached to Our Royal Person and Government, and affectionately disposed to maintain and promote the Welfare and Prosperity of the Whole Empire; And We being willing to confer upon Our Subjects of Our Said Kingdom a testimony of Our sincere love and affectionate regard, by creating an Order of Knighthood in Our Said Kingdom . . . This is Our Royal Will and Pleasure and We do hereby Authorize and Require You upon Receipt hereof forthwith to cause Letters Patent to be passed Under the Great Seal . . . for creating a Society or Brotherhood to be called Knights of the Most Illustrious Order of St Patrick'.[1]

Royal Warrants need to be read with great care and circumspection, and seldom, if ever, does their archaic language give the remotest hint of what personalities and situations lie behind an occurrence as rare as the foundation of a new Order of Knighthood. We are led to believe that peace and harmony reigned in Ireland, and that its relations with England were marked by great cordiality. As a result, the King had been moved to institute the Order as a reward for his loyal Irish citizens, all mindful of their duty to him and to the Empire. Nothing could be farther from the truth. Ireland in the late 18th century was a restless, turbulent country, chafing with increasing unrest against the political and economic control exercised over her by the British government in London. It would be futile to tell the story of the creation of the Order of Saint Patrick without giving some account of the events and mood of opinion in Ireland in the preceding 20 years, because the two are inextricably mixed.

Power in Ireland was nominally vested in the Lord Lieutenant, generally an English peer appointed by the government of the day, and changing with each administration. He ruled in the name of the King from Dublin Castle,

1

maintaining a smaller version of the royal court and household, and as far as possible, he represented the pageantry of the monarchy in Ireland. Below the Lord Lieutenant was a politician styled the Chief Secretary, who took care of day-to-day government business, and filled in Ireland a position at least as important as that of the Prime Minister in England. Like the office of Lord Lieutenant, the occupants of the post were usually Englishmen, who changed with English administrations.

One of the Chief Secretary's responsibilities was the conduct of government business in the House of Commons of the Irish Parliament. This body met in the impressive classical colonnaded building on College Green, opposite Trinity College, which still stands, though now housing the Bank of Ireland. In theory, it was the legislature of Ireland. Like the English Parliament, it was divided into two Houses, Commons and Lords, and its jurisdiction extended to the whole of Ireland, but there the similarity ended. By a series of Acts, beginning with Poyning's Law of 1494 and ending with the Declaratory Act of 1719, the freedom to legislate enjoyed by the Irish Parliament was substantially diminished. Heads of Bills arising in either House were first passed to the Irish Privy Council, which could either suppress them altogether or amend them as it pleased. It was then put into the form of a Bill and transmitted to the English Privy Council, which also had unlimited power of suppression or alteration. If this second ordeal was passed, it was returned with such changes as both Privy Councils had made to the House of Parliament from which it had originated, and then passed to the other House. Neither House had the power to alter the Bill; they could only accept it as it had been returned from England, or reject it altogether and start again. Furthermore, Acts of the British Parliament were binding in Ireland, and the supreme court of appeal was transferred from the Irish House of Lords to that of England. There was no Habeas Corpus Act, nor was there any Act obliging Members of Parliament to resign their seats when accepting places of profit, or pensions from the Crown. There was no national militia, no security of tenure for judges, and two-thirds of the country's revenue was outside the control of Parliament.

This was tolerated during the climate of civil war and unrest in the years after 1689, but from about the middle of the century a new atmosphere was beginning to pervade Irish politics, and to find its way into the debates of the Irish Parliament. The growth of a middle class, the evaporation of civil war passions, the decline of religious intolerance, and the sudden rise of a free press were significant factors. In addition a head-on clash between the Lord Lieutenant and the Irish peers became more likely after 1765, when a decision was made to make the holder of the post reside permanently in Ireland during his term of office. Hitherto, the Lord Lieutenant had spent only six months of every two years in the country, and the government was 'undertaken' by a few important Irish peers who possessed considerable parliamentary influence, on the condition of obtaining a large share of the disposal of patronage. From his appointment as Lord Lieutenant in October 1767, Lord Townshend tried to break the power of these 'Undertakers', complaining that the Lord Lieutenant had been reduced to a mere 'pageant of state'. He reported that their constant plan was to possess the government of the country and to lower the authority of the English government, both of which would destroy the dependence of Ireland on Great Britain. It is not without significance that at this stage we find the first mention of an Irish Order. On 31 May 1768 Townshend wrote to Lord Shelburne, urging the propriety of creating an Irish Order on the lines of the Thistle in Scotland.

Unlike modern parliaments, the Irish Parliament was not divided into clearly marked political divisions. Settled political parties had not yet developed, due to the nature of constituencies which gave a predominating influence to a few personal interests. Some of the numerous small boroughs were held by men who had purchased their seats; some were attached to the properties of moderately wealthy gentry; some were under the direct influence of the government, and some were connected to the Church. But the great majority belonged to a few rich members of the House of Lords, and it was considered a point of honour, that on important questions, the borough member should vote in accordance with the wishes of his patron. In ordinary business the government usually carried an enormous majority, but there were questions on which the strongest government saw its majority vanish overnight. Finance Bills, for example, which either originated, or were substantially modified in England, were almost always rejected. It was quite common for paid servants of the Crown, while in general supporting the government, to go into strong opposition on certain questions, and for others, who had been the most active opponents of the government, to pass suddenly into its ranks. There was a rapid fluctuation of politicians between government and opposition. In such a situation, it was almost inevitable that bribery and corruption became legitimate and accepted parts of government. Every kind of ecclesiastical, official, legal and civic office was used as a bribe to gain support for the government in Parliament. Peerages, baronetcies, knighthoods and pensions were widely distributed, and the large number of Irish peerages created from 1760 onwards caused considerable annoyance to the King, who rightly saw them as a devaluation of the peerage in general. In 1776, for example, 18 commoners were ennobled on 18 consecutive days, and 12 peers were promoted to higher peerages. In most cases the terms of the bargain were well known to be an engagement to support the government by their votes in the House of Lords, by their substitutes and their influence in the House of Commons. Horace Walpole (Last Journals) called them 'a mob of nobility', and added that the King in private laughed at the eagerness for such insignificant honours. In 1780, Lord Buckinghamshire wrote to the Prime Minister recommending eight commoners for peerages, 13 peers for advancement in the peerage, five appointments to the Privy Council, 17 persons for civil pensions, and several others for varying favours, adding that he had been driven to it by not having any other means of rewarding government supporters at his disposal. The Irish peerage was

systematically degraded by these profuse creations which grew more frequent
as the century drew on, reaching a peak in 1800, and the question of an Order
of Knighthood was again raised. Writing in 1777, Buckinghamshire expressed his
thoughts: 'I wish our gracious master would institute an Irish order of knighthood
. . . for Irishmen only. They certainly without invidious comparisons have as good
a right as others who enjoy those marks of distinction. The establishment should
not be too numerous, and, bestowed with propriety, would occasionally be
received in lieu of emoluments and lessen the necessity of lavishing those
hereditary honours which ultimately become burthensome to a country and
essentially weaken and embarrass government . . .'.[2] Nothing, in fact, was done
for a further five years until Lord Temple arrived as Lord Lieutenant, in
September 1782, in a very different political climate.

The period from 1760 to 1782 saw a gathering campaign by virtually all
sections of Irish opinion to free the Irish Parliament from all legislative
restrictions. Attempts by successive Lords Lieutenant from 1765 onwards to
break the power of the Undertakers and reassert Viceregal authority only served
to throw those who had previously supported the government into the opposition
camp. Lords Townshend, Harcourt and Buckinghamshire spent thousands of
pounds creating new offices or annexing salaries to old ones in their efforts to
maintain their powers of patronage.

The appearance of the Volunteers in 1778 only served to make the position
worse. War with France was beginning to appear inevitable at that time, and with
an empty treasury, the government found itself totally unable to raise a militia
of 12,000 men needed to defend Ireland against invasion. The Lord Lieutenant
therefore recommended that several companies of volunteers should be raised,
and the response he received was overwhelming. Within a short time the volunteer
force numbered some 42,000 men, and the government looked with some alarm
on this massive army, rising up independently of their control at a time when
discontent was simmering. With the army bogged down in America, the Volunteers had to be treated with great care. The doctrine that no laws were valid in
Ireland that had not been made by the King, Lords and Commons of Ireland was
rapidly becoming the dominant slogan in the country. News of the defeats
at Yorktown and Saratoga spurred on the opposition to demand total legislative
independence. Speaking in the Irish House of Commons, Henry Grattan, the
brilliant Irish orator, made a passionate declaration of the Irish position asserting
that while the Crown of Ireland was inseparably united to that of England, Ireland
was by right a distinct kingdom. In April 1782 the Duke of Portland, who had
succeeded Buckinghamshire as Lord Lieutenant, wrote that the government
could no longer exist in its present form, and the sooner England recalled her
Lieutenant, and renounced all claims to Ireland, the better. If, on the contrary,
concessions were made, then the Union of the two countries might be saved.

Faced with a serious and deteriorating situation, the government introduced a
resolution in the British Parliament stating that it was indispensable to the interest

and happiness of both kingdoms that the connection between them should
be established by mutual consent upon a solid and permanent footing. By a series
of measures the Irish Parliament was freed from all legislative restrictions and,
almost overnight, the whole constitution of Ireland was changed with virtually
no disorder or violence. Edmund Burke rightly described the events of 1782
as the Irish analogue of 1688.

Shortly afterwards, a new administration was formed in England under Lord
Shelburne. The Duke of Portland was replaced as Lord Lieutenant by Earl Temple
who arrived in Ireland in September 1782, and for the third and successful time,
the question of an Irish Order was raised.

During the 1780s, the period immediately before and after independence, the
whole spirit of Irish political life was completely opposed to anything which
might lessen the distinctive dignity of Ireland. As a result of the independence
campaign, a new pride in things Irish began to develop, and an Irish Order must
have appeared to Shelburne and Temple as a natural corollary, quite apart from
political considerations. England had the Orders of the Garter and the Bath, and
Scotland, with an insignificant degree of independence since the dissolution of
the Scottish Parliament in 1707, had the Order of the Thistle. A curious parallel
may be noticed here between the creation of the Thistle in 1687 (in the closing
years of the Scottish Parliament) and the creation of the Order of Saint Patrick,
only 17 years before the dissolution of the Irish Parliament. The foundation of
the Order seems in this light to be a simple case of redressing the balance—giving
to Ireland the status that had long been enjoyed by England and Scotland.

There was no demand on the part of Irish peers for an Irish Riband, and the
origins of the Order lie entirely in England. But here the picture becomes cloudy,
and ascribing the idea to any one individual becomes difficult. It may be useful
to recall at this point that Lord Shelburne had been the recipient of a letter
12 years earlier, urging the creation of an Irish Order, and it is conceivable that
given the increased difficulty in securing the passage of government legislation
through the Irish Parliament, he may have decided that an appropriate time had
come to implement the idea. There is no evidence, but he must certainly have
known about Temple's plans before the latter arrived in Ireland in September.

George Nugent-Temple-Grenville, 3rd Earl Temple, was one of the small
number of English Viceroys who was personally unpopular in Ireland. Hard
working, frugal, easily elated or depressed, he had an acute sense of his own
dignity and importance, and was alert to see (or imagine) and to resent any
slight. All his despatches to London refer to 'my Order', and we have to rely
largely on his papers for an account of what occurred in the months leading up
to the public announcement of the Order on 5 February 1783.

According to Temple's despatch to Thomas Townshend in November 1782,
the King had asked him before his departure from England, to raise the question
of instituting a new Irish Order of Knighthood and to consult the leading Irish
nobility on the subject. Temple spoke first to the Duke of Leinster, a haughty

young man of 33 whose power and influence were out of all proportion to his age and abilities. In March 1774, when only 25 years old, he wrote to Lord Harcourt, the then Lord Lieutenant: 'I do not expect to be a ruler or adviser; tho' my rank in life does not prohibit me from either, I might say entitles me, yet my age forbids me claiming that right at present. I shall however expect to be informed of intended measures'.[3] In May 1784 he was described as 'so fickle and unsteady in his opinions and so weak in all his public conduct that I hardly know how I shall be able to dispose of him. There seems to be a perpetual struggle in his mind between avarice, pride and ambition. His consequence is solely confined to his name and situation in this country'.[4] Nevertheless, Leinster was the obvious peer to consult. Not only was he the head of the Fitzgerald family, but he was also the greatest borough owner and the only Duke in Ireland. There being no Marquesses, the next rank of Earl was some way below him, giving him an increased sense of his own importance. He was flattered at being consulted and pronounced himself in favour, wanting to be assured at the same time that the new Order was to be strictly limited in terms both of rank and numbers, to ensure its exclusiveness.

Delighted at gaining the approval of one of the most difficult Irish peers, Temple wrote to Townshend outlining his plans: 'This idea will be productive of the best consequences by holding out honourable marks of distinction among the peers of this country who have hardly any objects to which they can look forward. I trust that whenever I may think it most adviseable for His service I may be permitted to send over for His Majesty's approbation any number of names not exceeding sixteen and at the same time submit for his consideration such a plan as may best suit the tempers and inclinations of those for whom this dignity must be intended'.[5]

Apparently the government were hesitant, for he wrote again a few weeks later: 'Pray let me have my Order of Knighthood as it is necessary for our House of Peers',[6] and again the following month: 'Pray likewise press my Order of St Patrick, as it will be very useful'.[7] By late December the government had finally decided to allow the institution of the Order, and Temple was requested to send over a list of names. Writing to his brother, William Grenville, on Christmas Day, he said: 'My idea is to give it only to peers . . . and this was strongly the King's wish. I will look over the list of names and think of limiting the numbers to sixteen: which, considering that we have 157 lay peers, of whom near 100 are resident in Ireland and others occasionally there will not be more than is absolutely necessary. I shall think myself at liberty to give one to private love and regard, and upon that footing, in confidence, offer one to Lord Nugent as the only testimony I can offer him of my sense of what I owe for him for contributing so largely to my happiness'.[8] Nugent was Temple's father-in-law.

Temple appears to have worked extremely fast, because the outline of the Order had been completed within a few days, and on 2 January 1783, he sent over a list of sixteen names for approval:

Duke of Leinster	Earl of Clanricarde
Earl of Antrim	Earl of Westmeath
Earl of Inchiquin	Earl of Drogheda
Earl of Tyrone	Earl of Shannon
Earl of Clanbrassil	Earl of Charlemont
Earl of Hillsborough	Earl of Mornington
Earl of Bective	Earl of Courtown
Earl of Ely	Earl Nugent

Nugent and Hillsborough both declined the Order, the latter with 'great civility', and, only days before the first Investiture of 11 March, the Earl of Antrim, when informed that he would have to surrender the Order of the Bath to which he had been appointed in 1780, announced his intention of retaining the Bath and surrendering the Patrick. The holding of more than one Order was most exceptional in the 18th century, and Antrim should have been aware that he would not be allowed to hold both Orders. The Bath was the more well-established and the more prestigious, but he expressed his mortification at having to decline the Patrick. He was quickly replaced by the Earl of Arran, and the other two stalls were filled by Prince Edward and the King, fixing the number of Knights at 15, excluding the Sovereign. None of the Founder Knights, as they became known, was below the rank of Earl, and this was Temple's idea, 'because if we go lower, I do not see what line can be drawn between numbers whose pretensions are equal, and the first institution being confined to Earls puts it on a higher footing. I mean that the Viscounts and Barons shall be informed that they will be equally candidates in the future'.[9]

An examination of the *curriculum vitae* of each Knight yields little evidence of why they were chosen, and in any case such a search would be futile. They were either supporters of the government in Parliament, or they were peers whose power and influence was such that the government needed their support. For example, the Duke of Leinster and the Earls of Ely, Shannon, and Tyrone between them controlled 62 members of the Commons, and their support or opposition could make the difference between victory and defeat for the government.

True to form, the Duke of Leinster was difficult when first offered the Order and said that he did not regard being placed without distinction in the Order as a sufficient mark of royal favour, and that his birth and rank entitled him to the Garter. Temple managed to sooth him, and assured him that he would be placed first in the list of Knights after Prince Edward, and that acceptance would not prejudice his claims on the Garter. The Duke was angling for the vacant Vice-Treasurership of Ireland and was indignant about the Order being a *full* reward for his services. Temple reported that 'he rode the high horse so truly for 3 days, that I doubted his acceptance, however it is now all right'.[10]

The Earl of Bective had three sons in the Commons as well as a borough, and had always supported the government; the Earl of Shannon had a following of about twenty M.P.s and three peers; and after Antrim's refusal, Temple recommended the Earl of Arran, 'whose borough influence is just strengthened by a marriage which gives him two more seats'.[11] Even the Officers of the Order were to be exploitable as 'the honor of wearing a badge in the mode proposed, joined to the Fees and to a small allowance upon the establishment would make them eligible, and consequently the disposal of them useful to government'.[12]

Temple found himself besieged by peers asking for the Order. He speaks of being 'plagued' by Lords Arran, Aldborough and Altamont, the last of whom renewed his application on the first occurrence of a vacancy in May 1783. Lords Bellamont, Clermont, Meath and Donegal and many others submitted claims, but Temple was adamant on the grounds for membership: 'Lord Bellamont, who ended last session the advocate of Mr Flood, must be objected to till he has expiated his offence'. As for Lord Clermont: 'I can have no plea to give the Order to the last upon the Earl's bench, who has reached that dignity by an extraordinary exertion of royal favour in five years from the House of Commons,' and Lord Meath, 'has almost always opposed'.[13] In his official despatch to London, Temple remarked rather ambiguously: 'I have endeavoured to select those people whose property and situation seem peculiarly to point them out',[14] but it is clear that he intended the Order only for those who would guarantee their loyalty to the administration. Lord Bellamont was not without his supporters and admirers, one of whom wrote an ode commemorating the foundation of the Order, doubtless assuming that the peer would be one of the first Knights.

> O may this day, from age to age
> 'Twixt Britain and Ierne prove
> The grave of all domestic rage,
> The bond that seals the sisters love;
> When great ST. PATRICK'S Knights are nam'd,
> By patriots good and warriors fam'd,
> Then let them say that Order high,
> By princely Brunswick was design'd,
> Like some blest edict of the sky,
> To give two nations but one mind.[15]

Temple hoped that the appointment of the young Prince Edward would add to the honour of the Order, by establishing an immediate connection between the Royal Family and the Government of Ireland. Apparently the Prince of Wales had desired to be the first royal K.P., and asked the King for the Honour, but on intimating that he would expect permission to go to Ireland for the Installation, 'those unfortunate jealousies, which have at all times subsisted between the King and the heir apparent, and some other obvious reasons, interfered, and induced his majesty to refuse his compliance with his son's desire'.[16] In good Hanoverian tradition, the King was suspicious of the motives of his heir.

Perhaps the most interesting of the Knights was the Earl of Charlemont, Commander-in-Chief of the Volunteers, whose numbers reached 80,000 at one point. No administration could afford to ignore him or do without his support. He was leader of the opposition in the Lords, in so far as there was one. Although its numbers naturally fluctuated, he was the leader of a small solid group of about six peers. A leading advocate of legislative independence in 1782 and highly respected by his fellow peers, he was as incorruptible as any Irish peer could be, and his motives for accepting the Order were probably more disinterested than the other Knights.

His story is best told in his own words: 'It seemed to be, and in my opinion really was a proper and honourable distinction to the kingdom, and might be considered as a badge and symbol of her newly-rescued independence. The time also most assuredly was . . . peculiarly favourable, since as such institutions usually take place in consequence of some signal success, the present period must be allowed of all others the most proper, as no events could possibly be more worthy of commemoration than those which had lately happened . . . As long as this honour was confined to the House of Lords, and more especially to the Earls' bench, I must confess that the Crown would not be likely to gain much additional influence by it, as nothing could possibly render my illustrious brethren better courtiers than I knew them already to be. But then, on the other hand, this very argument militated against my acceptance as it could not be very pleasing to me to be one of an order which must be composed of men who differed so essentially from me in every political principle, and whose association might not be advantageous to me as a public man . . . What effect could it have on me?—since I must candidly confess that was his excellency to suffer me to select fourteen peers from among the earls, I should not be able to find one half of that number with whom I would wish to class myself. This might appear somewhat impertinent, but unfortunately it was but too true. The honour besides would probably descend into the lower ranks of the nobility, and possibly into the Commons. Should that ever happen, as in the course of time, and change of governments was by no means improbable my former objection would remain in its full force. These inconveniences might, however, perhaps be outweighed by the honourable distinction resulting to Ireland from the institution, and, with regard to my determination the great and capital point was I must confess to discover if possible how the measure would be taken by the people . . . My principal objection . . . had been lest the people should consider my acceptance of any royal favour as a dereliction of their interests, and should on that account withdraw from me that unbounded confidence by which alone I could be useful. But every such danger was by [his] letter clearly obviated, since both the people and the Volunteers might therein at the first glance perceive that the honour was offered and accepted merely as a reward for services performed, not to the crown, but to them . . . It was certain that, had I refused, the order would have become unpopular, and possibly might have fallen to the ground; and this was an additional reason for my acceptance, as I did not wish to take upon myself the possible danger of depriving the kingdom of so honourable and so proper a distinction'.[17]

Whatever Charlemont thought he may have contributed to its success and popularity, the announcement of the new Order was greeted in Dublin with a high degree of enthusiasm. 'Our Order is wonderfully popular',[18] wrote Temple to his brother; and again on 5 February he said: 'half Dublin is mad about the Order'.[19] And in response to criticism levelled in England at the Order, he wrote: 'I am glad Fox abuses it, and I hope he will laugh at it in the House of Commons as it is universally popular with all ranks of people'.[20] Ignoring the fact that Temple was praising his own creation, the Order was, on balance, well received by the people, as newspaper reports bear out. But Dublin newspapers of the time need to be read with as much discrimination and discernment as do Royal Warrants; articles range in content from shrewd perception to total ignorance, and in style from excessive adulation to personal abuse. For example, in the last case, the Officers of the Order, particularly the Chancellor, the Secretary and the Usher, came under considerable attack over the large fees they were to receive.

The *Dublin Evening Post* expressed 'apprehension, that the Order of Saint Patrick . . . is not merely intended *honoris causa*; but is a subtle engine of Government wherewith to secure the interest of some leading men on questions of consequence that are expected soon to be agitated in Parliament. It is a fact too often experienced that the offer of a glittering bauble for personal ornament, has greater influence in subduing patriotic integrity, than any lucrative temptation'. And further, 'The Order of Saint Patrick is considered by many of the best friends of Ireland only as an additional lure, thrown into the hands of Administration, to take off such of our great men, as bare-faced corruption could not render subservient to their every purpose . . . If through the governing miraculous power of Saint Patrick no venomous animal can live in Ireland, pray heaven that the ribbon of this Order may never be worn by any man who has planted a sting in the bosom of his country'.[21] At the same time the *Post* was aware of how much a boost the Order would bring to the depressed Irish economy; remarking that no less than twenty looms were employed making the robes of the Knights, Esquires, and their numerous attendants. Temple had tactfully ordered that only Irish materials should be used, as a further gesture to Irish feeling.

Needless to add, the Earl of Antrim was repeatedly lampooned for what the *Post* saw as his unpatriotic refusal to relinquish the Order of the Bath in favour of the Patrick, and in an anonymous letter signed PADDY WHACK and addressed to the Earl of A-----, the author pronounced himself 'sick of so scandalous a subject, as your preference of the lowest Order of England, to the FIRST ORDER of ancient Ierne'.[22] A caricature depicted him trying on the blue riband in front of a mirror, and deciding against it as not becoming his complexion. The attitude of the *Post* made little difference to the position of the Order, which was now firmly established in Irish politics, and probably in the eyes of most, as an honoured symbol of Irish independence. Few in those exciting years could have forseen that the declaration of Irish independence in 1782 which brought the Order to life, was to be followed 140 years later by a similar declaration which ended its existence.

Chapter Two

INVESTITURE AND INSTALLATION

'Heaven appeared yesterday to beam down a plaudit
on the institution of the Order of Saint Patrick'
Dublin Evening Post,
18 March 1783

IT SEEMS STRANGE, with our 20th-century concern for efficiency and detail, that something as exalted and complex as an Order of Knighthood should have been put together so hastily in the space of a few weeks. Yet this is exactly what happened with the Order of St Patrick. Temple sent an outline plan of the Order over to London on 16 November 1782; the government communicated their agreement on 21 December; the Order was publicly announced on 5 February; and on 17 March the Knights were installed in Saint Patrick's Cathedral, the whole process taking only four months. Unfortunately, the result of their hastiness can be seen only too clearly in the Statutes. Given the short amount of time in which to put the order together, Temple had the Statutes copied from those of the Order of the Garter, making only the most necessary changes of name and place. No thought was given to writing a set of Statutes relevant to the distinctively Irish situation in which the Order was set, and there were a number of peculiar anomalies.

The whole complicated procedure for electing new Knights was a total farce. It was never, in fact, put into operation, the Lord Lieutenant merely recommending to the King the peer he thought most suitable for appointment. Probably the worst example of this lack of thought and imagination was Article XVIII, which stated that the Chancellor of the Order should have custody of the Seal of the Order, except on occasions when he was more than 20 miles away from the King. In such instances he was to surrender it to a junior officer. This arrangement probably worked very well in the Order of the Garter, but Temple had decided that the Chancellor of the Order of Saint Patrick was to be the Archbishop of Dublin, who was separated from the King not only by twenty miles, but also by the Irish Sea. He could not very well comply with the article, without either permanently surrendering the Seal, or residing in England. Not surprisingly the rule was never enforced, and along with the major parts of the Statutes, it was simply ignored. Amending warrants were issued throughout the 19th century, making corrections and additions as and when they became desirable,

11

but it seems a pity that the Order should have been governed throughout the greater part of its life by these archaic and inoperable rules. The Order evolved its own rules, and the extensive revision of the Statutes in 1905, was, in essence, a codification of existing practice.

With the question of the Knights finally decided, Temple turned his attention to the Officers. They were far too valuable a source of patronage to be treated lightly, and careful consideration was given to how they could best be allocated. Temple decided initially that there should be four Officers, two to be held by dignitaries of the Church of Ireland, and two by members of the House of Commons. However, objections from certain quarters within the Church, and, no doubt, realisation of just how valuable the places could be, caused the figure to soar to the unprecedented number of thirteen. No other Order, either then existing or subsequently created, was so well endowed with Officers as the Order of Saint Patrick. The 15 Knights, presided over by the Lord Lieutenant as Grand Master found themselves waited upon by almost as many Officers: a Prelate, a Chancellor, a Registrar, a Secretary, a Genealogist, a King of Arms, an Usher, two Heralds and four Pursuivants.

The office of Grand Master was the inevitable result of basing the Order in Ireland. No British monarch had visited Ireland since 1690 (and none was to do so until 1821), and thus the Grand Master was empowered to 'do all things and enjoy all privileges, rights and prerogatives, and do all manner of things touching the said Most Illustrious Order, in as ample a manner as We ourselves could have done as Sovereign . . . if we ourselves had been present . . .'.[1] As the Sovereign's deputy in the affairs of the Order, it was natural that the office should be held by the Lord Lieutenant, his deputy in the affairs of the state. But a striking inconsistency emerged. The Grand Master was not a member of the Order over which he presided, and on resigning the office of Lord Lieutenant he ceased to have any connection with the Order. Of the 40 Grand Masters appointed between 1783 and 1922, only two were made Knights of the Order: Lord Talbot (1817–1821) in 1821, and Lord French (1918–1921) in 1917. In attempts to correct this silly oversight in the Statutes, ex-Grand Masters were authorised by subsequent amendments to wear the Badge and Star of the office for their lifetime, which led to even greater anomalies which will be discussed later.

The appointment of a Prelate to the Order was not originally envisaged by Temple, and was apparently made solely as the result of a letter from the Archbishop of Armagh, asking for the office. In a despatch to London, asking for the King's approval, Temple mentions the Archbishop's 'merits and virtues', but a closer look at the hierarchy of the Church reveals the real reason. The Church of Ireland was the established Church of the Kingdom. It was Protestant, episcopal and very small but the fact of its establishment and its great wealth gave it a position of significance far greater than its membership justified. With 38 bishops and four archbishops, its episcopate was excessively numerous. The two senior archbishops, Armagh and Dublin, were styled respectively Primate of All Ireland, and Primate of Ireland, a compromise dating from a time of rivalry between the two for the primacy of the Church. From Temple's correspondence, the rivalry between the two archbishops apparently flared up again, over his decision to appoint the Archbishop of Dublin as Chancellor of the Order. Although the letter has not survived, we can safely say that the Archbishop of Armagh probably expressed his strong indignation at such an appointment, and pressed his own claims as holder of the senior archbishopric, not only to a position in the Order, but also to one superior to that held by the Archbishop of Dublin. The appointment of the latter as Chancellor was a natural choice, since the headquarters of the Order lay within his Province, but the Lord Lieutenant stepped on archiepiscopal pride in the process and aroused strong emotions. He described the Archbishop of Dublin as 'outrageous about the Primate's prelacy',[2] and the matter was still simmering a year later when his successor, the Duke of Rutland, wrote: 'A dispute has arisen between the Primate and the Archbishop of Dublin with respect to the precedence on the ceremonial of the Order of St Patrick. The Primate claims to walk single. The Archbishop claims to walk at the Primate's left hand. I ask for your opinion and decision as to what was understood and intended as to their particular ranks when you founded the order. The matter seems trifling but the dispute is conducted with great heat'.[3] The newly-appointed Prelate was also assigned the Chancellor's former duty of administering the Oath of new Knights at their Investiture. Alone of all the Officers, he received neither salary nor fees.

The Chancellor had the responsibility of keeping the Seal of the Order and of taking the votes at elections of new Knights, which never took place. The Office of Registrar was held by the Dean of Saint Patrick's Cathedral, Dublin, and it could be assumed that he was to keep a register of the transactions of the Order, though he never appears to have done so. It could be similarly inferred that the Secretary should conduct the correspondence of the Order, though again there is no trace that any holder of the office ever did. The Genealogist was to have custody of the Certificates of the Pedigrees of the Knights. No duties at all were assigned to the Usher. He generally led processions and acted as a door-keeper. At least two of the holders of the Office between 1783 and 1800 appear to have been also Ushers to the Irish House of Lords, much on the lines of the Usher to the English House of Lords who waited on the Order of the Garter. Both bore the designation 'Black Rod'. The Irish Usher is mentioned in the first printed Journal of the House in 1634, and it seems that he was intended to be modelled precisely on the English Black Rod. According to the Civil List of 1783 his salary was £355 11s. 1d., a figure that indicates responsibilities wider than his merely nominal attendance on the Order of Saint Patrick. There is no point in taking much notice of the nominal function, or lack of function, of these Officers. They were never intended to be anything more than decorative sinecures. When he was discussing them in a letter to his brother, Temple wrote, 'the details of these playthings . . . is hardly serious'.

Throughout the history of the Order, its day-to-day business was handled entirely by the King of Arms, a post annexed to the much older office of Ulster King of Arms. The first Ulster King of Arms, Bartholomew Butler, was appointed by Letters Patent dated 1 June 1552. Ulster now became responsible for ceremonies of investiture and installation, preparing the Banners and Achievements of the Knights, and the procurement, custody and repair of the insignia. He, rather than the Genealogist, signed the Certificates of Noblesse of the Knights and their Esquires. He, rather than the Registrar, kept a register of the Order's affairs, and he, rather than the Secretary, conducted all the Order's correspondence. Any decisions about the Order were made either by Ulster or on his advice.

The holder of this office in 1783 was one William Hawkins, who had been appointed in 1767. A shadowy figure of whom little is known, Hawkins had the misfortune to fail to live up to Lord Temple's high standards, since the latter was reluctant to entrust him with too much responsibility. The difficulties of arranging an Investiture and an Installation at such short notice may have been beyond Hawkins's abilities, but Temple had the annoying tendency to underrate the abilities of everybody except himself. 'Our Ulster is not equal to it'[4] he wrote to his brother, and requested him to ask Joseph Edmondson, Mowbray Herald Extraordinary, to come over to Dublin and superintend the ceremonies. William Hawkins, incensed at being pushed to one side, made his feelings clear, and a few weeks later Temple cancelled his request: 'Ulster has plagued me so completely, and Edmondson makes so enormous a demand, that I have determined to leave it to this Ulster'.[5]

Ulster had one other subordinate Office of Arms, known as Athlone Pursuivant, and the Statutes added a bevy of Heralds and further Pursuivants to form a little heraldic court around Ulster. There were two Heralds, styled 'Dublin' and 'Cork', and three more Pursuivants without any particular designation, known simply as Junior Pursuivants. Though they were sometimes listed as being on Ulster's staff, and some occupants of the posts may have engaged in heraldic or genealogical work, they were primarily Officers of the Order of Saint Patrick, and their only functions were to attend the ceremonies of the Order.

The matter of fees paid to the Officers may be mentioned here from interest, since by the middle of the 19th century they were so heavy that there was considerable difficulty in filling vacancies in the Order. Initially the three Church Officers—Prelate, Chancellor, and Registrar—received no fees, but the rest of the Officers were well paid for their non-existent duties.

The Secretary	£25 (£25)	Dublin Herald	£10 (£10)
The Genealogist	£25 (£25)	Cork Herald	£10 (£10)
The Usher	£20 (£20)	Athlone Pursuivant	£5 (£5)
The King of Arms	£15 (£15)	Three Junior Pursuivants	£5 (£5)

Note.—The first sum in each case was paid to the official in question by each Knight on his investiture; the second sum by each Knight on his installation.

This brought the cost of becoming a Knight of the Order to £250, quite apart from numerous additional expenses. The sum was less than half the cost of becoming a Knight of the Bath, but still a considerable amount of money in late 18th-century Ireland. It was a very clever way of endowing ten new disposable officers in the gift of the Lord Lieutenant, without asking the Treasury to provide money for salaries.

The first investiture of the new Order was originally set for 8 March 1783, but the refusal of Lord Antrim caused a delay until the 11th. The place chosen was the great ballroom in Dublin Castle. The word 'Castle' was as much a misnomer in 1783 as it is today. Anyone with an aerial view of Dublin would be hard pressed to find a castle in the traditional sense of the word. Of the square five-towered medieval building, only one tower remains, the rest having been systematically demolished between 1680 and 1750 and replaced by the present graceful collection of 18th-century buildings grouped around two courtyards. The ballroom, re-named Saint Patrick's Hall on the day of the first investiture, is situated in the State apartments on the south side of the Upper Castle Yard. Built after 1746, and decorated in an elegant colour scheme of white and gold, the Hall is certainly the most impressive room in the Castle. The ceiling, supported by richly-gilded Corinthian pillars, is decorated with three pictures. The centrepiece is an allegorical painting of the coronation of George III. On one side Saint Patrick is shown preaching to the native Irish; and on the other, the Earl of Pembroke receives the homage of the Irish chiefs during the reign of Henry II. They are the work of Vincent de Waldre, and were executed during Temple's second period as Grand Master, 1787–90. Although investitures were not always held there, it acquired a special relationship with the Order, particularly after 1871 when the banners of the Knights were hung around the walls.

Twelve of the 15 Knights were present for the investiture in Saint Patrick's Hall on 11 March, and had Temple not insisted on their presence, the number would have been smaller. The Earl of Drogheda and the Earl of Clanricarde both wrote asking to be excused from attendance, the latter because of 'a very precarious and infirm state of health with which I have been afflicted for many years'.[6] And when the Earl of Ely wrote on the same grounds of ill health, he was told that Lords Drogheda and Clanricarde had applied on the same grounds, but on being turned down they went to Dublin 'with great personal hazard from the singular inclemency of the season'.[7] If Lord Ely were granted a dispensation, they might take offence. We may forgive Temple's harshness since he was anxious to make the occasion a success. However, Ely does appear to have been seriously ill. He was not present at either the investiture or the installation, and he died at Bath on 8 May, uninvested and uninstalled. There was insufficient time to include the Earl of Arran, who had only been nominated three days previously to replace Lord Antrim, and Prince Edward was privately invested by the King in St James's Palace on the 16th, in view of his youth. The investiture was a small private ceremony compared with the great spectacle of the installation six days later, and attendance was restricted. The official account in the *London Gazette* records that 'St Patrick's Hall was elegantly fitted up for the occasion, and the galleries belonging to it were crowded with ladies of the first rank and fashion; and the whole ceremony was conducted with the utmost propriety and with the most splendid magnificence'.[8]

The appointment of the Dean of Saint Patrick's as Registrar, and the use of the Cathedral as the Chapel of the Order, followed closly on the precedent of the Order of the Garter, where the Dean of Saint George's Chapel, Windsor Castle— the Chapel of the Order—was also Registrar of the Order. The origins of St Patrick's Cathedral go back to the late 12th century when a church was first built on the site, next to a well at which Saint Patrick was supposed to have baptised converts. Enlarged and restored on several occasions, there is little left of the original fabric, but it remains the most famous Cathedral in Ireland. Since 1872, it has been styled the National Cathedral, outside the jurisdiction of any bishop, but having a common relation with all the dioceses of the Church of Ireland with canonical representation in the Chapter from each diocese.

The Installation ceremony was held naturally on Saint Patrick's Day—17 March. It proved to be both very splendid and very expensive. The total cost of £4,419 goes some way to explaining why installation ceremonies were held so infrequently. Only six were held before the disestablishment of the Church of Ireland in 1871, which rendered the ceremony inappropriate.

The ceremony was considered to be of the utmost importance, and only on the rarest of occasions were Knights excused from attendance. Between 1783 and the abandonment of the ceremony in 1833 only three Knights were given dispensations, and all were installed by proxy: Prince Edward in 1783, the Earl of Carysfort in 1800, and the Duke of Cumberland in 1821. When Temple announced his desire to use the Cathedral Choir as the Chapel of the Order, the Archbishop of Dublin ordered the precincts to be cleaned up in readiness for the event, provoking sarcastic comment from the *Dublin Evening Post*: 'Although frequenters of the Cathedral may for penance sake, be allowed to wade knee deep in mud to their spiritual exercises, it will be very unworthy for the Knights of St Patrick who are cloathed with temporal honour, to soil a single heel-piece'.[9]

The Dean and Chapter were at first delighted at the choice of their Cathedral for the ceremony, and expressed their gratitude to the Lord Lieutenant for such a mark of honour. He was given permission to use the Cathedral and 16 stalls on the day, and was permitted to erect scaffolding in the Nave, Choir and Aisles. But their enthusiasm was considerably dampened when Temple informed them that the scaffolding was to be erected at their own expense, and they expressed the hope that 'should there be a material loss his Excellency will not suffer the Chapter to be essentially injured'.[10] Temple proposed in reply that the Dean and Chapter should pay half the cost, and the Dean as Registrar of the Order should pay the other half. In the same way, profits arising from the sale of tickets for seats should be divided between the Dean and Chapter. This provoked a great deal of annoyance. The Chapter replied that each of its members had equal rights and consequently 'the aggrandizement of one can never with justice be promoted to the prejudice of the rest', and they were 'concerned and alarmed to find . . . so partial a distribution in favour of the Dean . . . We apprehend that . . . our sentiments of respect and acquiesence to Your Excellency had reference to the necessary preparations within our Cathedral and the mode of reimbursement of our several expenses not supposing that those indications of respect could operate to the emolument of one at the expence of 24 . . . We should consider it a breach of trust not to remonstrate upon such a measure as the precedent might be established in the injury of our successors'.[11] Whether the Chapter were concerned with their successors or not, the Dean communicated their decision to Temple on 4 March, reporting that he himself was unable to accept the plan because of 'jealous murmurings and discontent'.[12] Temple quickly realised that he was in danger of stirring up another problem, and agreed to pay the whole cost himself.

No other problem appears to have marred the colourful and spectacular ceremony. A carriage procession conveyed the Grand Master and the Knights Companions from the Castle to the Cathedral, through streets lined with cheering spectators and regiments of the army and the Volunteers. Each Knight was invested in the Choir of the Cathedral by the Chancellor and the Registrar with the Sword, the Mantle and the Collar. His Banner was unfurled by his Esquire, and the Ulster King of Arms proclaimed his titles. The *Post* could scarcely contain its excitement: 'Heaven appeared yesterday to beam down a plaudit on the institution of the Order of St Patrick. The sun rose in full splendour, and the whole day was uncommonly bright and serene. The magnificence of the ceremony, the crowds of spectators of the first distinction in the cathedral, and the myriads of all ranks of people in the streets to see the Knights, etc., pass and repass in their carriages to and from the Castle, with the animation that lit up the countenances of the public, formed a scene that is indescribable, and which will long be remembered with pride and satisfaction by thousands of the sons and daughters of Hibernia'.[13]

The day was closed with a banquet in Saint Patrick's Hall for the Grand Master and Knights, and though no representation of the Installation is known to exist, the atmosphere of the Banquet is captured in an oil painting by John Keyse Sherwin, painted in 1785. It depicts the Grand Master and the Knights, robed and hatted, standing around the table with their goblets raised, about to toast the King's Health. No longer thought worthy of display, it now (1981) reposes in the stores of the National Gallery of Ireland in Dublin.

Lord Temple left Ireland shortly afterwards. He had never been very happy in Ireland, and had expressed a desire to resign as early as 15 January: 'It would always have been a sacrifice to continue here . . . and no temptation shall again draw me from those enjoyments within my reach the value of which I truly know and sacrificed, when I took this splendid plaything'.[14] Only 29 years old at the time of his departure from Ireland, he was a proud young man who knew a great deal and was too fond of communicating the fact. He could be imprudent and headstrong, and the flattering letters he had to write asking Irish peers to accept the Order, some of which border on the obsequious, probably caused him great irritation. Writing to Lord Charlemont, he praised that peer's 'public services, so justly distinguished, and of a nature which this kingdom must ever most gratefully remember', adding, 'I cannot hesitate a moment in requesting your lordship's permission to place your name upon the list'.[15] He saw the Order of St Patrick primarily as an extension of the Lord Lieutenant's powers of patronage, a method of easing government business through the Irish Parliament, and he soon tired of the intricate details of setting up an Order of Knighthood. Writing to his brother on 20 February, he said: 'every one is mad about this nonsense, which I am tired to death of',[16] and he greeted the end of the installation with great relief: 'The Parade of our Knights is over much to my satisfaction'.[17] In February when he was considering a date for the dissolution of Parliament, he wrote: 'our installation will fill the void till the 17th March, and on the 18th I would dissolve if all is safe . . . and in the nonsense of the farce of the Order which will be attended from all parts of Ireland, tests will be forgot, and no regular system formed to meet so sudden an event'.[18]

Arriving as Lord Lieutenant, he left as Lord Lieutenant and Grand Master, handing over both Offices to the Earl of Northington at the beginning of June. He was created Marquess of Buckingham in the following year for his services, and he returned to Ireland for a second term of office in the winter of 1787 which lasted for only a little more than two years. He died in June 1813 at the age of sixty. As befits the Founder of the Order of Saint Patrick, a statue of him, arrayed in the Mantle and Collar of the Order, stands in the north aisle of Saint Patrick's Cathedral.

1. The Mantle of H.R.H. the Duke of Connaught (No. 84) K.P.1869.

2. (*top left*) The Genealogist's Badge. There
are no marks but the reverse is inscribed with
the word 'Genealogist'. (*top right*) The Grand
Master's Gold Badge made of gold and enamel
and set with rubies and emeralds. Made by
Rundell, Bridge and Rundell of London in
1830. (*bottom left*) The Usher's Badge, Made
by West and Son of Dublin in the period
1838-41, the reverse bears the elements of a
Dublin hallmark though there is no date letter,
and the makers mark E + JJ 18. The reverse bears
a miniature replica of the Usher's Rod set in a field
of white enamel. (*bottom right*) A Grand Master's
Star, late 19th century. No marks or inscription.

3. (*top left*) The Chancellor's Badge. Made
by Clarke and West of Dublin in 1819, it
bears the Dublin hallmark for that year.
(*bottom left*) The Secretary's Badge. No
marks or inscriptions. (*top right*) The
Badge of the King of Arms. (*bottom right*)
A gold Knight's Badge, early 19th century.

(*above*) A Collar and Badge made for the Royal Installation of 1821. It bears the Dublin hallmark for that year,
and the reverse of each rose is stamped with the name
'Browne'.

(*right*) The Riband, Star and Badge of a Knight. The
Star was made by West and Son c.1860-1880. The Badge
was made in the second half of the 19th century.

6. The Star of the 3rd Earl of Limerick (No. 112) K.P. 1892. Silver and enamel, no hallmark or inscription, probably made by West and Son. Size 82mm x 82mm.

The insignia worn by the Earl of Shaftesbury (No. 4) K.P. 1911. The Badge was made by West and Son of Dublin in 1910. The Collar probably of the same date.

8. The insignia worn by the 9th Earl of Shaftesbury (No. 134) K.P. 1911. A unique style of Badge, probably made for Lord Shaftesbury and worn by him as a Riband Badge.

9. (*above left*) A silver and enamel breast Star of the period 1820-1830. The reverse engraved 'Rundell Bridge and Rundell, Jewellers to His Majesty and the Royal Family.' Gilt pin.

10. (*above*) A plain round gold badge. No marks or inscriptions.

11. (*left*) The Diamond Star of the Earl of Granard (No. 131) K.P. 1909. No hallmarks, the reverse engraved, ' and Son, College Green, Dublin.'

2. A Grand Master's Badge, worn by the Earl of Eglinton and Winton (1852-3, 1858-9)

13. An early 20th century embroidered Mantle Star. Worn by the 2nd Lord Castletown, K.P. 1908. Embroidered Stars were replaced by silvered base metal Stars during the second half of the 19th century. This is an unusually late example.

14. The Crown, Collar and Sceptre of Norroy and Ulster King of Arms. The Crown was made for Norroy King of Arm and bears the London hallmark for 1936-7. The Collar of SS was made for Ulster King of Arms by West and Son of Dublin and bears the Dublin hallmark for 1893-4. The Sceptre was made for Ulster King of Arms by West and Son of Dublin and bears the hallmark for 1907-8.

Chapter Three

RISE AND DECLINE

'Transporting the imagination to the golden days of chivalry and romance'
Irish Times
29 August 1821

IF TEMPLE, OR ANY OF HIS CONTEMPORARIES, had foreseen that the Irish Parliament, the bribing of whose members was the principal function of the Order, was to be abolished 17 years later, it is doubtful if he would have spent so much time and energy bringing it into existence. Nevertheless, for the remainder of the 18th century, the Order continued much on the lines that Temple laid out. The Earl of Northington, Temple's immediate successor, was of the opinion that 'this Honour should be bestowed in the Channel of Great Parliamentary Weight, or to those who shall shew a disposition to support Government by their Activities and Abilities in Parliament'.[1] and accordingly he recommended Lord Carysfort (later 1st Earl of Carysfort) to succeed to the Stall vacant by the death of the Earl of Ely in May 1783. Carysfort was only 32 years old at the time of his appointment, but he was a steady supporter of the government, and in such circumstances, the age of the recipient was not deemed relevant to the award of an honour. Before making Carysfort a K.P. George III wanted a promise from the peer of continued support for the government. But on being told that Carysfort had already been informed that he might expect the honour, the King washed his hands of the business and Lord Sydney wrote to Carysfort telling him that his future support would be expected. The appointment also reveals the considerable influence of the Lord Lieutenant in recommending peers for the Order. In a letter to the King, Sydney urged compliance with Northington's request as it was 'necessary to keep the Lord Lieutenant in tolerably good humour'.[2]

This was typical of the pattern of appointments to the Order, until the end of the 18th century. Peers were selected either as a reward for their past support, or in return for a promise of future support. Very little is known about the internal organisation of the Order at the time. Sir William Hawkins, the Ulster King of Arms who had so successfully claimed his rights to supervise the ceremonial of the Order in 1783, died early in 1787. He was succeeded by one Gerald Fortescue, about whom even less is known. He was a close friend of

19

the Earl of Mornington, K.P., who wrote to the Lord Lieutenant, then the Duke of Rutland, thanking him, and mentioning that 'his appointment is understood to be intended as a provision also for Mr. Fortescue's brother, the naval officer'.[3] We cannot be clear about what exactly was meant by this strange statement, except to say that Gerald Fortescue died in October of the same year at the age of 36, and was succeeded by his older brother, Chichester (later Rear-Admiral Sir Chichester Fortescue), the first of a series of long-serving Ulster Kings of Arms. The post was a fairly lucrative one; the salary amounted to £228 9s. 9d. in 1788.

After much soul searching and long hours of debate, the Irish Parliament voted itself out of existence in 1800. Almost immediately the complexion of appointments to the Order of Saint Patrick began to change. There was now no longer any necessity of filling the vacancies with 'government supporters', and although the politics of the new Knights were inevitably those of the government which recommended them, such phrases such as 'Lord X looks after his tenantry' or 'Lord X is an excellent Irishman' began to greet appointments. The last two appointments to the Order before the enactment of the Act of Union were, as might be expected, supporters of the Union. One of them, the Earl of Altamont, it may be recalled, had pressed his claim to the Order as early as 1783. He was also made Marquess of Sligo, and was elected one of the first 28 Irish Representative Peers to sit in the House of Lords. Earl Conyngham was given £15,000 in cash for the loss of his borough influence, and also elected a Representative Peer. Four other Knights were given United Kingdom Baronies, enabling them to sit in the House of Lords in their own right, and two of them were given Irish Marquessates. But there was one casualty: Sir Richard St George, M.P. for Athlone since 1789, had been Secretary of the Order of Saint Patrick since 1793. He took a firm stand against the Act of Union, to the extent of declining a peerage, and was dismissed from office. He lived on for more than half a century, dying in 1851 at the age of 86, being then one of the few survivors of the Irish Parliament.

The Viceroy during these proceedings was the distinguished soldier, Lord Cornwallis, who found himself in the position of having to dispense patronage and shower honours to an extent that no Lord Lieutenant before him had had to do. He recorded his feelings with some asperity. In a letter to the Prime Minister he observed, 'The political jobbing of this country gets the better of me. It has ever been the wish of my life to avoid this dirty business, and I am now involved in it beyond all bearing . . . How I long to kick those whom my public duty obliges me to court! . . . My occupation is now of the most unpleasant nature, negotiating and jobbing with the most corrupt people under heaven. I despise and hate myself every hour, for engaging in such dirty work'.[4]

Either to distract himself from such unsavoury tasks, or to distract the people of Ireland from the loss of their Parliament, or perhaps because there were now five Uninstalled Knights of the Order, Cornwallis decided to hold an Installation ceremony. It was the first since the Installation of the Founder Knight in 1783, and the five Knights appointed since that date, beginning with the Earl of Carysfort from as far back as 1784, were still waiting to be assigned stalls in the Cathedral. The heavy cost of the Installations appears to have been the principal reason for the infrequency with which they took place. The practice grew up of holding the ceremony only after several Knights were waiting for their stalls. This meant that a period of up to 10 years might elapse between the appointment of a Knight, and his installation in the Cathedral. Were it not for the fact that many K.P.s were comparatively young at the time of their nomination, several might well have died before being installed. The Earl of Clermont, for example, was appointed and invested in 1795, at the age of 72, but not installed until 1800 at the age of seventy-eight. In practice, Installations were held roughly at 10-year intervals, in 1800, in 1809, and in 1819. The Installation of 1821 marked the occasion of the visit of George IV to Ireland; and, after a long period of dormancy, the sixth and last Installation was held in 1868. Apart from the cost, the ceremony also involved considerable interior reorganisation of the Cathedral, which argued against it being a frequent event. The Dean and Chapter, mindful of the dispute in 1783, were careful to state in 1800 that the alterations to the interior should be made 'without any expence whatever to the Chapter'.[5] They further stipulated that the government should restore the Cathedral to its original state, immediately after the Installation.

With minor amendments, the ceremonial on each occasion followed the pattern set in 1783. A carriage procession conveyed the Grand Master and the Knights from the Castle to the Cathedral, where they were received by members of the Chapter and the Officers of the Order. The Grand Master and the Installed Knights wore Mantles and Collars, the Uninstalled Knights wearing only Surcoats. The ceremony began with the choir singing 'Zadok the Priest', after which the Sword, Mantle and Collar of each of the Uninstalled Knights was brought in by Ulster King of Arms, and his attendant Heralds and Pursuivants. Each was invested in turn with the Insignia by the Chancellor and the Registrar, and then conducted to his stall. His titles were formally proclaimed by Ulster, and his Banner presented at the altar. After this had been completed, the choir sang a Te Deum (in 1800, Handel's 'Dettingen'), and the Knights returned to the Castle for a banquet. 'The forms of introduction, splendour of the habits and general pomp accompanying this grand spectacle (of which a description would give but a *maigre* and inadequate idea) rendered it interesting to a vast assemblage of the Nobility and Gentry'.[6]

The Third Installation of 1809 was apparently held at the request of the Uninstalled Knights, who jointly petitioned the Duke of Richmond—then Lord Lieutenant—requesting that an Installation should be held as soon as possible. The Duke, not wishing to make a decision on his own, referred the matter to the King. In itself the incident is probably not worth recording since the King readily granted their request, but the significance lies in the fact that this was the only occasion when the Knights, or at least a good number of them, acting together, petitioned the Grand Master to uphold their right to be installed. The event was unparalleled until 1908, when the Knights petitioned the Sovereign at the height of the Crown Jewels affair (see below, Chapter Five).

The conspicuous use of Irish materials for the habits of the Knights, and the dresses of their ladies, provoked a great deal of favourable comment from the press, which saw the occasion as providing much needed employment for the weavers of Dublin. The Duchess of Richmond was applauded for appearing in a sky blue tabbinet dress and a tiara of Irish diamonds. Even the correspondent of the normally critical *Dublin Evening Post* wrote, 'Nothing in the eyes of the spectators added more effect than the reflexion that all they saw was Irish—they looked upon the Duchess as the patroness of the Irish arts, as the benefactor of the decayed artists, as setting a truly patriotic useful example to the higher ranks of this country . . . A proud day indeed it was for Ireland—all the rank fashion and beauty of the country were contained within the walls of the Cathedral—and all dressed in the manufacture of their country . . . about 300 ladies vied each other in displaying the beauties of the Irish loom—never in our eyes did the beauty of our countrywomen appear to greater advantage to give an idea of the benefit conferred on our poor weavers'.[7]

The temporary seating erected for the Installation of 1809 so impressed the Dean and Chapter that they resolved that prior to the next installation, the Dean should ask the government to erect the seating 'in a permanent manner so to remain'.[8] The Cathedral Minutes record that this cost £446 1s. 11d. in 1809, with a further charge of £181 15s. 0d. for replacing the old pews after the ceremony, and the Chapter, concerned to save every penny, saw the opportunity to provide the Cathedral with new seating at no cost to themselves. Whether the Dean did approach the government in 1819 is not recorded, but it is probable that the request was received favourably. The government would have been spared an item of heavy expenditure on future occasions, quite apart from the benefit to the Cathedral.

Rear-Admiral Sir Chichester Fortescue (who had succeeded Sir William Hawkins as Ulster King of Arms in 1788, after his brother Gerald had briefly occupied the post for six months) died in March 1820 at the age of sixty-nine. He had not been active in the affairs of the Order for some time, and his successor, Sir William Betham, Athlone Pursuivant and Deputy Ulster King of Arms since 1807, had supervised the arrangements for the installation in the previous year. Betham's appointment as Athlone began a connection between his family and the Order which lasted until 1890. He was the first Ulster King of Arms to appoint members of his family to the junior offices of the Order, initiating a policy which was to be continued by his successor, Sir Bernard Burke. His sons, Molyneux and Sheffield, were made Junior Pursuivants, and they rose through the ranks to become Cork Herald and Dublin Herald respectively. Molyneux was appointed a Junior Pursuivant in 1820 at the age of seven, and promoted first to Athlone Pursuivant and subsequently to Cork Herald in 1829 at the age of sixteen. His younger brother, Sheffield, was appointed Dublin Herald in 1833, also at the tender age of sixteen.

The visit of George IV to Ireland in 1821 provided Betham with the responsibility of organising another Installation, only two years since the last. It was to be the only one at which the Sovereign of the Order presided in person. Furthermore, it was the first visit to Ireland by a reigning monarch since 1690, and the King's presence provoked great demonstrations of loyalty. The *Post* recorded that the balconies of houses along the route of the procession to the Cathedral 'were filled with lovely females, in the bright blue costume, one of whom moved a flag as the Procession passed, bearing the following inscription in gold letters:—The Sons and Daughters of Erin hail their King'.[9]

A total of nine new Knights were appointed on this occasion; three to fill the existing vacancies, and a further six Extra Knights to celebrate the King's visit. The plan was that they should be absorbed into the ranks of the regular Knights as vacancies arose. One of the six was the Lord Lieutenant and Grand Master, Earl Talbot, a rather inept administrator whose service in Ireland from 1817 to 1821 was rendered personally difficult by the deaths of first his son, and then his wife. His sole legacy seems to have been a large stock of Ayrshire cattle, store sheep and horses which were auctioned off in Dublin after his departure. He was the first of only two Grand Masters to be appointed Knights of the Order. The King being present, Talbot's presence as Grand Master was not needed, and he took his place as one of the Knights. A measure of Talbot's inefficiency can be seen in the fact that Betham was forced to write to him only 10 weeks before the Installation, asking who, exactly, was to be installed.

As with preceding Installations, the Dean and Chapter formally surrendered the Cathedral to Sir William Betham. Unfortunately, the ceremony was marred by one or two upsets, and by the end of the day, Betham's patience had been sorely tried.

The Lord Mayor of Dublin wrote to Betham claiming the right to be present *ex-officio*, attended by his Sheriffs and Chaplain, without tickets. He demanded a particular seat—which happened to be the one Betham had assigned to the Lord Chancellor of Ireland, as head of the temporal nobility. The Lord Mayor had consulted the Dean who had evidently given his approval, because Betham maintained later that 'the Dean had no right whatever to assign places to any one or to give the slightest order on the subject of the preparations further than concerned his own closet'.[10] Betham held that the Church was in the County of Dublin, and therefore outside the jurisdiction of the Lord Mayor. On the day before the Installation, Betham sent word that he opposed the Lord Mayor's desire. His Lordship and the Sheriffs had been sent ordinary tickets of admission and that was that. However, by some means the Lord Mayor gained admission and seated himself in his desired place. Betham was furious. He was determined that the Lord Mayor's action out of his jurisdiction should not set a precedent. 'I was under the painful necessity', he wrote later, 'of remonstrating on the spot with His Lordship upon his intrusion and to declare to him openly before the whole assemblage there collected that his being there was an intrusion, that he had no right to be in that honourable situation or to take precedence of the peers. His Lordship refused to go away, stating that the Liberty of St Patrick's, although in the County was part of the Liberties of the City of Dublin'.[11] Who won this battle of words is unfortunately unrecorded.

On the morning of the Installation the congregation started to arrive at the Cathedral before 7.00 a.m., although the Service was not due to begin until three hours later. At 9.00, one Chief Constable Farrell discovered a man, apparently a bricklayer's labourer, taking two tenpenny pieces to admit a person into the Cathedral by a door which was reserved for the King, his Household and the Knights. He promptly turned the person so admitted out, and got Mr. Maguire, the sexton, to place an authorised person in charge of the gate.

The ceremony must have been one of the most spectacular sights ever to be seen in Dublin, and was the nearest Ireland ever came to having a coronation. Somewhat surprisingly, a number of Knights asked to be excused attendance— the Earl of Carysfort pleaded his very advanced age (70 years) and a severe chronic disorder; the Earl of Shannon was unable to be in Ireland; the Marquess of Ely begged to be excused; the Marquess of Sligo wrote from Paris that he had a severe indisposition; and the Marquess of Waterford was also ill.

It is a matter of great regret that there are no surviving illustrations of the occasion. The fancy Under Habits ordered by the King for the occasion sound more appropriate to a comic opera, in an age accustomed to functional clothing. The King wore a richly trimmed silver tissue coat, shoes of white kid skin with large white rosettes and diamond clasps, trunk silk hose and large knee rosettes of light blue ribbon and silver points. He wore a black velvet hat, with a diamond button and loop, and black and white plumes of feathers, and over all this, the Collar of the Order and the Mantle, which the *Post* remarks was 'of great extent'.[12]

The Knights wore Mantles with large trains 'which rendered their stepping backward gracefully, and without tripping, a matter of some difficulty',[13] and Hats covered with a profusion of crimson, blue and white ostrich feathers. This Installation was the last occasion on which these cumbersome things were worn. They were never worn at Investitures, and although the revised Statutes of 1905 still mention them, they passed into oblivion after 1821, never again to be seen at a ceremony of the Order. We have a good idea of what they looked like from the illustrations of the King of Hanover, and Earl Talbot, but none of them have survived the passage of time.

Despite, or perhaps, even because of all these frills and fripperies, Dublin was charmed by the whole affair. The presence of her King, with her Knights, in her Cathedral, not to mention the presence of Prince Esterhazy, the Austrian Ambassador, overawed the Dublin newspapers, one of which declared: 'It is

impossible to conceive of a more powerfully impressive combination of the
Religious and State ceremonial than that afforded at this moment. The glitter
and variety of rich and splendid dresses—the Military Uniforms, and various
Orders, worn by Officers and others—the precious jewels which sparkled in
Ladies' headdresses, pendant to their ears, and on their snowy necks and bosoms—
the glare of the dresses of the Knights and their Esquires—the profusion of
feathers to be seen on every side moving in graceful curves, delighted the eye,
whilst the pealing of the organ, the finest toned in Europe, mingling celestial
sounds with the vocal harmony of the Choir, charmed the ear even to satiety.
The ceremony was of matchless splendour and magical effect, removing for a
moment the curtains of Time, and transporting the imagination to the golden
days of Chivalry and Romance'.[14]

The King's visit was preceded a few days earlier by the death of his wife,
Queen Caroline. The history of their unfortunate marriage is too well known to
need repeating, but after the report of her death in black-edged newspapers,
the following announcement appeared on 18 August in the *Post*: 'It is not
expected by his Majesty that Persons shall appear in mourning on the day of his
Public Entry into Dublin, nor on any of the days of Public Ceremonials or
Festivities during the period of his Majesty's residence in Ireland'.[15]

After the service was over there was such chaos that an investigation was
ordered into the arrangements made by the police. Betham complained that
the police had neglected the printed regulations, and attributed responsibility
for the confusion and disorder to them alone. Alderman Darley, the Head
Police Officer, replied that the magistrates had not received the printed regulations,
and therefore could not give official orders to the police about the arrangements
for the carriages. The real cause was identified when the dependable Chief
Constable Farrell reported that on the departure of the King from the Cathedral
'all the Knights were anxious to get to their carriages which could not be done
readily as every avenue leading to the church was so blocked with carriages and the
servants being heated with liquor and anxious to get their families into the
coaches that I had a great deal to do to prevent many of the reins being cut'.[16]
Thinking it might be needed, Betham had left his carriage at the south entrance
to the Cathedral during the Service, only to find that four mounted police had
attacked his servants and beaten them. It is hardly to be wondered that the Chief
Constable adds to his report, 'the language of Sir William Betham to me was most
abusive and insulting'.[17]

After this great peak in 1821, the Order entered into what can only be
described as a period of decline, which lasted for more than 30 years. The
appointments of the six Extra Knights by George IV, and their gradual absorption
into the Order, prevented any further appointments during his 10-year reign, and
at the time of the accession of William IV in 1830, two still remained—the Earl
of Roden and the Earl of Courtown. The King, emulating his predecessor,
appointed a further four Extra Knights on the occasion of his coronation, raising

the number back to six, and the total number of Knights of the Order to twenty-one. In view of his age, the probability of more than six vacancies occurring in his reign was remote and he was faced with the likelihood that he would appoint no further Knights. Accordingly, little more than a year later, a decision was made, probably by the King, though this is not certain, partially to revise the Statutes and to end the anomalous situation whereby the Order had half as many Knights again as it was supposed to have.

By a Warrant dated 24 January 1833, the maximum number of Knights was permanently increased from 15 to twenty-two. One Extra Knight having succeeded to a vacancy in 1832, this left a total of 20 Knights, and two vacancies, which were filled by the appointments of Marquess Conyngham and the Earl of Leitrim. The same Warrant also ordered that Knights might be dispensed from the ceremony of Installation, yet wear all the insignia and enjoy all the rights and privileges of Installed Knights. William IV enjoyed the reputation of being a thrifty and cost-cutting King, anxious to avoid the extravagant behaviour of his brother. His coronation, costing a fraction of that of George IV, was the most notable example. Indeed, the King is known to have wished to do without a coronation altogether. The Installations were very costly to stage, and there is good reason to suppose that this archaic and colourful ceremony was a casualty of the King's economy drive. Although the language of the Warrant is permissory rather than mandatory, the precedent was set, and with the exception of the Prince of Wales in 1868, all further Knights received a dispensation from Installation until 1871, when the ceremony was finally abolished. Article 5 of the Statutes was amended a few months later to give recognition to the fact, and at the same time, cosmetic changes were made to four other articles relating to the duties of the Grand Master and Genealogist, and the method of electing new Knights. It seems a pity that no thorough-going revision of the Statutes was attempted at this stage when a good opportunity presented itself, and the Order drifted on with this collection of unworkable rules ignored by Knights and Officers alike.

With the disappearance of the Installation ceremony, there was now no established method of investing new Knights with the Collar. Instead of including this in the ceremony of investiture, the new Knight was simply provided with a Collar at a later stage by Ulster King of Arms, and by the Warrant dispensing him from Installation, he was granted full power to wear it.

For the next 20 years or more, the Investiture ceremony was also shorn of something of its grandeur. With rare exceptions, the ceremony was usually held at the more comfortable and intimate surroundings of the Viceregal Lodge in Phoenix Park, or even dispensed with on occasions, and it was not until the popular viceroyalty of the Earl of Carlisle (1855-1858) that it was restored to its traditional setting in Saint Patrick's Hall. Appointments to the Order were still generally made from among the friends of the government in power, but the recognition of merit was beginning to play a small part in the choices.

There were two vacancies in March 1833, and, writing to the Lord Lieutenant, the Marquess of Anglesey, the Prime Minister, Lord Grey remarked: 'I have determined one in favour of Lord Conyngham who will be invested on Wednesday—the other I will take time to consider but I incline to Lord Kenmare—Nothing can be better than Lord Leitrim, but he has lately had an Irish peerage, and we should look to an equal distribution of the good things among our friends'.[18] Most appointments were greeted favourably and without cynicism. On the appointment of the Earl of Clare and Marquess of Ormonde, *The Times* commented that 'both are excellent landlords, and, as far as practicable, constant residents in their native country'.[19]

The King initiated a custom, which appears to have lapsed at his death in 1837, of entertaining the Knights and Officers of the Order of Saint Patrick to dinner at Saint James's Palace, together with the Knights and Officers of the Order of the Thistle. The dinner was generally held in May of each year, the last occasion being 7 May 1836, and the King appeared wearing the Collar and Star of each Order. Past Grant Masters of the Patrick were invited, and in 1834, four of them were present. A complicated series of toasts in strict order of precedence were given at the end of each dinner:

1. The King
2. The Queen and the Royal Family
3. The Duke of Cumberland, K.P. (senior Royal Knight of the Patrick)
4. The Duke of Sussex, K.T. (senior Royal Knight of the Thistle)
5. The Knights of the Thistle (drunk by the Knights of Saint Patrick)
6. The Knights of Saint Patrick (drunk by the Knights of the Thistle)
7. The Grand Master of the Order of Saint Patrick
8. The Past Grant Masters of the Order of Saint Patrick
9. The absent Knights of both Orders
10 The Prelate, Chancellor and Registrar of the Order of Saint Patrick
11. The Earl of Kinnoull, Lord Lyon King of Arms
12. Ulster King of Arms and Sir William Woods, Acting Secretary of the Thistle

No doubt considerable joviality ensued from such an excessive number of toasts.

Little else of note appears to have taken place in these quiescent years. The Register of the Order preserved at the Central Chancery of the Orders of Knighthood has nothing but blank pages for the years from 1821 until 1853, being the period during which Sir William Betham was King of Arms. An interesting item in the appendices to the Statutes records that a certain John O'Flaherty, one of the Junior Pursuivants, was removed from office in 1823, 'having taken Holy Orders'. Of him and his subsequent ministry, nothing further is known.

Chapter Four

DISESTABLISHMENT AND SECULARIZATION

'It is now reconstituted with a more intelligent perception of the great
social and political changes which the world has since experienced'

The Times
4 August 1871

THE APPOINTMENT OF Sir Bernard Burke as Ulster King of Arms and Knight
Attendant of the Order in 1853 began a connection between the Burke family
and the Order of Saint Patrick, which lasted until his son, Sir Henry Farnham
Burke, Genealogist from 1889, died in 1930. Burke, who was only 39 years
old at the time of his appointment was a scion of a family distinguished for its
genealogical and heraldic attainments, and probably best remembered for the
massive red and gold volume *Burke's Peerage,* which appeared annually from
the 1840s until the beginning of the Second World War. Burke was without doubt
the most distinguished of the seven Kings of Arms of the Order. Apart from
being a prolific author, he was a prominent and indispensable figure in the
arrangement of the ceremonies and pageants of the Viceregal Court, and had a
grasp of his subject perhaps greater than any of his predecessors. The investitures
of the Order which had sagged in dignity and ceremonial since the 1830s were
revived and restored to their proper setting in Saint Patrick's Hall; a new
atmosphere of efficiency began to pervade the office of Ulster King of Arms.
There was little he could do to remove the sons of Sir William Betham from their
offices in the Order, had he wanted to, and Molyneux and Sheffield Betham
continued as Cork and Dublin Heralds until their deaths in 1880 and 1890.
However, when the post of Athlone Pursuivant fell vacant in 1883, on the death
of the 90-year-old Captain Robert Smith, Burke appointed his second son,
Bernard Louis, to the post, and on the death of the latter in July 1892, his
youngest son, John Edward. His eldest son, Henry Farnham, already Somerset
Herald in the College of Arms in London was appointed Genealogist of the
Order in 1889. This nepotism was not without parallel—the Woods family
virtually ran the day-to-day business of the Order of the Bath for most of the
19th century. But it presented difficulties for his successors, Sir Arthur Vicars,
who was faced with the unpleasant task of removing John Edward Burke from
office in 1899, on the grounds that he could not be relied upon to attend investitures of the Order, even when summoned. The two most significant events

28

in the history of the Order during Burke's reign as King of Arms were the Installation of the Prince of Wales in 1868, and the secularization of the Order resulting from the disestablishment of the Church of Ireland in 1871.

Analysing the root causes of the Irish problem in 1844, Benjamin Disraeli had defined four areas: 'a starving population, an absentee aristocracy, and an alien church, and in addition, the weakest executive in the world'.[1] The position of the Church of Ireland, the 'alien church', was growing steadily weaker. Realistically assessing the needs of the Church, Parliament had sharply reduced the numbers of Archbishops and Bishops in 1833. By the late 1860s demands from increasingly important quarters for the disestablishment and disendowment of the Church of Ireland grew louder. At the same time, the Irish Administration received a severe battering in terms of publicity from the ill-organised and ill-equipped Fenian Rising of March 1867. The result of both was that the sixth and last Installation of the Order of Saint Patrick was held on 18 April 1868, after 37 years of dispensations.

The Marquess of Abercorn (Lord Lieutenant, 1866–1868) conceived the idea that the residence of a member of the Royal Family in Ireland, for at least part of the year, would provoke demonstrations of loyalty; provide a focal point for unity; and give a kind of moral support for the administration in the wake of the Fenian troubles. The only problem standing in the way of this solution was the Queen. Queen Victoria was not well disposed towards Ireland and the Irish, and she was decidedly antipathetic to the question of a royal residence there. Furthermore, there was no question of her visiting Ireland, or anywhere else for that matter, since the death of the Prince Consort seven years earlier which had sent her into virtual seclusion. The whole matter therefore had to be handled very carefully if the Queen's strong opposition was not to be aroused. Abercorn settled on the plan of inviting the Prince of Wales to Ireland for a week, with the intention of persuading the Queen to allow a longer visit later in the year should it prove successful, and he wisely enlisted the support of Disraeli, to whom the Queen was devoted. And what better a culmination to this visit than the appointment of the Prince as a K.P., and his Installation in Saint Patrick's, the National Cathedral of Ireland? After years of neglect and decay during which it had fallen into a near ruinous state, the Cathedral had been carefully restored in the 1860s at great personal expense, by Sir Benjamin Guinness of the brewing family. To admit the Prince to the National Order in the National Cathedral could prove to be an enormously valuable exercise in public relations.

The first step was to approach the Prince of Wales directly on the subject. Abercorn went to see him and explained his plans: 'I spoke to him very strongly indeed on the good that it would do . . . I spoke to him about the Patrick Ribbon and the function in the Cathedral. He seemed quite pleased with the idea and said he had not got the Patrick, and would like to have it'.[2] He planned to exploit the visit to the full. 'I should think a day's hunting, 2 days Racing,

The Installation of H.R.H. the Prince of Wales (later King Edward VII) as a Knight of Saint Patrick on 18 Ap
1868 in Saint Patrick's Cathedral, Dublin. The Prince is standing on the left, the Marquess of Abercorn, Lord
Lieutenant and Grand Master, is seated in the Dean's Stall on the right. (From the *Illustrated London News*)

the Installation, and a Review would pretty nearly do him'.[3] With the Prince in favour, Abercorn wrote to the Queen telling her that an Installation in the newly-restored Cathedral would give enormous pleasure to the Irish people. Disraeli supported his request, saying that there was 'a great yearning in Ireland for the occasional presence and inspiration of royalty',[4] adding that the Sovereign had spent only 21 days in Ireland in the last two centuries. He ended by cautiously suggesting that the Prince might take up residence in Ireland for a longer period, later in the year, avoiding all mention of a permanent residence. But the Queen was not to be persuaded. Although she pronounced herself in favour of a week's visit, and the Installation, she firmly rejected any idea of a royal residence in Ireland, on the grounds that similar pretentions might be aroused in Wales and even the Colonies. Furthermore, no one would dream of going to Ireland for health and relaxation, although thousands went to Scotland. Ever suspicious of the Prince's activities, she cautioned that 'any encouragement of his constant love of roaming about and not keeping at home or near the Queen, is most honestly and seriously to be deprecated'.[5] When the Prince was foolish enough to mention that his visit coincided with the annual races at Punchestown, she insisted that he should not be seen to sanction or encourage them as they had 'ruined so many young men, and broken the hearts thereby of so many kind and fond parents'.[6]

The date was set for 18 April, and for the sixth and last time, Saint Patrick's Cathedral was turned upside-down for an Installation of the Order. Services were held intermittently, and public worship on Easter Day was limited to a celebration of Holy Communion at 8.00 a.m. The Choir was temporarily transferred to the rival Christ Church Cathedral, some 200 yards away, where sung services were held daily at 3.00 p.m. The usual galleries were erected in the Choir and the Nave to allow greater numbers to attend and, rather theatrically, the west doors of the Cathedral were removed and replaced by a scarlet curtain. The disruption to the life and work of the Cathedral were considerable, but, as the *Clerical Journal* observed: 'No-one, however, grumbles at the Dean of St Patrick's for abdicating his functions temporarily in favour of Sir Bernard Burke. The latter gentleman is well known for his skill and taste and is eminently popular . . . and the public in general is so rejoiced at the Prince's visit as to wink at any ecclesiastical enormity'.[7]

Not every one was pleased with the venue. The *Daily Telegraph* remarked condescendingly that the Cathedral looked 'naked, cold and cheerless. The proportions are good and the nave is long; and when you have said this you have have said pretty well all that need be about it. Owing to the recentness of the restoration, the church has no air of antiquity; and the two mouldering banners, which have been carried by British troops in the wars of Marlborough and which floated in their tatters over the north transept, seemed well-nigh the oldest objects in that modernised shrine'.[8] But for the ceremony itself there was fulsome praise on all sides, and it was conducted with as much magnificence as its five predecessors. The Prince was enthusiastically praised for his desire to identify himself with something as 'truly national, and therefore most highly prized by the Irish people',[9] as the Order of Saint Patrick. The train of Lord Abercorn's Mantle was borne by three young pages, one of whom, Lord Frederic Hamilton, recalled the event in his memoirs published 52 years later: 'I remember it chiefly on account of the bitter north east wind blowing. The five pages drove together in an open carriage, and received quite an ovation from the crowd, but no-one had thought of providing them with overcoats. Silk stockings, satin knee breeches and lace ruffles are very inadequate protection against an Arctic blast and we arrived at the Cathedral stiff and torpid with cold'.[10]

Though there is no evidence that it played any part in the desire to hold an Installation, the question of the future of the Church of Ireland was beginning to cast a shadow over its relations with the Order. Throughout the 1860s, calls were repeatedly heard for the disestablishment and disendowment of the Church, and the results of the census of 1861 confirmed what many had long suspected. In a population of 5¾ million, adherents of the Church of Ireland numbered just under 700,000, with the Roman Catholic Church accounting for 4½ million. The change had long been wanted by the Catholic Church and the nonconformist minority, and it was rapidly becoming a hot political issue. The government of Benjamin Disraeli was defeated on a proposition by Gladstone to end the privileged state of the Church of Ireland, and the ensuing election was fought on the issue of disestablishment. So strongly did the Roman Catholic Church feel on the matter that the Archiepiscopal Vicariate of Dublin felt it necessary to issue a statement before the Installation, saying that the diocesan authorities considered the ceremony as purely civil in its character and object, and therefore not coming within the prohibition against Catholics assisting at acts of religious worship other than those of the Catholic Church. The exclusively Protestant nature of the Order had ended with the appointment of the 8th Earl of Fingall in 1821, and a small number of Catholics had been appointed in succeeding years. There were two Roman Catholic Knights in 1868, the 9th Earl of Fingall, and the 7th Earl of Granard, and the increasingly interdenominational nature of the membership of the Order made the continued presence of *ex-officio* Anglican Officers something of an anomaly.

The passing of the Irish Church Act in 1869 disestablished and disendowed the Church of Ireland from 1 January 1871, reducing it to the status of a voluntary body. Within six months, Abercorn's successor, Earl Spencer (Lord Lieutenant, 1868–1874) wrote to Gladstone proposing the inevitable changes in the constitution of the Order: 'It is clear that for an Irish State Order, these Heads of the Protestant Episcopalian Church have no longer any special right to hold office: nor can the Protestant Cathedral be the official place for the Stalls of the Knights. The difficulties of introducing clerical Officers from the different sects in Ireland are so great that the only course to pursue is to follow the precedent of, I think, the Order of the Thistle, and certainly of the Star of India, and have only lay Officers in the Order'.[11]

The Royal Warrant giving effect to this 'secularization' of the Order bears all the marks of Sir Bernard Burke's desire for efficiency. As well as the removal of the Church Officers, several other Offices were dispensed with or amalgamated. The Warrant guaranteed the rights of all the existing Officers, but decreed the following changes in the event of the death or resignation of the existing holders: the Office of Chancellor was to be transferred to the Chief Secretary of Ireland; the Office of Registrar was to be amalgamated with the Ulster King of Arms; and the Offices of Prelate, Genealogist, Cork Herald, Dublin Herald, and Junior Pursuivant were abolished outright. The ceremony of Installation was discontinued (though by special desire of the Queen, the Banners of the Knights existing at January 1871 were to continue hanging in the Cathedral). The 'home' of the Order was transferred to Saint Patrick's Hall, Dublin Castle, where the banners were to be hung in future.

One by one the named Officers of the Order died, beginning with Sir William Leeson, the Genealogist, in March 1885, and ending with the last of the Junior Pursuivants, George Frith Barry, in 1891. Information relating to the Junior Pursuivants is less than satisfactory. There is no complete list of them, and in several cases their complete names and dates of office are unknown. They appear to have been little more than messengers appointed at extremely early ages by Ulster King of Arms, and their disappearance made little difference to the Order. Burke himself felt it to be a nominal and superfluous office: 'It was perfectly useless and very troublesome. No duties were attached and there was no connection whatsoever between it and the heraldic staff in Ireland. In point of fact it had nothing to do with heraldry and genealogy'.[12] Burke no doubt considered the Heralds to be equally superfluous, and the amalgamation of the office of Registrar with Ulster was only a belated recognition of a situation which had long existed. Why he maintained the Office of Secretary when he was cutting out everything else is not clear. Ulster had always conducted the correspondence of the Order, and the post could safely have disappeared without any noticeable loss. But the office of Genealogist was missed after the death of Sir William Leeson in 1885, and four years later, Henry Farnham Burke, Sir Bernard's eldest son, was appointed Genealogist and Deputy Ulster. The necessity of having a second High Officer of the Order, who could fill the place of Ulster in case of absence or illness, had become apparent.

At the same time, Lord Spencer recommended to Gladstone the necessity of taking some action on the question of the fees paid by Knights on admission to the Order. The fees now totalled more than £500 (quite apart from the cost to each Knight of providing himself with a Mantle and a Star) and the government was experiencing 'difficulties' in filling vacancies in the Order due to the heavy charges. The Fees were made up as follows:

(*See Table at top of next page*)

	£	s.	d.
The Registrar	25	0	0
The Secretary	25	0	0
The Genealogist	25	0	0
The King of Arms	25	0	0
The Usher	20	0	0
Two Heralds	20	0	0
Four Pursuivants	20	0	0
Similar fees on dispensation	160	0	0
Queen's Letter and Sign Manual fees of, application for, registration	21	0	0
Certificate of noblesse of blood	10	10	0
Helmet and Crest in Stall	8	8	0
Sword in Stall	3	13	6
Banner over Stall	21	0	0
Plate of Arms in Stall	6	16	6
Ulster for superintendence	21	0	0
Fees to the Officers of Arms and His Excellency's Household on receiving the Honor of Knighthood	75	0	0
Purse, to the Dean of St Patrick's for the Poor	21	0	0
	£508	7	0

In future it was decided that each Knight should pay a flat sum of £300 to the Treasury, who would give yearly allowances to the Officers instead of the individual fees on the appointment of each Knight. The Officers pronounced themselves satisfied with this arrangement, but they claimed that a vacancy in the Order on the death of the Earl of Roden in 1870 had been deliberately left unfilled for nearly 18 months until after the introduction of the new system. They addressed a petition to the Grand Master, claiming that they were entitled to receive the usual fees on the appointment of Roden's successor, Viscount Powerscourt, in August 1871. Burke was the only Officer who did not sign, but he agreed to forward the letter. The Treasury, realising that its position was untenable, agreed to pay the Officers their fees, less a 3½ per cent. deduction.

The papers were quick to applaud the abolition of the religious side of the Order. *The Times* remarked rather pompously that the original religious foundation had been a 'mistake', and the Order was now placed on a wider and more popular basis, being no longer limited to any sect or creed—not that it had been for several decades, the first Roman Catholic being admitted in 1821. 'It is now reconstituted with a more intelligent perception of the great social and political changes which the world has since experienced, and is made more in harmony with the liberal spirit of the times'.[13] The disappearance of the religious ceremonial left the Investiture as the only ceremonial admission of Knights to the Order. For most of the history of the Order, it had been overshadowed by the pomp and circumstance of the Installation, and during the 1830s to 1850s it was scaled down to a very informal gathering at the Viceregal Lodge in Phoenix Park. Burke had done a lot to revive its formality, restoring it to its proper setting in

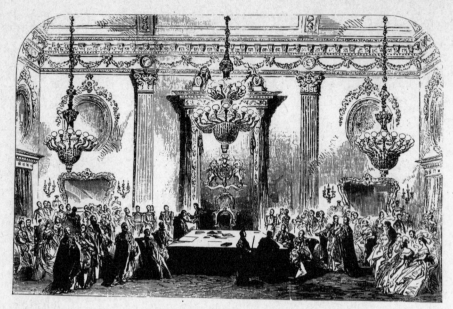

The investiture of the Earl of Gosford and Lord Cremorne (later Earl of
Dartrey) in the Throne Room, Dublin Castle, 21 April 1855.

Saint Patrick's Hall, and after 1871, both he and Spencer decided to elevate
its status, to the extent that it would replace the old Installations in popular
esteem. The first investiture after the passing of the Church Act was held on
2 August 1871, and Burke did his utmost to make the occasion interesting and
imposing. All the resources of the Castle were expended in the production of a
brilliant ceremony.

The investiture was preceded by a sumptuous banquet, the menu of which
has happily survived. Dublin was not London, and Castle banquets were rarely
vehicles for the display of culinary skill or imaginative *haute cuisine*. Food and
style differed very much from one Viceroy to the next. Lord Dudley (1902-5)
was rich, and hated any form of economy. He maintained a brillaint and
extravagant court, spending £80,000 of his own money during his first year of
office. Lord Londonderry (1886-9) hated lengthy dinners and instituted short
meals lasting no more than half an hour. A footman stood behind nearly every
chair, and plates were often whipped away from the guests before they had
finished. If guests stopped to talk, there was every chance they would get nothing
to eat at all. The Knights and their guests were given a choice of stuffed fillets
of turbot, boiled salmon with lobster sauce, souffles of poultry, sweet bread,
fillets of duckling, young turkey, venison, mutton, roast beef, quails, hare,
artichokes, pineapple, and raspberry meringue glacés.

The dinner must have been quite long, since the investiture began at the
nocturnal hour of 11 p.m. It was decided to hold the investitures at night, when

its pomp and splendour could be displayed to best effect. A large table covered with a blue cloth was placed before the Viceregal throne in the Hall. Evergreens and flowers were placed at intervals around the walls. Festoons and garlands looped with blue ribbon were suspended along the galleries and from the chandeliers, and a band of the Grenadier Guards, stationed in the gallery, played a triumphal march as the Knights entered and seated themselves around the table. The new Knights, Viscount Powerscourt and Viscount Southwell, were led in by the Ulster, knighted by the Grand Master, and invested with the Riband and Badge of the Order. The Chapter was then dissolved, and the Knights left the Hall in procession to the sound of the band playing 'St Patrick's Day'. The public investiture of the Order continued, much on these lines as laid down by Burke, up to and including the Royal Investiture of 1911.

After several years of failing health, Sir Bernard Burke died in December 1892 at the age of 78, to be succeeded two months later by Arthur Vicars, a comparatively unknown young man of twenty-nine. Vicars, the son of an English colonel, was born in Warwickshire in 1864. His mother, a member of the Gun-Cunninghame family of County Wicklow, had previously been married to Peirce K. Mahony of Kilmorna in County Kerry. She had two sons by this marriage, and although Arthur was educated in England, he spent his holidays at the Irish country houses belonging to his half brothers, and developed a longing to identify himself with the old Ireland that they represented. His interest in genealogical matters came to the notice of Sir Bernard Burke as early as 1890. Sheffield Betham, the son of Sir William Betham, who had been appointed Dublin Herald as far back as 1833, died on 2 July 1890, and 10 days later, Vicars wrote to Arthur Balfour in somewhat precocious terms applying for the office, despite the fact that it had been scheduled for abolition by the Royal Warrant of 1871. 'The duties of the office are such as I believe I am competent to discharge, requiring as they do, a knowledge of heraldry and the usages of state ceremonials. To this branch of study I have applied myself for several years and I believe I am the only person in Ireland who not being an official has steadily and most exclusively given his attention to the study of heraldry' . . .'[14] Vicars was told that the emoluments to the office had been abolished, and, in any case, the Royal Warrant of 1871 had specifically abolished the office. A less pertinacious man might well have given up in the face of this official negative, but Arthur Vicars was not to be put off so easily, and he pursued the matter over the next three years with a dogged and slightly naïve perseverance. He wrote back saying that he was quite willing to accept the office without any emolument, and as far as the Warrant of 1871 was concerned, the discontinued office of Genealogist had been revived in the previous year. Flustered by this unexpected persistence, the Lord Lieutenant's Private Secretary wrote back stating firmly that His Excellency saw no grounds for reviving any of the offices abolished in 1871.

There the matter rested for eight months until early 1891, when the last surviving Junior Pursuivant, George Frith Barry, died. Vicars wrote again to Balfour on 4 March, asking to be appointed to the post which he called 'St Patrick Pursuivant of Arms'—a quite incorrect description. Again he offered to accept the post without any emolument, and again he quoted the office of Genealogist in regard to the 1871 Warrant. He also added that the Office of Arms in Ireland was lacking in 'dignity and efficiency' compared with the considerable number of Officers in England and Scotland, and that two (Ulster King of Arms and Athlone Pursuivant) was an insufficient number to discharge the duties connected with the Office of Arms. 'I may add', he finished, 'that I am the only professional herald in Ireland not officially connected with Ulster's Office'.[15]

The Private Secretary was irritated by the fact that Vicars was refusing to take no for an answer, and in his reply he enclosed a memorandum by Burke describing the office of Junior Pursuivant as 'nominal and useless'. Vicars wrote back with an astonishing degree of naïvety which bordered on foolhardiness, accepting Burke's opinion, and saying that he could not assume it applied to the post of Dublin Herald as well! The government replied that since Vicars was so keen to be appointed to one or the other of the posts, could he furnish further reasons why the posts should be revived. Vicars listed seven: Sir Bernard Burke was an invalid, unable to attend any of the ceremonies connected with his office, and had had to appoint his eldest son as his deputy, and his younger son, Athlone Pursuivant, never attended the investitures of the Order; the Irish Heraldic establishment had dwindled to two Officers, whereas there were 11 in Scotland and many more in London at the College of Arms, which made the Dublin staff appear insufficient; he was not asking for any emolument so why should there be any objection to revival; the office of Genealogist had been revived, so why not Junior Pursuivant or Dublin Herald, which were more important; Ulster's office was a source of profit to the Exchequer and existed of necessity for public convenience; such offices should be maintained to encourage those studying a branch of knowledge as rare as heraldry—'the state has always recognized its duty to do so';[16] he had made heraldry and genealogy his profession, and was the only such person in Ireland. Vicars continued on a personal note which, on reflection, he might well have excluded. He had reason to believe that Sir Bernard Burke was antagonistic towards him because he felt that to give Vicars any heraldic appointment would encroach upon the monopoly of the Burke family. It appears that two or three years earlier, Vicars had applied and been accepted for the post of Secretary in the Office of Arms. Some days later after his testimonials had arrived, Burke cancelled the appointment saying that he felt they were so extraordinarily high that he did not think he was justified in offering Vicars such a low post.

The government must have been adamant, since Vicars was not appointed to either post. But he was not without influence. He was able to name Lord

Rayleigh, the Attorney General, the Solicitor General and the Chief Secretary in his letters as referees. The government were clearly impressed by his persistence if nothing else. On 23 February 1893, two months after Burke's death, Vicars was appointed Ulster King of Arms, Registrar and Knight Attendant of the Order of Saint Patrick. His only desire was to make the Office, which had run down in the last years under Burke, as efficient as possible. He could not remove Henry Farnham Burke from his office as Genealogist of the Order, but his post as Deputy Ulster was terminated. He also had to endure John Edward Burke, Sir Bernard's youngest son, as Athlone Pursuivant for the next seven years. John Edward Burke had been appointed to the office in July 1892, six months before the death of his father. We know little of his relationship with Vicars, but it cannot have been easy since in 1899 the latter reported to Lord Cadogan (Lord Lieutenant, 1895-1902) that Burke had failed to attend the investiture of Lord Lucan in March, though duly summoned, without giving any reason for his absence. He said that Burke 'cannot be relied upon to efficiently discharge duties in the future',[17] and recommended his removal from office. Vicars could not have foreseen that his own efficiency would be called into question nine years later on a much more serious matter, and that his own dismissal would result.

Chapter Five

ALL CHANGE

'I am very sorry for poor Ulster and should like to do anything I could to help him, but I think appealing to the King against the decision of the Grand Master of the Order is a very serious matter, and would not tend to his advantage.'

Lord Clonbrock
November 1907

IN 1905, A DECISION WAS TAKEN to revise the Statutes of the Order, and at the moment we can say no more, since the files relating to the episode are still closed at the time of writing. It was the first important change in the rules governing the Order since 1871, and the first thorough-going revision of the whole body of Statutes since they were promulgated in 1783. We do not know why or when the decision was taken to embark on such a major upheaval, but there are indications that Vicars influenced the process, which may well have been carried out under his supervision. The original Statutes of 1783, copied from the Statutes of the Order of the Garter, contained so many archaic anomalies that they were virtually inoperable from the moment of their publication. Furthermore, they had been so tampered with over the course of the 19th century that they needed to be read, if at all, in conjunction with a large number of amending Warrants and Ordinances. They were hardly fit documents to govern an Order of Knighthood, and they must have irritated a man like Arthur Vicars, with a preoccupation with tidiness and precision in every detail. Given that nobody except Ulster King of Arms was really affected or bothered by the Statutes, it seems likely that the revision was begun on his initiative.

The new Statutes, published on 29 July 1905, generally codified in print what was already happening in practice. There were very few innovations, and the whole process is best seen as a gigantic tidying-up operation. Technically, the Sovereign was empowered to appoint and nominate Knights to the Order for the first time. This had been the practice since the beginning, although the original Statutes provided a complicated machinery of election by the other Knights. The Grand Master was now officially allowed to wear the Badge of the Order, and his magnificent diamond insignia were fully described in Article XII. Dispensations from investiture were now officially allowed, and the Knights were no longer financially penalised for non-attendance at investitures or non-wearing of insignia. Provision was made for the safe storage of insignia, which had caused so much trouble in the early years of the 19th century, and new Knights were required to sign a receipt for insignia entrusted to their care. Ulster King of Arms was defined as the 'executive Officer' of the Order, and the list of his functions (Article XXVII) made it abundantly clear that he alone was responsible for the care and arrangement of the Order, its insignia and its ceremonies. Only one anomaly was retained: Article X dealing with the robes and insignia of the Knights described in detail the cumbersome Hat, and the elaborate Surcoat and Under-habit, none of which had seen the light of day since George IV prescribed them for the great Installation in 1821. Why these comical costumes should be retained when everything else was being cut out is not clear.

The few innovations may be mentioned quite briefly. Provision was made (Article V) for the appointment of foreign princes as Honorary Knights Companions, although none were ever appointed, and it is extremely unlikely that any would have been, had the Order survived. Foreign Heads of State are invariably given the Garter, the G.C.B., the G.C.M.G., or the G.C.V.O. None have ever been appointed to the Order of the Thistle, with the sole exception of King Olaf V of Norway, due to the historic connections between Norway and Scotland. Such appointments to the Saint Patrick would have been almost inconceivable. Explicit recognition was given to the possibility that commoners might one day be made K.P.s (Article IX), although again, none were ever appointed. Article XXIII made provision for the degradation of Knights who were convicted of treason, cowardice or felony, or 'of any crime derogatory to his honour as a Knight or a Gentleman'.[1] Article XXXVI reduced the sum paid by each Knight on appointment, from £300 to £50. The figure of £300 had been fixed in 1871 when the separate fees payable to each Officer were abolished. It was still an unwarrantably high figure, and Lord Aberdeen (Grand Master, 1905–1915) proposed its reduction. There was some delay before the Treasury eventually authorised the reduction in August 1908. The fee remained at £50 until 1916 when it was raised to £65, to cover the cost of presenting each Knight with a Star, in addition to a Collar and Badge. Article XXIV revived the defunct posts of Dublin Herald and Cork Herald. Perhaps Vicars recalled his own efforts to revive the post of Dublin Herald some 15 years earlier; perhaps he saw them as useful training posts in the world of heraldry and genealogy; or perhaps he simply wanted to increase the size of his little heraldic court, to give it greater dignity. Whatever the reason, he continued the nepotistic practices of his predecessors and appointed his nephew, Peirce Gun Mahony, as Cork Herald, and his close friend, Francis Richard Shackleton, as Dublin Herald.

Within two years of the setting up of this little court over which Vicars, still only 43 years old, had confidently expected to preside happily for many years to come, an event occurred which resulted in the destruction of his career, his ignominious dismissal from office, and his death as an embittered recluse 14 years

The Diamond Star and Badge of the Grand Master. Both are composed of rubies, emeralds and Brazilian diamonds mounted in silver. Made by Rundell, Bridge and Co. of London, in 1830. They were stolen from Dublin Castle in 1907 and have not been recovered.

later. The event has gone down in history as the theft or disappearance of the 'Irish Crown Jewels', and the facts are briefly these. On 6 July 1907, the Messenger of the Office of Arms, one William Stivey, was asked by Vicars to take the Collar which had been worn by the recently deceased Lord de Ros, and lock it in the safe in the Library of the Office. The safe contained five other Collars, and the Grand Master's Diamond Star and Badge. On finding the safe door closed, but unlocked, Stivey reported the matter to Vicars, who came to check the situation. An examination of the contents of the safe proved that the diamond insignia of the Grand Master and the five gold Collars were all missing. The press seized on the description of the diamond insignia as 'Crown Jewels' in Article XII of the Statutes, and referred to them ever after as the 'Irish Crown Jewels', a phrase which by its implications of a fabulous mysterious treasure, had a far greater popular appeal than the correct description, 'Insignia of the Grand Master of the Order of Saint Patrick'. Talk about the latter, and most Irishmen will look at you blankly; talk about the former, and most of them will recall something.

The disappearance of the Jewels has been the subject of three books, one of which reconstructs the theft, the circumstances surrounding it, and the lives of the people involved with considerable detail. There is little to be gained here by exploring the story again, or any of the lurid scandals surrounding it. As far as the stolen items are concerned, it is sufficient to say that they have never been recovered. But the theft had repercussions on the Order and particularly the staff of the Office of Arms. The discovery that the Jewels were missing occurred only days before a state visit to Ireland by King Edward VII, who intended to personally invest Lord Castletown as a Knight of the Order. The King, who was by all accounts extremely angry at the loss of the Jewels, cancelled the ceremony, and it was not held until February 1908, after Vicars had been dismissed. King Edward was determined that blame should be affixed to someone, and he refused to be pacified by the letters of the Earl of Aberdeen (Lord Lieutenant, 1905–1915) assuring him that everything that could be done was being done. 'He is not I am afraid satisfied with your explanation and he desires me to let you know that there is a mystery and an apparent lukewarmness about the enquiry and in fact the whole of the proceedings which he does not understand . . . H.M. also says that somebody must have been careless in their care of the Crown Jewels, and if so he would be glad to know whom, and whether, whoever it may be, anything in the way of punishment or reprimand has been given to him'.[2] This was the first indication that the King was out for blood, and by 17 September he had quite settled in his own mind that Vicars was the person responsible, and that he should be suspended from office. At the beginning of October, after a conference between himself; Augustine Birrell, the Chief Secretary; Sir James Dougherty, the Assistant Under-Secretary; Sir John Ross of Bladensburg, Chief Commissioner of the Dublin Metropolitan Police; and Mr. W. V. Harrel, the Assistant Commissioner, Aberdeen, wrote to the King. He recommended that the Office of Arms should be reconstituted. All the staff should be requested to resign, and in the event of their refusal, they should be dismissed. Aberdeen, however, reckoned without Ulster's tenacity. Vicars had fought hard to get into the Office of Arms and he now fought harder to stay in. On 23 October, Dougherty wrote to Vicars indicating that the King had decided to reconstitute the Office, and that his services were no longer in regard. Vicars replied, recording his hitherto unblemished record in office, and asked for an official inquiry to be held into all the circumstnaces surrounding the disappearance of the insignia. He enlisted the aid of his elder half-brother, Peirce O'Mahony, a colourful and adventurous figure who had fought against the Turks in the Bulgarian War of Independence.

O'Mahony urged his brother not to resign under any circumstances and entered into a vigorous correspondence with the Irish Government on his behalf, announcing that Vicars was being sacrificed in order to shield those really responsible. O'Mahony realised that he must have powerful supporters if his brother's cause was to succeed, and he took the very unusual step of drawing up a petition and asking all the Knights of St Patrick to sign it. The petition recorded that Ulster had 'invariably discharged his functions for the last fifteen years in a manner which has called forth the special approbation of the various Grand Masters of the Order under whom he served',[3] and that an enquiry should be held into all the circumstances of the affair before any steps were taken to dismiss him. Of the 21 existing Knights, excluding members of the Royal Family, 16 signed the petition; the Marquesses of Ormonde and Waterford, the Earls of Gosford, Carysfort, Bandon, Mayo, Listowel, Dunraven, Rosse, Lucan, Longford, Enniskillen, Meath, Erne, and Roberts, and Lord Monteagle of Brandon. Of the remaining five, the 80-year-old Earl of Howth was too ill to be approached; Viscount Wolesley was abroad; and the Earl of Kilmorey, Lord Clonbrock, and Viscount Iveagh declined to add their names. Kilmorey was quietly pursuing Vicars' cause through other channels, and thought it best not to approach the King in such a way. Iveagh had been warned by Knollys that the presentation of the petition would be distasteful to the King, and he refused, adding 'I am in a different position to that of the other knights',[4] without elucidating. Of the three, only Lord Clonbrock showed any regard for the internal structure of the Order and its bearing on the affair: 'I am very sorry for poor Ulster and should like to do anything I could to help him, but I think appealing to the King against the decision of the Grand Master of the Order is a very serious matter, and would not tend to his advantage'.[5]

Clonbrock was right, the petition was a very serious matter. The majority of the Knights were taking a stand on behalf of an individual for whom the King had developed an intense dislike, an event without parallel in the history of the Order. The King was extremely angry with the signatories, as witnessed by Field Marshal Earl Roberts, who sent a telegram from Windsor on 15 November, 10 days after signing the Petition, asking for his name to be withdrawn. The great soldier must have felt uncomfortably aware of the King's displeasure. Clonbrock was less accurate in his reference to the Grand Master. Aberdeen was a kindly, sensitive man, who appears to have tried hard to shield Vicars from the King's anger. He proposed that Vicars should be allowed to resign, and that the functions hitherto exercised by Ulster King of Arms should be split between two offices. The office of Ulster should continue to exist as before, but its functions should extend only to the fields of heraldry and genealogy. All his duties relating to the Order of Saint Patrick should be taken over by a new official who was to be styled Registrar of the Order, thus reverting to the position existing before 1890, with the exception that the new Registrar rather than the King of Arms was to be the executive Officer of the Order. This would enable Vicars to continue working in the field he loved best, while removing him from all further connection with the Order as a punishment for his negligence in the care of the insignia, which the King had sought.

The plan foundered for four reasons. Firstly, the Statutes would require alteration with the King's personal authority, thereby implying that the King had reasons for making the change. Secondly, altering the Statutes for the benefit of the King of Arms when two subordinate Officers had been dismissed (Shackleton and Francis Bennett-Goldney, Athlone Pursuivant, had both resigned on request in November 1907) would be a travesty of justice, and might invite criticism and hostile comment. This would be difficult to answer without involving the King. Thirdly, Vicars' act of gross negligence would be revealed, and condoned by his reappointment. Fourthly, Vicars would occupy a position which would bring him into frequent contact with the Lord Lieutenant and, on more important occasions, the King.

The King was reluctant to deny Vicars the opportunity of an enquiry, and agreed in principle, but made it clear that he washed his hands of the whole business. He refused to allow the enquiry to have the status of a Royal Commission, which would give the appearance by its constitution that he had surrendered. A compromise was reached in the appointment of a Viceregal Commission which, as it emanated from the Lord Lieutenant, would free the King from all responsibility. The government initially decided that the enquiry was to hold its meetings in private, arousing the annoyance of O'Mahony and Vicars, and the surprise of Herbert Gladstone, the Home Secretary. 'If there is no publicity you will have to face an awkward position with the King, and a real flare up when the House meets. It may be too late to undo all the mischief. But I think in any case you must make the whole thing public. Publish the evidence already given and admit the Press . . . It's a very ugly business, and you will have, as things are, Nationalists and Unionists against you'.[6] The Commission first met on 10 January 1908, and published its report on 25 January. It came to the conclusion that Sir Arthur Vicars 'did not exercise due vigilance or proper care as the custodian of the regalia',[7] quoting extensively from the Statutes to emphasise Vicars's culpability. Articles 12 and 20 stated clearly that the insignia should be deposited in a steel safe in the strong room of the Office of Arms, which had been ignored. When the Office of Arms was transferred to the Bedford Tower in 1903, the safe which housed the Regalia and some of the insignia was found to be too large to pass through the door of the new strong room, and Vicars agreed to the safe being left in the library, until the Board of Works could provide him with a safe small enough to be admitted to the strong room.

The Report of the Commission confirmed what the government had already decided—that Vicars was guilty of negligence, and that he would have to go. On 30 January he received a letter from Sir James Dougherty, informing him that the Letters Patent appointing him had been revoked, and that his successor had been appointed. The letter came as a shattering blow to Vicars who after an unblemished record of 14 years in office, was deprived of his job and his career. Angry and bitter, he retired to Kilmorna House in County Kerry, the home of his half brother, to spend the remainder of his life. He never accepted the possibility that he was in any way to blame for the theft and his feelings of hurt and injustice lingered on. He continually referred to his successor, Captain Nevile Rodwell Wilkinson, as a 'usurper', and that his career had been 'purposely shattered by a heartless government'.[8] As late as September 1911 he wrote: 'I was simply made a scapegoat to save Ross of Bladensburg and the Board of Works, and Shackleton's wicked threats of a scandal (which were and are all bunkum and lies) were utilised to frighten the late King and make him hush it up'.[9] For a while he nurtured vain hopes that when the Home Rule Liberal government was replaced by a Conservative and Unionist one, he might be reinstated, but the hope was only a dream, and no Conservative government came to power in his lifetime.

In 1917, Vicars married his old friend, Miss Gertrude Wright, who did much to erase any residual feelings of bitterness in the last years of his life. The end came on 14 April 1921. The I.R.A. had initiated a policy of burning the great country houses of Ireland, and occasionally shooting the occupants before the blazing ruins. Arthur Vicars and Kilmorna fell victim. A gang of armed raiders surrounded the house and set fire to it after allowing the occupants to leave, except Vicars, who had been ill in bed, and who was taken out and shot. The I.R.A. took the almost unprecedented step of announcing that the murder had not been carried out on their instructions, and it was generally agreed that the raiders were local men.

The plaintive tone of his Will shows that Arthur Vicars died a confused and unhappy man: 'I am unconscious of having done anyone wrong and my very misfortune arose from my being unsuspicious and trusting'.[10]

The tragedy is that Vicars failed to understand the mentality of those who were responsible for his dismissal. Victorian and Edwardian court officials were drawn from the ranks of the armed forces, almost to a man. The principle of senior responsibility is basic in the military machine. If a junior officer fails in his duty, his senior commander is held responsible, even though he may not have been directly involved himself. Vicars was probably innocent of anything directly to do with the theft, but it was almost certainly perpetrated by one of his staff. He was accused, not so much of being personally guilty, but of being *responsible,* and for this reason he was fired. Not having a military indoctrination, the whole concept of the senior officer's responsibility was beyond his comprehension. All he could see was what he regarded as the injustice of the whole thing. His judges took a different view, understanding him as little as he understood them.

The bitterness of the whole episode, and the tragedy of his death should not obscure the fact that Arthur Vicars was a herald of great attainments, and a worthy successor of Sir Bernard Burke. His whole life had been wrapped up in the maintenance of the efficiency and dignity of his office, and until the catastrophe of the theft, he had performed his duties impeccably.

Of the Grand Master's Diamond Star and Badge, and the five gold collars, no trace was found, and no further reference to their location or existence was generally known until 1976. In that year, a file of the Irish government was opened to the public for the first time, and contained the following intriguing memorandum, dated 1927:

'IV. The President would not like them to be used as a means of reviving the Order or to pass into any hands other than those of the State.

'V. He understands that the Castle Jewels are for sale and that they could
    be got for £2,000 or £3,000. He would be prepared to recommend
    their purchase for the same reason.'[11]

The memorandum is signed by the Assistant Secretary of the Executive Council,
Michael McDunphy, and the President referred to is William Cosgrave, Prime
Minister of the Irish Free State from 1922 to 1932. It raises the interesting
possibility that the Jewels were still in existence in 1927, and might still be
so today. We have no way of knowing.

The investiture of Lord Castletown had been postponed since June 1907,
and it was important to fill up the vacant offices as quickly as possible,
to enable the Office and the Order to continue functioning. The scandal
surrounding the loss of the Jewels, and the dismissal of Vicars, made the
office of Ulster a rather controversial one, and three individuals are known
to have declined the appointment, before it was offered to and accepted
by Captain Nevile Wilkinson, a son-in-law of the Earl of Pembroke. Apparently Pembroke suggested Wilkinson's name at a Privy Council meeting
presided over by the King, who brushed aside any question of Wilkinson's
knowledge of heraldry, wishing only to be assured that he was honest. Captain
Guillamore O'Grady was appointed to the vacant office of Dublin Herald,
and Mr. George Burtchaell, who had worked in the office for some years
under Sir Arthur Vicars, was made Athlone Pursuivant. All three were invested
with their insignia of office on 4 February 1909, at the investiture of Lord
Pirrie.

Pirrie's appointment to the Order had been met with considerable antipathy
by the other Knights. They resented the appointment of this upstart, and
declined to take part in his investiture. Born in Quebec of Irish parents, Pirrie
joined the Belfast shipbuilding firm of Harland and Wolff at the age of 15, and
rose to become a partner at the age of twenty-seven. He had been given a
barony only 18 months before his investiture, and the admission of this
self-made man to their most illustrious Order caused some offence to the
aristocratic members. Aberdeen suggested that Pirrie's investiture should either
be delayed, or there should be a public investiture whether the other Knights
were present or not. The King, however, was firmly against the idea: 'The King
considers that to have a public investiture with only one Knight of St Patrick
would make the ceremony an absurdity, and he must ask that Lord Pirrie shall
be privately invested by you immediately on your return to Ireland. The King
feels that he has been placed in a very false position by Lord Pirrie having been
recommended to him for the St Patrick when none of the other Knights will
meet him in order to be present at his investiture'.[12] Pirrie was a shrewd
businessman, and closely identified with all the developments in naval architec-
ture and marine engineering. He transformed Harland and Wolff from a family
company into a large industrial organisation in the space of 50 years, and it is

doubtful whether he would have taken much notice of the prejudices of his fellow Knights, let alone be affected by them.

On taking office, the new Ulster was faced with a problem. Sir Arthur Vicars, still smarting from his abrupt dismissal, refused to hand over the keys of the strong room to his successor. Wilkinson tactfully ascribed this to the suddenness of the blow which had deprived Vicars of his career, and thrown him for the moment off his equilibrium, rather than to malice. Apart from the remaining insignia of the Order of Saint Patrick, the strong room contained the silver maces and the Irish Sword of State which were carried before the Lord Lieutenant on ceremonial occasions, and all three were needed at a forthcoming Levee. There was no option but to break into the room, and Wilkinson chose the two hours that guests at the Castle spent in assembling and eating dinner on Sunday evening. 'Shortly before the dinner hour, I had collected a select band of conspirators, including a representative each from the Dublin Metropolitan Police, the Board of Works, the office of the Treasury Remembrancer, and the Chief Secretary's Office. This band I admitted into my office under cover of darkness; then, with the assistance of the crowbars wielded by a couple of lusty labourers supplied by the Board of Works, all obstacles were overcome and entrance into the inner sanctuary obtained. Then, my quest accomplished, I quietly joined the guests as they sat over their coffee, and pointed out the recovered symbols of state to His Excellency as we passed through the Throne Room on our way to join the ladies'.[13]

After his succession to the throne George V followed the custom of his predecessors, and appointed a number of Extra Knights to the Order on the occasion of his coronation, intimating that he would visit Dublin to conduct the investiture in person. The new Knights were Field Marshal Earl Kitchener of Khartoum, and the 9th Earl of Shaftesbury, Chamberlain to Queen Mary. At the time of his death half a century later, Shaftesbury was the last surviving non-Royal Knight of the Order. The news of the impending royal visit and investiture provoked a suggestion that the Order of Saint Patrick should once more have a chapel, the obvious choice being Saint Patrick's Cathedral. The suggestion came from none other than Viscount Iveagh, K.P., third and youngest son of the same Sir Benjamin Guinness who had so carefully restored the Cathedral at his own expense in the 1860s. Iveagh appears to have discussed the whole matter with the Dean of Saint Patrick's, and proposed the idea directly to the King. He may have been motivated partly by the recent completion of a chapel for the use of the Order of the Thistle, attached to Saint Giles's Cathedral in Edinburgh, the result of a generous donation from the Earl of Leven and Melville. Lord Knollys, the King's Private Secretary, consulted Augustine Birrell, the Chief Secretary of Ireland, and Chancellor of the Order, who advised strongly against any action. Firstly, any attempt to renew the connection between the Order and the Church of Ireland would provoke objections from the Presbyterians and the Roman Catholics, and it would in any case be difficult to defend the connection of the Order with one particular religious body out of several, none of which had any connection with the State. Secondly, although Roman Catholic Knights of the Order had attended the installations of 1821 and 1868, the rules of the Church on the attendance of Catholics at acts of worship in other Churches were now much more rigorous, and no Catholic Knight would be allowed to attend a ceremony in a Protestant Church in Ireland.

The visit of the King and Queen at the beginning of July 1911 was an enormous success in a country which did not often see its monarch—the last royal visit had been four years earlier. The announced intention of the Liberal government to introduce a Home Rule Bill produced feelings that total independence could not be far off, and enthusiastic demonstrations of loyalty greeted the arrival of the King and Queen. The investiture on 10 July was a brilliant and picturesque affair. All the Knights were present with the exception of the two oldest members—the 78-year-old Viscount Wolseley, and the 81-year-old Earl of Lucan—for whom the lengthy ceremony would have been too exhausting. The King personally invested Kitchener and Shaftesbury with the Riband and Badge of the Order, and for the last time, the traditional admonition was heard in public:

An Investiture of the Order in Saint Patrick's Hall, Dublin Castle, c.1888.

Sir, the loving Company of the Order of Saint Patrick hath received you as their Brother, Lover, and Fellow, and in token and knowledge of this We give you and present you this Badge, the which God will that you receive and wear from henceforth to His praise and pleasure, and to the exaltation and honour of the said Most Illustrious Order and yourself.

Though none of those present had any inkling, the days of the Order were numbered and the ceremony was to be its last trumpet call. The failure of the government to implement the provisions of the Home Rule Bill which reached the Statute Book in 1914, the stupid mishandling of the Easter Rising of 1916, and the appalling atrocities committed by the Black and Tans after the War, ushered in a new age in which the Order of Saint Patrick had no role to play. Nobody could have foreseen in that hot summer of 1911 that the days of British domination in Ireland were nearly over. Nor could King George have guessed that neither he nor his successors would ever again ride in state through the streets of Dublin as Kings of Ireland.

1. George Nugent-Temple-Grenville, 3rd Earl Temple and 1st Marquess of Buckingham (1753-1813).
Founder of the Order of Saint Patrick. Grand Master March-June 1783 and 1787-1790.

2. The Collar may well be an original 18th century example, judging from the poor standard of workmanship. It seems that several links have been removed since a full Collar would consist of seven roses and six harps.

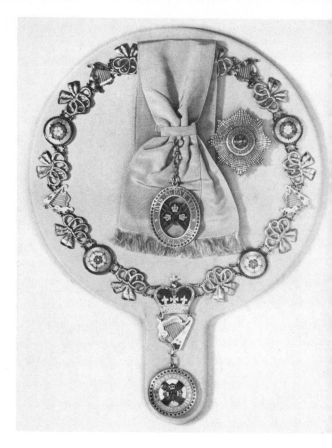

3. Silver breast star, c.1800, worn by Arthur Saunders, Earl of Arran, one of the Founder Knights of the Order, who died in October 1809.

The Duke of Kent's Badge in gold and
enamel. The reverse inscribed, 'The gift of
his Majesty George III to Prince Edward
Duke of Kent April 1804.' It is the oldest
Royal Badge known to exist.

5.   The Star of H.R.H. the Duke of Kent (No. 1) K.P. 1783.
Made c. 1806-10 and bearing the following inscription on the
reverse, 'Gilbert, Jeweller to their Majesties Cock Spur Street.'
The rings on each of the eight points indicate that it was
intended to be sewn on a coat.

Small Sovereign's Badge in gold, diamonds
and enamel. Made for George IV in 1812.

7.   Gold and enamel Badge made by Clarke and West of
Dublin in 1819. May have belonged to George IV.

8. Early 19th century Sta[r] probably of Irish manufact[ure] pre 1825.

9. Small silver breast Star by Tnycross & Son of Dublin, with gold and enamel centre, c. 1830.

A Sovereign's neck Badge made for William IV
[...]30 and worn by succeeding Sovereigns from
[...]to time. Gold and enamel.

(*below*) Queen Victoria's small St Patrick
[...]ar, made in 1837 of 22 carat gold and bearing
[...]naker's initials 'W.C.' The central Imperial
[...]vn is engraved 'Rundell, Bridge & Rundell,
[...]llers and Goldsmiths to the Queen'.

12. Small unofficial Badge of the period 1833-45, unmarked. 13. Small silver breast Star by Storr and Mortimer c.18[...]

14. The Prince Consort's Star in silver, gold and enamel. The reverse is engraved 'West and Son' and the inscription 'Belonged to the Prince Consort'. The elements of the Irish silver mark and the maker's initials 'E&JJ' are also stamped but the date letter is missing. Probably made in 1842 it is an unusually convex piece.

15. The Duke of Connaught's small oval Badge, K.P.[...] 1869. The edge is stamped with the maker's initial 'W.N.' and the figure of 18 for the fineness of the metal. It bears the London hallmark for 1842 which suggests that it may originally have been acquired by the Prince Consort who received the Order in that ye[...]

16.   The 1st Earl of Charlemont, K.P. 1783.

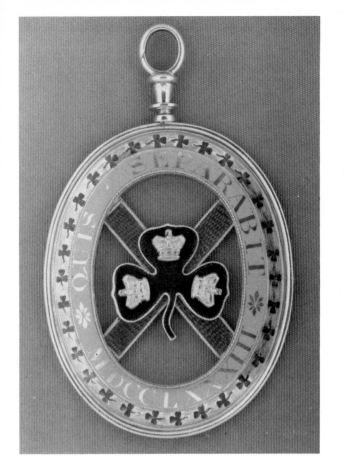

17. (*above*) An official Oval Badge, 1840-1850. The edge of this Badge is stamped with most of the elements of the Irish hallmark including the maker's initials 'E.J.' and the figure 18 for the fineness of the metal. There is no date letter and the Dublin crowned harp is missing. The style of workmanship, particularly the outer border of trefoils running clockwise and the plain gold crowns, assigns this Badge to the period 1840-50.

18. (*above right*) A Collar made during the reign of William IV. The reverse of each rose is stamped with the King's head, the Dublin town mark, the gold standard mark and the figure of 18 indicating the fineness of the metal, and the maker's initials 'E.J.'. There is no date letter. The Star is of silver, *c.*1820-7. The reverse is engraved 'Hamlet, Jeweller to His Royal Highness the Duke of York, Princess Augusta Hesse Homburg, Duchess of Gloucester, Princess Sophia and His Serene Highness the Prince of Hesse Homburg Frances Street Berkeley Square London'. The Badge is of the period 1825-1832.

19. (*right*) A mid-19th-century Star set with paste stones. No marks or inscriptions. A rather ugly piece.

20. The Collar Badge of the Duke of Connaught, K.P. 1869. The reverse is engraved 'West and Son, Dublin, Jewellers to the Order of St. Patrick, 1871'. Though made in 1871, this Badge is of the type of 1819 though differing in small details of workmanship. It would appear that West and Son when required to furnish a Badge for a regency Collar provided one closely resembling the original.

21. (below) The central portion of the short Collar of the Duke of Connaught. The Collar is unmarked and consists of a total of 23 links, four short of the normal complement of 27. Two knots and four harps have been removed from the back section to reduce the length. It is unlikely that this Collar is the one originally received by the Duke on his appointment to the Order in 1869 since the appendant Badge is dated 1871. It may well be an additional piece made specially for use during his command in Ireland from 1900 to 1904.

22. A Star made by West and Son of Dublin for the 4th Earl of Dunraven and Mount Earl, K.P. 1872. The acute angles and fluted rays make this Star a unique piece. There are no hallmarks but the reverse is engraved 'WEST AND SON.'

23. (*above right*) The Collar, Star and Badge of H.R.H. the Duke of Windsor K.P. 1927. The Collar and Badge are of 18 carat gold and were made by West and Son of Dublin. They bear the Dublin hallmark for 1887-8 and the reverse of the Badge bears the following incription, 'WEST AND SON DUBLIN COLLEGE GREEN'. The Star is unmarked though probably of the period 1860-90 and bears the following incription on the reverse, 'WEST AND SON DUBLIN'.

24. (*right*) A jewelled Star in the possession of the National Gallery of Ireland. Donated as part of the Milltown Gift in 1902. Composed of diamonds, rubies and emeralds, set on a silver base and backed with a sheet of nine carat gold. Inscribed 'R. & S. Garrard & Co./Jewellers to the Crown/25 Haymarket/London. No hallmark, but probably made for the 6th Earl of Milltown (No. 108) K.P. 1889.

25. The 3rd Earl of Kilmorey K.P. 1890.

26. (*right*) The Star of Field Marshal Earl Roberts K.P. 1897. Silver and enamels.

27. (*left*) The Badge and Riband of Field Marshal Earl Roberts K.P. 1897.

28. The Mantle Star of Field Marshal Earl Roberts, K.P. 1897. Made by Robinson and Steele of Dublin.

29. Field Marshal Earl Roberts, K.P. 1897, in Field Marshal's full dress, dismounted order, *c.*1902.

30. The 12th Earl of Meath, K.P. 1905.

A Star made by West and Son of
blin for the 12th Earl of Meath,
P. 1905. No hallmarks, the reverse
graved 'WEST AND SON'.

32. The Star of Field Marshal the
Earl Kitchener of Khartoum, K.P.
1911. The reverse is engraved 'TO
FIELD MARSHAL VISCT. KITCH-
ENER, K.P. FROM HIS A.D.C.'s
CORONATION 1911'. There are no
other marks.

33. The Star of the 2nd Duke of Abercorn, K.P. 1922. Made by W and Son of Dublin.

34. A late example of a Star in silver and enamel. The body of the Star has been crudely cast and highly burnished but the rays are neither chipped nor pierced. The word QUIS of the motto does not conform to the circular base on which it is set. The first four letters of SEPARABIT are similarly badly set. Both words have been hand cut from a flat sheet of metal. The reverse bears elements of a London hallmark, though there is no date letter. The Star was almost certainly made after 1922 by a London firm which had no familiarity with the techniques of making St. Patrick insignia.

35. King George V when Duke of York wearing the robes and insignia of a Knight of Saint Patrick, 1897.

36. Three examples of early 19th-century Knights' Badges. The centre Badge is pre-1825. The Badge on the left is of the period between 1825 and 1832. The Badge on the right dates from the period 1833-1845.

The Badges of the Prelate. The Badge, with original riband, f 18 carat gold and enamel. The mitre is set with small els. The Badge was made by Clarke and West of Dublin, bears the Dublin hallmark for 1819. The miniature badge a personal gift of King William IV to Lord John George esford, Archbishop of Armagh 1822 to 1862. Made of 18 t gold and enamel, it is heavily jewelled with diamonds, ies and emeralds. It was made by Rundell, Bridge & Co. in 4 and bears the London hallmark for that year.

38. The Badge of the Registrar. Gold and enamel. Probably early or mid-Victorian, there are no marks or inscriptions. It was not worn after the death of Dean John West of St. Patrick's Cathedral in 1890 when the office of Registrar was united with Ulster King of Arms.

39. Edmund Bernard Fitzalan-Howard, 1st Viscount Fitzalan of Derwent (1855-1947), 40th and last Grand Master of the Order of Saint Patrick, 1921-1922.

40. A Grand Master's Badge, the winged Irish harp surmounted by an imperial crown topped with a single pearl and with the band set with small emeralds and rubies, c.1817, with original neck riband and gold clasp. Originally the property of Charles Talbot, 2nd Earl Talbot, Lord Lieutenant of Ireland (1817-21) and Grand Master of the Order of Saint Patrick.

A Grand Master's Badge c.1850.

42. The Chancel of Saint Patrick's Cathedral, Dublin. The symbolic Swords and Helmets of the Knights are still in position above their Stalls, as are the Banners of the Knights existing at the time of the disestablishment of the Church of Ireland in 1871.

43. The Bicentenary Service in Saint Patrick's Cathedral: The Rt. Revd. Bishop George Simms, former Archbishop of Armagh, and the Very Revd. Dr. Victor Griffin, Dean of the Cathedral.

. The Bicentenary Service in Saint Patrick's Cathedral: the Cathedral Choir singing the anthem 'Quis Separabit' at e beginning of Service.

45. The Bicentenary Service in Saint Patrick's Cathedral: descendants and relatives of Knights of the Most Illustrious Order of Saint Patrick. Standing (*left to right*): Miss Caroline Gough, Miss Rosaleen Gough, Miss Cynthia Gough, Mr. John Gough, The Earl of Meath, Viscount Ardee, The Honourable Dominick Browne (representing The Lord Oranmore and Browne), Brigadier Denis Fitzgerald (representing The Duke of Leinster), The Viscount Gough, The Earl of Rosse (standing behind Lord Gough), The Earl of Bessborough, The Earl of Limerick, The Dean's Vicar, The Viscount Massereene and Ferrard, Dr. Brendan O'Brien (representing The Lord Inchiquin), The Earl of Shaftesbury, The Lord Monteagle of Brandon, The Marquess of Waterford, Viscount Elveden, The Marchioness of Waterford, Lady Louisa Guinness. Seated (*left to right*): The Countess of Wicklow, The Countess of Meath, Lady Hyacinth Gough (representing The Earl of Kilmorey), The Countess of Iveagh (representing The Earl of Iveagh), The Rt. Revd. Bishop George Simms (former Archbishop of Armagh), The Very

Chapter Six

CAUTION AND DELAY

*'It is very difficult to go leaving the Order in suspense merely to avoid
raising troublesome questions, with the Free State'*
Sir John Anderson
March 1927

WITH THE PLACING of the Home Rule Bill on the Statute Book in 1914, the Liberal government decided that the appropriate moment had arrived to make a change in the Viceroyalty, and the Earl of Aberdeen, who had been Lord Lieutenant since 1905, longer than any of his predecessors, retired in February 1915. His departure was greeted with considerable regret and the streets of Dublin were crowded for his state departure on 15 February. The Aberdeens were an earnest, kindly, and well-intentioned couple; but like so many people who went over to Ireland imbued with a desire to show their appreciation of and sympathy with Irish nationalism, they were more Irish than the Irish themselves, a condition of mind which, when displayed by English people, generally amused rather than impressed the Irish Nationalists.

Preceded by Ulster King of Arms in his tabard, Lord Aberdeen rode on horseback with his Staff, followed by Lady Aberdeen and others in carriages. According to custom, Lord Aberdeen wore black morning dress with a black silk top hat, the sombre appearance being relieved only by the Star of the Order of Saint Patrick on his coat. Journeying by train from Westland Row Station to Kingstown (now Dun Laoghaire), accompanied by the Lord Mayor, the Lord Chancellor, and the General in Command, they set sail for Scotland. It was the last ceremonial departure of a Lord Lieutenant from the shores of Ireland. Though Aberdeen was not the last Lord Lieutenant (as he had expected with the passage of the Home Rule Bill), none of his three successors ever again held Court in Dublin Castle, or rode out of the city in State.

Aberdeen was succeeded by Ivor Churchill Guest, 1st Lord (later 1st Viscount) Wimborne. He was an impetuous man with an active mind, who much resented the fact that as Lord Lieutenant he had no real power, except to give effect to the policy of the government as laid down by the Chief Secretary. Some weeks after he took office, the Earl of Bessborough was nominated to fill a vacancy in the Order, and the question of his investiture arose. At the beginning of the War, the State Apartments in the Castle including Saint Patrick's Hall, had been

51

converted into a hospital for wounded soldiers, which precluded the Hall from being used for ceremonies of the Order for the duration. Wimborne proposed that investitures should take place instead at the Royal Hospital, Kilmainham, and issued summonses to the Knights to attend accordingly. In spite of the War, he pressed for a full public investiture which 'would furnish me with the opportunity of entertaining as spectators many prominent Dublin people which . . . would be in itself desirable . . . I may say that all addresses and public utterances since my arrival here have been animated . . . by a distinct tendency towards concord which I am much anxious to foster and I regard the investiture as offering an opportunity for this purpose'.[1] The King agreed with Wimborne's motives, thinking that it would be a good opportunity to gather together those 'who, during the late regime, had studiously absented themselves from the Castle'.[2]

But public attitudes towards the War were beginning to change in the face of the use of poisonous gases, the *Lusitania* tragedy, and the publication of the report of the Bryce Commission. The original cry of 'business as usual' was being replaced by the view that the country was not taking the War sufficiently seriously. 'His Majesty, therefore, thinks that it would be incongruous to summon the Knights of St Patrick, many of whom are engaged in matters connected with the war, to Dublin, to be arrayed in their full dress robes and to assist in a function, which, even held privately at the Vice Regal Lodge, would be of a distinctly ceremonial character . . . Whenever the war comes to an end His Majesty feels you will have ample opportunity to hold a State Investiture, and he hopes by that time in St Patrick's Hall'.[3] This decision ended all possibility of any more formal investitures while the War continued, and though Wimborne again wrote to the King In February 1916 on the subject, he was firmly rebuked. With the exception of Lord French, who was invested personally by the King at Buckingham Palace in June 1917, all the war investitures were held privately at the Vice Regal Lodge. The Officers suffered a similar fate. Henry Duke, who succeeded Augustine Birrell as Chief Secretary in 1916 was never invested with his Badge as Chancellor, nor was Sir John Olphert, who was appointed Usher of the Black Rod in May 1915 two years after the death of his predecessor. When Olphert died in March 1917, the post was left vacant for 19 months, the government deciding that there was no urgency in filling it.

The tragedy of the Easter Rising of April 1916, and the insensitive way in which it was handled, swung moderate Irish public opinion against the government and led to a sharp upturn in civil disturbance. Wimborne was not held responsible for the rising—he would in any case have had a very good answer to any such charge, since he was never given the opportunity of exercising any responsibility, and there was no question of his resignation until the necessity for a military Lord Lieutenant became apparent by 1918. Recent evidence has shown that the leaders of the rising were not so unshakeably committed to the ideal of a republic, as previously thought. A number of them, including Patrick Pearse, who was named first President of the Republic, seriously considered the possibility of inviting a German Prince to be installed as King of Ireland in the event of Germany winning the war, and they went so far as to name Prince Joachim, one of the Kaiser's sons, as a possible candidate. The concept was vague and visionary, and the eventual outcome of the war ended all thoughts of a German monarchy in Ireland.

The appointment of Viscount French (later Earl of Ypres) as Lord Lieutenant in May 1918 was the second and last occasion on which a Grand Master of the Order was also numbered among its Knights. In honour of his Irish ancestry, French had been made a K.P. in 1917 as a reward for his services, first as Commander-in-Chief of the British Expeditionary Force in France, and subsequently as Commander-in-Chief of the Home Forces. It was thought that he might win the respect of the Irish as an Irishman with a considerable military reputation, but such hopes were quickly disappointed. Events in Ireland had moved too far. An increasing polarization between the people and the government negated the effect that the appointment of an Irish Viceroy might have had in earlier years, and French's heavy-handed attempts at enforcing the law produced a mood of dangerous irritation. Matters went from bad to worse; the struggle degenerated into a campaign of aggression and punishment, of outrages and reprisals, and his position only grew more unsatisfactory with the passage of time. The 'Black and Tans', an auxiliary force to aid the Royal Irish Constabulary, became infamous for their brutality and a synonym of terror. They were mostly young men who found it difficult to settle down after the war, after becoming accustomed to a life of adventure and bloodshed. Their ruthlessness and contempt for life and property stemmed partly from the brutalising effect of four years of trench warfare, and partly from the intense strain imposed on them by service in Ireland, surrounded by enemies who could not be identified. Appalling atrocities were committed by both sides in the three years up to 1921.

The Order was scarcely affected by these occurrences, shielded by the walls of Dublin Castle from events outside. Two new Knights were appointed during French's viceroyalty, Lord Oranmore and Browne in 1918, and the Earl of Desart in 1919—the last two before the constitutional changes of 1921/2. But the situation was changing rapidly. The government, recognising the failure of force, replaced French with Lord Edmund Talbot, subsequently created Viscount Fitzalan of Derwent. Fitzalan was faced with a task which required very little initiative, simply the oversight of the partition and the transfer of power. He is chiefly remembered as the only Roman Catholic to hold the post of Lord Lieutenant and, for our purposes, the last Grand Master of the Order of Saint Patrick. Like all his predecessors, he was received by the Lords Justices in the Council Chamber of Dublin Castle, and solemnly invested with the Grand Master's insignia on 2 May 1921. His magistracy lasted only until December 1922. Under the new constitution, the office of Lord Lieutenant was to cease to exist and its functions were to be divided between a Governor-General for the new Irish

Free State, and a Governor for Northern Ireland. This created something of a problem. Which of the two new Viceregal representatives was to be the new Grand Master, and, in any case, what was to be the future of the Order?

The King made his feelings on the matter of the Grand Mastership quite clear when he received the Duke of Abercorn in audience as the new Governor of Northern Ireland on 21 December 1922. The Duke was invested with the insignia of a Knight of the Order of Saint Patrick, indicating that the King considered the new Governor to be the Grand Master, in practice, if not in name. Mr. Timothy Healy, the new Governor-General of the Irish Free State, had no interest in the ways of the Viceregal Court which preceded him, let alone the Order of Saint Patrick, and his views were expressed in an interview with *The Times*:

Q.   Will there be any Viceregal State?—
A.   I hope not.
Q.   Any Court?—
A.   That is the last thing I should think of.
Q.   You will still be Mr. Tim Healy?—
A.   I hope so—to my friends at all events (*laughing*).
Q.   Are you likely to take any other rank?—
A.   Never.
Q.   It will be usual to address you as 'Your Excellency'?—
A.   I hope not, but I cannot prevent any man from being courteous.
Q.   How would you dress for State functions?—
A.   As I am now.
Q.   The old State ceremonial goes, as far as you are concerned?—
A.   That will be a matter for the Irish Cabinet to determine. In that respect I am entirely in their hands, but my own wish would be simplicity itself.[4]

Timothy Healy was a strange echo from the past. Sixteen years earlier, even then a distinguished Irish barrister, he had defended Sir Arthur Vicars in front of the Commission of Enquiry into the circumstances surrounding the loss of the Crown Jewels.

Within five weeks the future of the Order came under close scrutiny in the Irish Office in London, and problems had to be faced. Was the office of Grand Master to be abolished, or continued under a new system? Similarly, with the disappearance of the office of Chief Secretary, what was to become of the office of Chancellor? Was it necessary to retain both offices? Should the Chancery of the Order remain at the Office of Arms in Dublin Castle, and could the status of Saint Patrick's Hall be maintained? Sir Nevile Wilkinson was consulted, and a conference was called at the Home Office on 30 April to discuss the matter. Those present included Sir Douglas Dawson, the State Chamberlain; Sir James Masterton-Smith, Under Secretary for the Colonies; and Sir Mark Grant-Sturgis, Assistant Under Secretary for Irish Affairs. Wilkinson advised them that the provisional government had intimated that nothing should be done which might draw public attention to the existence of his office and the Order, which they were anxious should continue in due time. Considering the strong opposition to the Order expressed by the Irish government in the late 1920s, this is a very curious statement. It is possible that Wilkinson was misreading the signs of the times as far as the Order was concerned. Whatever his assumptions, he wrote to Sturgis saying that it would be injudicious to raise any questions regarding the property and status of the Order.

The Conference reached seven conclusions. Firstly, the Irish Free State would in time come to regard the Order with the same respect in which it had been held in the past. Secondly, that if this came about, it would prove to be a valuable link between Ireland and the Crown. Thirdly, that subject to the safeguarding of the insignia, no change should be made at the present, and certainly that no step should be taken which might imply that the Order was to be transferred to Northern Ireland at some future date. Fourthly, the United Kingdom Prime Minister would continue to be responsible for all appointments to the Order. Fifthly, although the Statutes were obsolete in several respects, they should not be changed at present. Sixthly, Wilkinson should be asked to arrange the transfer of the regalia, insignia and the most important records to London for safety. Lastly, the Chancery should remain in the Office of Arms, and that no action should be taken with regard to the banners hanging in Saint Patrick's Hall. In short, everything was to be left alone except for the cautious removal of the insignia.

In spite of Wilkinson's emphatic insistence that the insignia and records were probably far safer where they were, the King was firm on the point that they should be transferred to London for safe custody. Ulster warned that the danger of them being stolen in transit was far greater, and that 'Ireland being what it is, any attempt to move them would almost certainly get known and would cause protest, and in a word bring upon the whole question the attention which the Free State government and everybody else wishes at the present time to avoid'.[5] When he was asked whether he could bring over the Irish Sword of State, he remarked that it would be extremely difficult as it was nearly four feet long and it would be a tragedy or a farce or both, if he were caught trying to smuggle it through Customs. Cosgrave would have no choice but to intervene and claim it for the Dublin Museum rather than sit by and see it carried off to London.

The position of Ulster King of Arms and his Office was the subject of much discussion between London and Dublin throughout the 1920s, '30s, and early '40s. Wilkinson himself was convinced that the Irish Free State government were anxious that his office should continue, and that nothing should be done to draw attention to its existence, hoping and believing that he would be able to return to Dublin in a short time and carry on with his duties without protest, and with growing popular approval. The question mark hanging over Ulster was the same that hung over the Order of Saint Patrick of which he was the executive Officer. While there was any possibility of the Order being maintained, even in a modified form, nothing should be done to jeopardise the continued existence of Ulster King of Arms. As conscious of economy in 1923 as they still are

60 years later, the Treasury raised the matter of the cost of the Office in view of its diminishing duties. There was no longer any viceregal ceremony for Ulster to supervise, nor any connected with the Order, and there was a comparatively heavy deficit on the working of the Office. In 1920/1 the receipts totalled £461, and the expenditure £1,998. In 1923/4 the expenditure fell to £1,610, and the receipts increased to £945, but the Treasury proposed that Ulster's salary should be reduced from the high figure of £600, to about £300–£400. The Colonial Office agreed that for work done by Wilkinson himself, £600 was an over-payment, but in view of their decision to maintain the Office, they recommended that nothing further should be done until Wilkinson's resignation or death. The Office of Arms was the only department left which served the whole of Ireland, and from this aspect alone its retention was desirable.

Few people in government at the time thought very highly of Captain Sir Nevile Wilkinson. He left all routine matters of heraldry and genealogy to his deputies, George Burtchaell (until 1921), and Thomas Sadleir, preferring to spend the majority of his time at his London home off Portland Place. In the days before partition, he had the ingenious theory that he could do his work equally well from his home in London, and had to be summoned to Dublin and told to carry out his official duties at the Castle. He is perhaps best remembered as the creator of the 16-room model house called 'Titania's Palace', and took it abroad on several occasions in the '20s and '30s, exhibiting it to raise funds for handicapped children. On each occasion he wrote punctiliously to the Governor-General in Dublin and the King in London, asking for permission to go on leave of absence. When he visited the United States in 1926, the Home Office suggested to the Treasury that he should take unpaid leave, 'although you will discover that Wilkinson has influential friends who will probably bring pressure to bear on you with a view to continuing his salary'.[6] During his absences, the Office continued as smoothly as it had always done, under the careful supervision of his deputy, Thomas Sadleir, a hard-working and conscientious man who had succeeded George Burtchaell as Deputy Ulster, though not as Athlone Pursuivant on the latter's death in 1921.

The decision of the meeting of April 1923 was followed faithfully. Nothing was done to draw attention to the Order and no further appointments were made for some years. No attempt was made to fill the posts of Athlone Pursuivant and the Secretary of the Order, when they fell vacant in 1921 and 1926 respectively, and the Office of Arms continued to function quietly in Dublin Castle under the nose but not under the jurisdiction of the Free State government. But by early 1927, it was clear that serious consideration of the future of the Order could not long be delayed. Seven Knights had died between April 1924 and December 1926, leaving only 15 out of a maximum of twenty-two. Never in the history of the Order had there been so many vacancies at any one time, and the longer the matter was left, the more difficult it would be to make new appointments to an Order which many considered to be defunct. The King kept an active interest in the Order, publicly wearing the Star at the wedding of his son, the Duke of York, in 1923, and by the early months of 1927 he was being pressed by peers resident in Northern Ireland, to fill the vacancies and save the Order from extinction. As a prelude, the King favoured conferring the Order on the Prince of Wales and possibly also the Duke of York and communicated his decision to the Prime Minister, who felt that he could no longer oppose this 'reiterated desire'[7] on the King's part, and asked the Home and Dominions Offices to examine the whole problem.

Leopold Amery, the Secretary of State for Dominions, was far more cautious than his colleague, Sir William Joynson-Hicks, the Home Secretary, who was all for bringing the Order over to England, reviving it, and ignoring any protestations from the Free State government. Amery showed great sensitivity for Irish feeling and constantly urged restraint to avoid provoking a dispute which might cause unnecessary damage to Anglo-Irish relations. The ruling Fine Gael government in Ireland was facing a serious threat from the nascent republican Fianna Fail party of Eamonn de Valera. The Home Office felt that one or two appointments of members of the Royal Family would publicly indicate that the Order was still alive and it might therefore be possible to defer the question of further Irish appointments for some years, although it was obvious that sooner or later that matter would have to be faced. 'Our view here is that it is very difficult to go on leaving the Order in suspense merely to avoid raising troublesome questions with the Free State . . . and I think that Mr. Amery will have to make up his mind now whether he desires to press the Prime Minister to urge upon the King a further postponement of the appointments which His Majesty has it in mind to make'.[8]

Amery agreed, but felt that there should be no revision of the Statutes until it could be effected with the concurrence of the Free State government on the basis that the Order was an 'all-Ireland Order'. If not it would certainly mean the severance of all connections between the Order and the Irish Free State. He also pointed out that as no revision had been deemed necessary before the appointment of the Duke of Abercorn in December 1922, doubts might be raised as to the validity or propriety of that appointment. He considered it very important to wait until the Free State was prepared to take an active interest in the Order before appointing Irish peers, because the Order would either become exclusively associated with Northern Ireland, or it would lose any connection with Northern Ireland at all, both of which were to be deplored. His view was echoed by the Earl of Granard, K.P., a distinguished Irish politician, who had been nominated a member of the Senate of the Irish Free State in 1922 by Cosgrave. His name had also been suggested for the new post of Governor-General at the same time, and he proved to be a useful intermediary between the British and Irish governments. Granard wrote to Lord Stamfordham, the King's Private Secretary, indicating that many would regret the passing of the Order, 'but I think that the general opinion would be that it would be better if it came to an end than that its character should be changed and we, in the south, would greatly deplore if this great order was conferred only on Irishmen resident in Northern Ireland'.[9] Granard had certainly consulted Cosgrave by 23 March 1927, and told him that plans were afoot to revive the Order, when the latter indicated to him that such a move would be 'most undesirable'.[10]

Amery recommended that Cosgrave should be informed before any royal appointment was made and assured him that no non-royal appointments were being considered at the present. But whether or not this was done, the Prince of Wales was appointed a Knight of the Order of Saint Patrick on 3 June 1927. The reaction of the press was one of general astonishment since there was a widespread belief that the Order was to be allowed to lapse, and the *Belfast News Letter* reported that the announcement had caused 'a good deal of speculation'.[11]

The appointment broke an important psychological barrier, jolting the government into sorting out the details of how to reconstitute the Order, and how it would function when reconstituted. An informal committee was established, consisting of representatives of the Dominions Office, the Home Office, the Secretary of the Central Chancery of the Orders of Knighthood, and the Prime Ministers's Principal Private Secretary.

The first meeting on 5 July concluded that there was nothing to be gained by simply amending the Statutes of 1905. The situation in Ireland had changed so drastically that nothing less than new Letters Patent and a completely new set of Statutes would do. Sir John Anderson of the Home Office pointed out that the existing Statutes provided for a maximum of ceremonial and an excessive number of Officers, more than any other Order. It was agreed that the new Statutes should be as simple as possible, and provide for a minimum of ceremonial, giving the widest possible discretion to the Sovereign in such areas as investitures. It was also agreed that the Irish character of the Order should be retained, not as formerly by the provision of an Irish habitat and by the Officers being holders of Irish Official posts, but by the appointments themselves, which should be limited as before to persons having a close connection with Ireland. The large number of Officers should be reduced to six: a Grand Master, who should be a member of the Royal Family appointed by the Sovereign; a Chancellor, who should be a Knight of the Order, again nominated by the Sovereign; a King of Arms, a post to be filled by Ulster as before; a Registrar, who should be the Secretary of the Central Chancery of the Orders of Knighthood; a Secretary, and a Gentleman Usher of the Black Rod. Some discussion took place as to whether a Genealogist was strictly necessary, and it was resolved to investigate the reasons for the original appointment of such a Officer, before coming to any decision. The Home Office was to prepare the new Letters Patent, and the Ulster King of Arms was to draw up the new Statutes.

At the second meeting of the Committee on 13 July, Sir Nevile Wilkinson was present by invitation, and he put forward a rather cranky and unworkable suggestion that the Office of Chancellor should be held jointly by the

Governor-General of the Irish Free State, and the Governor of Northern Ireland. The idea was overruled on the grounds that great objections might be made to mentioning the Irish Free State in the Letters Patent. There was the question of the implied equality between the Governor-General and the Governor, and as the whole matter of Dominion honours was shortly to be raised, the adoption of Ulster's suggestion might raise an awkward precedent. Wilkinson recommended that though the functions of the Genealogist were obsolete, the post should be left alone during Sir Henry Burke's lifetime (he died in 1930). The number of Knights was to remain at 22, though some members of the Committee favoured a reduction to the original fifteen. It was felt that any reduction might lead to the undesirable inference that the reduction was a consequence of the Irish Free State having come into being. Wilkinson objected to the impingement on his rights by the appointment of the Secretary of the Central Chancery as Registrar, on the grounds that it might offend national feeling in Ireland and lead to the general supposition that the administration of the Order was to be absorbed into the Central Chancery. Furthermore, all the records were in Dublin and it was inconvenient to remove them. Sir John Anderson pointed out that the Central Chancery was already involved through the custody of the insignia (which had been transferred to London in 1923 in accordance with the King's wishes) and that there was no intention to reduce Ulster's rights. But in deference to Wilkinson's feelings, it was decided that all reference to a Registrar should be omitted, and the Central Chancery should keep only a register of appointments.

By the time of the third and final meeting of the Committee, six days later, Wilkinson had produced a completely new set of Statutes incorporating all the decisions of the first two meetings. The Statutes were, as desired, a model of simplicity, but they were also extremely vague in places and show signs of having been put together without adequate thought or preparation. Article XXVIII, for example, ordered Ulster King of Arms within a year from the investiture of each Knight to make an escutcheon of his armorial bearings on a plate of metal, and a Banner, 'which shall be disposed of as shall be directed by the Sovereign'.[12] Wilkinson copied this injunction directly from Article XXXIV of the 1905 Statutes with the exception of the last phrase. Since Saint Patrick's Hall was no longer available for the erection of the Banner and the plate, the matter should be left entirely in the hands of the Sovereign. The Grand Master was described as 'First or Principal Knight Companion' to end the strange anomaly begun in 1783 and confirmed in 1905, of the Grand Master not being a Knight of the Order. The insignia of the Order were to be deposited in a 'place of safety' rather than 'a steel safe in the strong room'. New Knights were to be invested 'at such time and in such place' as the King should direct. And it was decided not to particularise the source from which a new Knight receive his insignia. Apart from these areas of vagueness, the Statutes of 1927 represented a sensible and workable revision, given that the Order was now without a home and in a state of limbo. The next step was to present the result to the Dublin government and hope for a favourable reaction.

The person chosen for the task was Bernard Arthur William Hastings Forbes, 8th Earl of Granard. Lord Granard had the double distinction of being an Anglo-Irish peer, highly trusted and respected by the British government, and President of the Senate, the Upper House of the Irish Free State Parliament, which gave him easy access to the Irish government. He was also, appropriately, a Knight of St Patrick. At the time of his death in 1948, he was a member of the Irish Council of State, and his funeral was attended by the President of Ireland and Mr. Eamonn de Valera. Some years ago his son, the 9th Earl, presented his father's Star of the Order for permanent exhibition to Saint Patrick's Hall, where it still remains (1981).

Granard was sent to Dublin in March 1928 to try to assess the reaction of the Irish government to a revived Order of St Patrick. He was to make it clear that 'the King and the British Government intend that the Order should continue in being as a live Order, preserving a distinctive Irish character, but that the Government are anxious to proceed in the manner least likely to cause embarrassment to the Free State Government'.[13] Had the British government proceeded with appointments immediately after the creation of the Irish Free State, the Order might have continued without interruption, but because they cautiously hesitated for five years, and then took the step of asking the Irish government for its opinion, they lost both the initiative and the Order. In 1922/3, the Cosgrave administration was facing a bitter civil war, and they would have taken very little notice of something so trivial as an Order of which most Irishmen knew little or nothing. But the situation in 1928 was such that Cosgrave could only say 'no'. Any other reply would have jeopardised his political future. The republicans had formed a strong political party under de Valera's leadership, which contested the 1927 general election for the first time, winning 44 seats, with the Fine Gael party of Cosgrave winning 47, holding on to power by an alliance with the 22-seat Labour Party. The growth of support for the republican Fianna Fail party throughout the 1920s, leading up to its victory at the 1932 election, meant that Cosgrave could not afford to make any concession to the British government without bringing trouble upon himself by losing electoral support, and there was never any possibility that he would agree to the Order's revival. Any attempt would have been met with strong opposition.

Cosgrave called for a report on the Order and its history by the Attorney-General, who returned a lengthy 14-page report on 18 May 1928. The Attorney-General reviewed the history of the Order, and went on to discuss the award of titles of honour by the Crown in countries of the British Empire with Dominion status, paying particular attention to Canada, because it seemed to him to be 'very relevant to and vital for the determination of the problems now presented in the case of the Order of Saint Patrick, that the principles at present governing the grant of such honours and dignities should be ascertained with some degree of precision'. 'The Order of K.P. is, in my opinion, clearly a "title of honour" within the meaning of Article 5 of the Constitution. That Order cannot, therefore, be conferred on a *citizen* of the Irish Free State without the approval or advice of the Executive Council . . . if the Order is granted in respect of services rendered in or in relation to the Irish Free State . . . I would go further and say that the grant to a person not a citizen of the Free State but who was domiciled or ordinarily resident in the Free State would not be proper without the same approval or advice'. The Attorney-General further recommended that the position of Northern Ireland was irrelevant since neither its government nor its Parliament had any jurisdiction over titles of honour, and, having opted out of the Irish Free State, it should be regarded for those purposes as part of Great Britain. 'In fact everything connected with the Order, its further existence or non-existence, its reconstitution and all other matters connected with it would be for the Executive Council to decide and advise . . . In all matters in reference to this order the King would be bound to act on the advice of Irish Ministers without the intervention of any British Minister.'[14]

The report has been quoted at length, since it has formed a basic attitude of every Irish government to the Order of Saint Patrick since 1928. Cosgrave and his colleagues discussed the matter at a Cabinet meeting, and Granard was furnished with a reply: 'We have formed a very strong view that in all the circumstances the most appropriate manner of dealing with the Order is that it should be allowed gradually to lapse. We could not think of advising His Majesty to reconstitute the Order, and of course without our advice and concurrence no purely British peer could be made a Knight of St Patrick'.[15] Cosgrave quoted the example of the Canadian House of Commons, which in 1919 had set up a select committee to consider the position of honours awarded to Canadian citizens. The result was an address to the King urging him to refrain from granting any titles of honours to Canadian citizens. Cosgrave added that report of any committee of the Dail 'would be couched in even stronger terms than the Canadian'.[16]

Granard duly reported back to Baldwin, taking Cosgrave's memorandum with him. The government were divided on how to proceed. Sir William Joynson-Hicks, the Home Secretary, took the view that Cosgrave should be disregarded, the Order brought over, reconstituted, and any further objections ignored: 'It seems to be perfectly ridiculous that a good Order of this kind should be allowed to lapse, merely because Cosgrave and Co. have an objection to it'.[17] Leopold Amery, the Dominions Secretary, who was backed up by Granard, took a more cautious view: 'In view of the action we have already taken, it may be impossible to avoid proceeding to the extent indicated: if so, I am prepared to acquiesce, provided we go very slow. But personally, I should prefer the Order to remain for the time being with its Statutes unchanged, new appointments being restricted to the Royal Family, and, like appointments to the Victorian Order, being made by His Majesty without ministerial advice. If this were adopted, there is, in my opinion, just a chance that the Free State might come in later'.[18] The government decided to adopt Amery's view, and Granard was authorised to tell Cosgrave that his views were not shared by the British government.

The further sequence of events then becomes rather cloudy. We certainly know that on 1 September 1928 the Irish government decided to take over the Office of Arms from 1 October, perhaps with the intention of halting any plans to revive the Order by taking control of its headquarters. There was some delay, however, and it was not until 10 November that the Irish Minister for External Affairs addressed a letter to the Dominions Office announcing his government's intention of taking control of the Office as soon as possible, and hoping for the full assistance of the British government. Initially, the letter made no difference to the plans for the Order's reconstitution, since the Clerk of the Crown in Chancery was preparing the Warrant for Letters Patent giving effect to this on 7 December. But the Letters Patent, and the Statutes which had carefully been drawn up by Nevile Wilkinson in July 1927, were not published and the Order was not reconstituted. It seems likely, therefore, that sometime in December 1928 the government decided to suspend all further action on the question of reviving the Order, and deal instead with this new problem.

Nine months elapsed, before in August 1929, the new Dominions Secretary, Lord Passfield, replied that Ulster was, like the College of Arms in London and Lyon King in Scotland, a servant of the Crown, and exercised his functions by Royal Warrant. In this sense, he was not under the control of the British government and he could not therefore be 'transferred' to the government of any other Dominion. They had no objection to the Free State authorities being responsible for paying the salaries of the Office staff. 'It would not appear, however, that this would give to His Majesty's Government in the Irish Free State any greater control over Ulster that is at present or has in the past been exercised by His Majesty's Government in the United Kingdom.'[19] The despatch was passed to the Minister of Finance who described it as an 'official concoction . . . Its bamboozling tone is very objectionable.'[20] The policy of the Irish government was again delivered to the British government on 29 January 1930: 'The Office (of Arms) performs purely Irish functions and the performance of some of these functions involves the exercise of the Royal Prerogative. The performance of all such functions and the exercise, whenever necessary, of the Royal Prerogative in connection therewith are all matters which must be performed and exercised respectively under the direction and control of the Executive Council.'[21] This was followed by yet another despatch from another new Dominions Secretary, Mr. J. H. Thomas, in July; 'The functions of Ulster extend to the whole of Ireland and are not limited to the area of the Irish Free State. It would seem constitutionally proper that, in the exercise of Ulster's jurisdiction in relating to persons belonging to, and matters arising in Northern Ireland, any Ministerial action should be taken by Ministers in the United Kingdom and not by Ministers in the Irish Free State'.[22] On that note, the matter was allowed to rest, each government agreeing not to raise it again until Sir Nevile Wilkinson either died or retired.

All files relating to the Order from this point onward are unfortunately still closed, so we have no way of knowing exactly what happened, except to say the government probably shelved all plans for the reconstitution of the Order some time in 1930. A memorandum dated 2 September is our only clue to what might have occurred: 'If the Order was reconstituted independently of the Irish Free State, the immediate reaction would certainly be to prohibit the taking of the honour by an Irish Free State citizen. Were so large a part of Ireland thus rendered ineligible for the Order, the essentially Irish character of the Order would be so diminished as practically to have changed the Order out of recognition, and it is open to question whether Irish sentiment would not be more affronted by this than by letting the Order run the risk of lapsing altogether'.[23] The government were still clinging to the hope that the Irish Free State might come to regard the Order as part of its heritage, and agreeing to preserve it from oblivion. It was far better to allow a further period of dormancy and to re-examine the matter at a more propitious time.

So ended the first, and probably the most serious attempt to revive the Order. The government decided to adopt Amery's view, to wait until the Irish Free State were prepared to 'join in', and in the meantime, not award the Order outside the Royal Family, and drop all plans for publishing the revised Statutes.

Chapter Seven

THE END IN SIGHT

'The Order continues to exist but with diminishing numbers and will
tend to disappear as new members cannot be appointed except on the
advice of the Executive Council of Saorstat Eireann, which advice will
not be given'
Irish Government Memorandum
December 1936

LIFE IN THE OFFICE OF ARMS was hardly disturbed by the events of 1922. Wilkinson and his staff went about their business as usual, paid by the Treasury in London, though occupying premises in the heart of Dublin, which belonged to the Irish Free State government. Sir Nevile spent very little time at work in the Office, and was more often to be found at his home in London, much to the annoyance of the Treasury. He made several trips abroad exhibiting 'Titania's Palace', one, oddly enough, to Argentina, before which he took lessons in Spanish. He presided over the Office as a ceremonial figurehead, leaving the day-to-day work in the care of his loyal deputy, Thomas Sadleir, who was undoubtedly underpaid for his workload. Sir Nevile received a salary of £600 p.a., and a clerical assistance allowance of £590. The latter sum was distributed between three officials: Thomas Sadleir received £300 as Registrar and Deputy Ulster; £170 went to a herald painter; and the sole secretary/typist received £120. The staff of the Office was minute, and far below what was needed to maintain standards of efficiency. The frequent and prolonged absences of Sir Nevile hardly justified his salary, and staff who worked for him recall that he used to take 'gentlemanly' week-ends off, sometimes Thursday evenings to Tuesdays. When the practical Edward MacLysaght took over the Office as Chief Genealogical Officer in 1943, he was appalled at the state of arrears. Sadleir confided that he had been too worried to ask for extra staff, in case the Office was closed down.

Although there were the two Heralds, Dublin and Cork, they had no duties or responsibilities within the Office of Arms at all. They were present at formal investitures of the Order in attendance on Ulster King of Arms, and they made their appearance at other Viceregal ceremonies, but no heraldic or genealogical work or knowledge was required of them. Captain R. A. L. Keith, the Cork Herald, was A.D.C. to the Countess of Aberdeen at the time of his appointment in 1910, and a retired officer of the Seaforth Highlanders. Seriously injured in the

First World War, he seems to have spent the remainder of his life in England, holding on to his nominal office until 1952, three years before his death.

In May 1920 Captain Gerald Burgoyne was appointed Deputy Cork Herald and it appears that he undertook some work in the Office. The following month a Writ was prepared for the King's signature by Wilkinson, allowing the appointment of a Junior Pursuivant to the Order, reinstating yet another office abolished by the Royal Warrant of 1871. No nomination appears to have been made to this Office as such, although in 1924 Burgoyne was given the title of Cork Pursuivant, a title hitherto unknown in the history of the Order. He went to Ethiopia in 1936 at the outbreak of the war with Italy, and offered his services to the Emperor. Given command of a Red Cross mule train, he was killed in March during an Italian bombing raid, and his office was not filled.

At the general election of 1932, the Fine Gael party of William Cosgrave, which had held power for 10 years, was defeated by the Fianna Fail party of Eamonn de Valera. De Valera's attitude to the Order is not on record, but there is every reason to suppose that he was as intransigent as his predecessor. Violently opposed to the settlement of 1922, and strongly committed to a 32-county republic, he set about dismantling the constitution he had inherited. By 1937, he could argue that it had been subjected to so many amendments that it was no longer a fit document by which to govern the country, and a totally new constitution was needed. If he was even aware of the continued shadowy existence of the obsolescent Order, it would have scarcely concerned him. He had more important matters to attend to, and in any case, the Attorney-General's memorandum of May 1928 clearly stated government policy towards the Order. Only one appointment had been made in 10 years, and there was every reason to suppose that the British government was respecting the Irish decision of 1928. In fact, he was so concerned with other issues, that neither he nor his government noticed the appointment of the Duke of Gloucester as a Knight of Saint Patrick on 29 June 1934!

The true circumstances surrounding the Duke's appointment are, like most of the recent history of the Order, contained in closed files. There was nothing particularly sensitive about the Order itself, but all government files relating to honours are closed for 50 years, and those relating to Anglo-Irish relations in the 1920s are generally closed for 100 years. Unfortunately, this does not facilitate the study of the recent history of the Order, and for the period from about 1930 onwards we are forced to rely on odd notes which have escaped the censor's net, newspaper articles, rumour, and speculation. Using such sources with care, we can, however, form a reasonably accurate picture of the last years of the Order's life.

In May 1934, the Duke of Gloucester, the King's third son, paid a visit to Northern Ireland, one of the few royal visits there since 1922. On the 31st of the month, the Duke of Abercorn, the Governor, wrote to the King describing the tour as a 'tremendous success', and urging his appointment to the Order as a just reward. The letter was written with the full knowledge and approval of the Prime Minister of Northern Ireland, Lord Craigavon, and may possibly have been written on his advice. Lord Wigram, the King's private secretary, wrote back to the Duke on 2 June, reminding him that the Patrick was only given on the King's initiative. Nevertheless, the Duke's wishes prevailed, and the appointment was announced in the *London Gazette* four weeks later.

What exactly happened in those four weeks? There was no mention of the appointment in the Irish government file dealing with the Order, and the appointment passed unnoticed in Dublin until 1948. This would indicate that there was no negotiation or consultation with the Irish government on the matter. Certainly there must have been considerable discussion in London on the propriety of making another appointment, and we may assume that the King played a significant role in the episode. He had appointed the Duke of Abercorn a K.P. in 1922 after the partition of Ireland, and we know that he was responsible for initiating the attempt at reconstitution in 1927, pressing for the appointments of the Prince of Wales and the Duke of York. He may have recalled the occasion 23 years earlier, when he himself had personally invested Lords Kitchener and Shaftesbury in Dublin Castle, the last occasion on which an English monarch rode in state through the streets of Dublin, and pressed the government to allow the appointment of his son to keep the Order alive.

The Duke's appointment was in full accordance with the 1927 recommendations that no one but members of the Royal Family should be appointed for the time being, and everything possible was done to avoid causing any offence to the Irish Free State government. The appointment was linked to the Duke's successful visit to Northern Ireland, and 'official authorities' stressed that it was being conferred upon him in his capacity as Earl of Ulster. He was invested quietly and privately by the King at Buckingham Palace, probably on 29 June or shortly afterwards. The *Belfast News Letter* greeted the appointment with 'great satisfaction': 'Where, I wonder, will the Duke be invested? Circumstances seem to rule out Dublin Castle. It would create tremendous enthusiasm in the loyal province with which the Duke is so closely associated if the ceremony could take place here, and thus preserve the association of the Order with Ireland'.[1] Despite the paper's strong advocacy of associating the Order with Northern Ireland, voiced on several occasions, particularly at the time of the passing of the Ireland Act in 1948/9, the policy of avoiding such a situation was maintained. The government continued on these lines until 1943, by which time it was generally accepted that the partition of Ireland was permanent, and that Southern Ireland would not participate in any plan to revive the Order.

A similar policy was followed on the appointment of the Duke of York as a K.P. in March 1936. George V, the last King of Ireland, had died in January of that year, to be succeeded by his eldest son, who became King Edward VIII. The new King was unmarried, and his next brother, the Duke of York, became heir presumptive to the throne. In such a situation, the King may have considered it anomalous that the heir to the throne should not possess the third of the three great national Orders, which was already held by their younger brother, the Duke of Gloucester. The Duke's appointment on 17 March (Saint Patrick's Day) added a note of irony, since no ceremony of the Order had been held on the feast day of its tutelar saint since the installation of the first 15 Knights in 1783. The *News Letter* trumpeted the appointment as heralding a visit by the Duke to Northern Ireland in the summer, and announced that the people of Northern Ireland would receive the news of the appointment with feelings of 'deep satisfaction'. In an editorial, the *News Letter* pointed out that the appointment was a welcome announcement and that 'for some years after the constitution of the Irish Free State many people thought that the Order was to be allowed to die out . . . The Order was complete with twenty-two Knights so lately as 1924, but as no successors were appointed on the deaths of Lords Enniskillen, Bandon, Listowel, Pirrie, Ypres, Dunraven and Monteagle the opinion grew that there were to be no new Knights . . .'.[2] The *Irish Independent* carried the investigation a stage further: 'The appointment of the Duke of York . . . indicates the King's intention to preserve this Order . . . His own appointment to the Order in 1927 came as a surprise, as it was believed that King George, in view of the changed status of Ireland, intended to let it lapse . . . Nor are any more appointments likely unless it were thought suitable to appoint a Knight whose connection was with Northern Ireland only. The Government is very anxious not to offend Free State susceptibilities in such matters'.[3] The paper was obviously mistaken about the King's intentions towards the future of the Order. Evidence has shown that he had no intention of allowing it to lapse. It is possible that had King Edward not abdicated in December 1936, he might have appointed his youngest brother, the Duke of Kent, as a Knight of Saint Patrick in due course.

The Duke of York's appointment was the last ever made to the Order of Saint Patrick, bringing the total number of Knights to three Royal and nine non-Royal. The senior Royal Knight was the Duke of Connaught, a son of Queen Victoria and the King's great uncle, who had been appointed as far back as 1869. The senior non-Royal Knight was Lord Castletown, appointed in 1908. One by one, the elderly Knights and Officers died. The offices of Grand Master and Chancellor had lapsed with partition in 1922, and the offices of Secretary, Genealogist and Usher were allowed to remain unfilled on the deaths of the holders in 1926, 1930 and 1933 respectively. Whatever limited functions they still possessed passed to Sir Nevile Wilkinson, who was functioning under the nose of the Irish government in Dublin Castle. He travelled to London with Major Guillamore O'Grady, Dublin Herald, to attend the Coronation of King George VI in May 1937, the Irish government apparently raising no objections. It was probably the last major public appearance of the last Ulster King of Arms, before increasing mental incapacity resulted in his withdrawal to a nursing home.

The continued presence of the Office of Arms had not been forgotten by the Irish government. After letting the matter lie dormant for six years, they raised the question again in the autumn of 1936, and an interesting reference to the Order appears in the lengthy memorandum detailing the duties of Ulster: 'It may be mentioned that the Ulster King of Arms is *ex officio* an officer of the Order of the Knights of St. Patrick under the title of King of Arms, as well as Registrar. [The Order] continues to exist but with diminishing numbers, and will tend to disappear as new members cannot be appointed except on the advice of the Executive Council of Saorstat Eireann, which advice will not be given. This aspect of the matter is consequently of little live interest at the moment'.[4] This would surprisingly seem to indicate that the Irish government had no knowledge of the appointment of the Duke of Gloucester, and that of the Duke of York only months previously. The Dominions Office still insisted that nothing should be done until after the death of Sir Nevile Wilkinson, although he was 'taking an unconscionable time to die . . . To raise the question seriously now might bring a proposal for division of functions, and perhaps it would be better to leave it as it is until we make some further progress on the unity issue. It is, after all, a good thing to have at least one office in Dublin with functions for the whole of Ireland'.[5]

Sir Nevile lingered on for another two years, dying in December 1940. His mind had begun to fail and death came as a release both for himself and his family. If he was ever aware of the political wrangling over the future of his Office, he gave no indication, believing to the end that the great majority of Irishmen were basically conservative at heart with a deep reverence for the institutions of the past, and therefore that his Office would continue. He was not a great herald, and his publications show that his major interest lay in the field of artistry which the love of arms inspires. He was a talented artist, as shown by the immaculately painted Roll of the Knights of St Patrick, which now hangs in the Robing Room of Saint Patrick's Cathedral. In the days of the British administration, Sir Nevile had introduced the custom of hanging three coloured paintings, mounted on dark cloth, from the parapet of the balcony of the Office of Arms, on ceremonial occasions. The paintings depicted a Badge and a Star of the Order, hanging either side of a lozenge-shaped painting depicting the Coat of Arms of the Office itself. In all probability they were the work of Sir Nevile himself. At least one of three survives, in private hands, and shows the Badge of the Order beautifully executed on a canvas measuring 520mm. by 470mm. With the disappearance of Investitures, Levees, Drawing Rooms, and the other ceremonial events of the Viceregal Court the paintings were wisely put into store. There they remained until 1938 when, as a gesture of courtesy, Sir Nevile had them hung out again for the installation of Dr. Douglas Hyde, the first President of Ireland. No-one could fault Ulster on courtesy, but the gesture was scarcely tactful; incensed officials of the republican government ordered him to remove the paintings.

Little more than a month after his death, the question of the future of the Office was raised for the final time. Towards the end of January 1941 the Director of the National Library wrote to the Secretary of the Department of Education, claiming the valuable collection of books and manuscripts held at the Office. The Irish government informed the Dominions Office that the time had now come to end the anomalous status of Ulster King of Arms, once and for all. Seeing that there was now no room for manoeuvre or further delay, the Dominions Office consulted Sir Alexander Hardinge, the King's Private Secretary, the Earl Marshal, and various other interested parties on the best way to proceed. They came to the obvious conclusion that it would be impossible to appoint a new Ulster King of Arms on the old basis, with jurisdiction relating to the whole of Ireland, given the present status of the Irish Free State. But in deference to the general feeling that the historic office should not be allowed to disappear completely, they proposed that the office of Ulster should be amalgamated with one of the three existing Kings of Arms in London. The jurisdiction of the new combined office would then be extended to cover Northern Ireland. The Irish government would then be free to make what arrangements it pleased in relation to the continuance of the functions of the Dublin Office. 'I should add that Ulster King of Arms is, by virtues of his office, the Registrar of the Order of Saint Patrick. In view of the fact that since 1922 no appointments have been made to this Order apart from members of the Royal Family, it is not considered that any practical difficulties would arise as regards the Order . . .'.[6]

The records of the Office initially presented something of a problem as those of the Irish Free State and Northern Ireland were inextricably intermingled. On 30 December 1941, Sir John Maffey, the United Kingdom Representative in Dublin (the title of Ambassador being considered inappropriate), wrote to the Department of the Taoiseach (Prime Minister) proposing the amalgamation plan, adding that the British government would expect *all* the records to be transferred to London. The request was greeted with disbelief by the Minister of External Affairs who described it as preposterous: 'If we acquiesced, there would be a clear implication that we accepted partition as permanent. Moreover the documents are undoubtedly ours, and the British have not a shadow of right to them. In fact the whole proposal is particularly audacious'.[7] There was some concern that the British government might begin to remove the records clandestinely, but de Valera decided that there was no urgency and the matter could safely be left until the war was over, on the strict understanding that no new Ulster should be appointed in the meantime. The Dominions Office, however, was adamant that the whole matter should be resolved without further delay. Thomas Sadleir, who carried on running the Office, derived any powers which he had from a delegation by Ulster, and with the death of Wilkinson, he no longer had any authority to carry out functions peculiar to a King of Arms. It was a very unsatisfactory position which had already lasted longer than it was easy to justify, and·it was necessary to take some definite step to regularise the position without further delay. Maffey discussed the amalgamation proposal with de Valera, who accepted it with some reluctance, and 1 April 1943 was agreed as the date of the transfer of the Office to Irish control.

The last two months saw a hurried tidying up of loose ends. The Office had been clearly understaffed for many years, and the Grant Books, for example, were months in arrears, much to the wrath of Dr. Edward MacLysaght, who was appointed to head the reconstituted Office. Confirmations and new Grants of Arms had to be entered and illustrated in the Grants Book as a record by the Office Painter, a Miss McGrane. Her work was of the highest quality, and inevitably time-consuming. Pedigrees for clients were copied by hand, and arrears were almost certain to develop. The newspapers only made matters worse by using such headlines as 'Ulster King of Arms Ancient Office to be Wound-up' and 'Office of Arms Passes', or, slightly more emotive, 'Eire Takes Over Office of Arms'. When the *Irish Times* announced in late March that the Office of Arms was about to close, the shock waves spread throughout the Commonwealth and the Office was inundated with letters and telegrams from all over the world making last-minute requests to have heraldic or genealogical work done under the old regime. The last request for a Coat of Arms came from Australia, and the last request for a family tree came from a Professor in the University of Allahabad in India. Tom Sadleir was a meticulous and thoughtful man, and the situation clearly worried him: 'What bothers me most is that the Grant Book and Pedigree Register have yet to be brought up to date, since I feel we could not hand over imperfect records. The fact that poor Sir Nevile was nearly two years in a Mental Home caused arrears, and with a small staff it has been impossible to overtake them'.[8]

Sadleir was an expert in heraldry and genealogy and undoubtedly the foremost authority on both subjects in his time. He was offered the chance of heading the reconstituted Office under a different title at the generous salary of £600 p.a. but declined from sentimental loyalty to the Crown. In his place the Irish government appointed Dr. Edward MacLysaght, the distinguished genealogist, to the new post of Chief Genealogical Officer, a title subsequently changed to Chief Herald of Ireland. MacLysaght arrived in the Office on 1 March to familiarise himself with the place before the formal transfer of responsibility on 1 April. While the two men were quite friendly to each other personally it was almost inevitable that the brisk and efficient MacLysaght would become impatient with the rather deliberate and conscientious Sadleir. To MacLysaght, Sadleir was unco-operative, old-fashioned, and slightly cranky, a lingering relic of the authority of the Crown when all else had been swept away. In his memoirs he described Sadleir as 'an unrepentant Unionist in politics, having nothing but ascendancy contempt for the new regime, and he had a pseudo-English accent delivered invariably in a raucous bark not unlike that of a sea-lion'.[9] Sadleir quite naturally resented the fact that his place should be taken by a rebel, a

Sinn Feiner, and a representative of the upstart republican government, who knew little and probably cared nothing for the intricate ways of heraldry and genealogy in which he had immersed himself for more than 30 years.

A slightly old-fashioned figure, Tom Sadleir had been trained as a barrister at King's Inns at the beginning of the century and was called to the Bar in 1906, spending 10 years on the Leinster Circuit before entering the Office of Arms as Registrar in 1916. On the death of George Dames Burtchaell in August 1921, he was appointed Deputy Ulster King of Arms in succession. Had times been other than they were, he might also have expected to succeed to Burtchaell's other post of Athlone Pursuivant. But the government had already taken the first steps towards a transfer of power and the dismantling of their administration in Ireland, and the historic office of Athlone, dating from 1552, quietly disappeared. He was always conscious of his status as a barrister and wore his gown over a suit at work, which lent him a rather schoolmasterly appearance. Badly paid by the Treasury, he was often very hard up and his frugal lunch consisted of a pot of tea and a bun at Bewley's Oriental Cafe in Grafton Street. He had every right to feel aggrieved at the way Sir Nevile Wilkinson expected him to run the Office without commensurate pay, but he remained consistently loyal and made a point of visiting Wilkinson once a week when the latter was confined to an asylum for the last two years of his life.

Sadleir was full of interesting stories and anecdotes, and his knowledge was both encyclopaedic and legendary. Until his death he kept in touch with a wide range of correspondents in the Commonwealth and the United States. His colleagues and friends testify to his great courtesy and generosity and his unrivalled knowledge of Irish heraldry, and also to his willingness to teach others everything he knew. Had the two governments been able to agree on the course, he would certainly have succeeded Wilkinson as Ulster; as it was, his deeply ingrained loyalty to the Crown cost him his job of more than 20 years, and it is difficult not to feel touched by the pathos of his last years. As compensation he was formally offered the post of Rouge Dragon Pursuivant at the College of Arms in London, by the Earl Marshal, but the offer was rescinded by Garter King of Arms, who discovered that Sadleir was in serious financial difficulty and that his name had appeared in the register of debtors.

It proved impossible for him to clear all the arrears of work by 1 April, and he was still working at the Office in early July. His financial difficulties were exacerbated when the Treasury refused to pay him a salary after 31 March, and he was forced to write letter after letter to try to obtain some recognition and compensation for his work after that date. For a man who was so loyal a Unionist that he would rather leave the Office where he had worked for nearly 30 years, rather than run it under another government, his treatment by the British government was disgraceful, and the sum of £250 that he eventually received was paltry and mean. His letters to the Treasury make sad reading: 'I am seriously worried at the turn of events, particularly as I have had no regular income since the 31 March, though I have continued to work daily at clearing the arrears of work . . . I had been offered a post at the College of Arms, but Garter's objections to my lack of means are insurmountable so I must seek other employment. But after 30 years service, I do not think I should be left penniless'.[10]

Eventually he was offered the subordinate and badly-paid post of Assistant Librarian in the Library of King's Inns. The Librarian was a certain Miss Walsh, a woman of pronounced republican sympathies who had little liking for anyone loyal to the Crown and she treated Sadlier with unpleasantness and contempt. His salary of £250 p.a. was less than he had received at the Office of Arms, but after representations to the Home Office by his friends the Earls of Shrewsbury and Wicklow, he was awarded a pension of £300 p.a. from the Civil List for services to scholarship. It was the largest Civil List pension since that awarded to Dr. Johnson. Tom Sadleir died in 1957 at the age of seventy-five.

MacLysaght recorded in his memoirs that he had been told by de Valera to carry on all the activities of the Office of Arms, now renamed the Genealogical Office, except matters relating to the Order of Saint Patrick, which would continue to be under the direct authority of the Sovereign. It is doubtful if de Valera would have issued this directive had he realised how widely MacLysaght would interpret it. Several items relating to the Order still remained in the Office, and they were all removed by the loyal Sadleir and handed over to Sir John Maffey without any interference by MacLysaght. Perhaps the most important item, the Seal of the Order, was handed over on 9 April, an event which was to cause much annoyance five years later. It was followed by two silver collars; two volumes of the register of the Order; a copy of the statutes bound in blue leather for the King's use; a silver and enamel badge, and a miscellaneous collection of such peculiarities as a large blue tablecloth, a blue satin hassock, and a red velvet cushion.

There was now no longer any legitimate base for the Order in Dublin, and it was clear that the Irish government would not allow any further appointments. The hope that Dublin might eventually be persuaded to co-operate over the Order, which had governed the developments and decisions of 1927/8, was not going to materialise. In the light of these developments, there was no further reason to prevent the association of the Order with Northern Ireland alone. The matter was strongly pressed by the new Northern Ireland Prime Minister, Sir Basil Brooke, who came to power on 6 May. He tried to persuade the government to revive the Order, and to transfer its base to the North. Again the files on the episode are still closed, so we have no way of knowing definitely what happened in 1943, but we can assemble an outline of the events.

The transfer of the Office of Arms to the Irish government and the effective abolition of the Office of Ulster probably gave rise to further discussion about the fate of the Order. With de Valera in power in Dublin and Southern Ireland a republic in all but name, there cannot have been anybody of any influence left who still believed that any action should be deferred until Eire was prepared to co-operate in maintaining the existence of the Order. If it was to survive, it would have to be transferred to England or to Northern Ireland. To transfer it to England and reconstitute it independently of Ireland with which it would cease to have any territorial connection, would make a nonsense of the whole ethos of the Order. The most sensible suggestion would be a base in Northern Ireland. With the abandonment of the Dublin office, Eire had no further lever to prevent the British government taking action. Plans were drafted, including a public announcement, and even names of possible K.P.s were mentioned. Generals Dill, Montgomery, Alexander, and Alanbrooke, all distinguished field commanders, and all having connections with Northern Ireland, were proposed. Sir Basil Brooke was pressing the government from Belfast not to let the Order die, and it seems that the plans to revive the Order in 1943 were as serious and far-reaching as those of 1927–30.

Why, then, were they dropped? We have a clue in a note recording a discussion between officials of the Dominions Office and Sir John Maffey. Maffey pronounced himself opposed to the plans as being prejudicial to Anglo-Irish relations. The time was not propitious for such a step. He thought that a time might come when it would be possible to revive the Order of Saint Patrick, as an award for men of Irish origin who had rendered service to the British Commonwealth. 'While the Eire Government could not very well raise objection to the award of British Honours to Irishmen who had rendered valuable war service as members of the United Kingdom Forces, they would, in view of Eire's present position of neutrality, certainly resent the use for this purpose of an Order which in its origin and history, was essentially Irish. The revival of the Order as one for award to persons connected with Northern Ireland only would be unlikely to raise difficulty in relation to Eire, but he wondered whether such a limitation would not be likely to detract from the value of the Order in the eyes of possible recipients'.[11] Maffey's views would certainly have carried weight in London, and he may have been instrumental in stifling the last serious attempt to revive the Order.

Chapter Eight

THE TWILIGHT YEARS

'Is the Order of Saint Patrick to go on or is it not?'
Sir Hugh O'Neill
11 May 1949

IN JULY 1946, King George VI spoke to Clement Attlee, then Prime Minister, about the possibility of conferring the Orders of the Garter, the Thistle, and the Saint Patrick, on his own authority, without any reference to the Prime Minister. The King felt that these three national honours had been considerably devalued by being used for political patronage, an irony when one considers the origins of the Patrick, and he was anxious to raise their status by assuming personal responsibility for appointments. It seems possible that once again the government toyed with the idea of reviving the Patrick, but highly improbable that it was given any serious consideration. A draft announcement was prepared, to be made at the time that any appointments under the new procedure were announced. 'You will note that . . . no reference is made to the Thistle and the Patrick . . . The object of this procedure is to avoid the possibility of the Eire Government raising difficulties about the Patrick. If questions were asked about the Patrick, it would merely be said that the matter did not arise as no appointments were being made at the present moment.'[1] We might infer from this that the government was anxious to keep all options on the Patrick open without seriously intending any action. The King himself records in his diary his feelings of delight at having the Garter and the Thistle returned to his personal control, but makes no mention of the Patrick, perhaps implicitly recognising its loss.

The Order of Saint Patrick was passing into the shadows. With the exception of the Sovereign and the two Royal Dukes—Windsor and Gloucester—there were only seven Knights still alive: Lord Granard, who had tried so hard to keep the Order alive in the 1920s; Lord Arran, the Liberal philanthropist; Lord Shaftesbury, former Lord Mayor of Belfast and Chamberlain to Queen Mary; Lord Donoughmore, the Conservative politician; Lord Powerscourt, who had declined the Viceroyalty in 1916; Lord Cavan, the distinguished soldier; and the Duke of Abercorn, first Governor of Northern Ireland. When the latter retired as Governor in 1945, the King significantly did not feel able to follow the precedent set by his father and appoint the new Governor, Earl Granville, a Knight of Saint Patrick.

One by one, the elderly Knights died, and as the Order faded from living memory so, too, did its chances of survival. The question of maintaining the Order at full or even half strength had exercised the minds of three government departments in the 1920s, but by 1946 there were few people left in office who could remember the great days of the Order in the first decade of the century. There was nobody left to fight for the future of an Order, whose shadowy existence was now an anachronistic, embarrassing survival of a long vanished culture. The glittering social world of Viceregal Dublin and the Anglo-Irish aristocracy, in which the Order had once figured so prominently, was drifting from fond memory to the history book, and the announced withdrawal of Ireland from the Commonwealth in 1948 finally severed the last tenuous links binding Southern Ireland and Great Britain. At the same time, a series of deaths brought the Order to the brink of extinction. Lord Cavan died in August 1946. Lord Powerscourt died in March 1947, followed two months later by Viscount Fitzalan, the last Grand Master. Viscount Greenwood, who had briefly occupied the office of Chancellor in 1921-2 died on 10 September 1947, the same day as Lord Granard. Granard had become a distinguished and respected politician in the Irish Free State after partition, and his funeral in Northern Ireland was attended by President O'Kelly and Prime Minister de Valera. The death of the 6th Earl of Donoughmore in October 1948 evoked a strange memory of the beginning of the Order. His ancestor, John Hely-Hutchinson, Prime Serjeant of Ireland, later 1st Earl of Donoughmore, had read the Royal Warrant creating the Order to the assembled Knights in Saint Patrick's Hall on 11 March 1783. The present Lord Brookeborough recalls that his father again made strenuous efforts at the time to keep the Order alive by transferring it to Belfast, but to no avail; the government were adamantly opposed to his plans. By the end of the 1940s, the Order of Saint Patrick had been permanently confined to the limbo of the lost, a graveyard it shares with hundreds of other defunct Orders of greater or lesser repute.

In May 1948, a certain Dr. Nolan, an official in the Department of the Taoiseach, was perusing a copy of *Thom's Directory*. He noted that the list of the remaining Knights included the name of the Duke of Gloucester, and 1934, the year of his appointment, 'an interesting fact—not disclosed by the previous papers on this file'.[2] How the Irish government could have overlooked the appointment of the Duke, 14 years earlier, which was widely reported in Dublin newspapers, is incomprehensible. Reading the Attorney-General's minute of May 1928, Dr. Nolan noticed first that the appointment had breached Irish government policy, and, secondly, that appointments were made by warrant under the royal sign manual and the Seal of the Order. He concluded rather pedantically that if this Seal was still kept at the Office of Arms in Dublin Castle, since its affixing to warrants was necessary for the appointment of new Knights, 'we would have in our hands an effective weapon with which to kill the Order . . . for, having the seal under our control, we could decline to permit it to be used for the purpose of sealing the warrants of appointments of any further Knights'.[3] On making enquiries at the Genealogical Office, he was informed that the Seal had been handed over on request to a member of the staff of the British Representative in Dublin on 9 April 1943. His annoyance at having his plan ruined is barely concealed: 'It was, in my view, a mistake of the first magnitude for the Genealogical Office to part with this seal in the cavalier fashion in which they evidently did . . . The question for us to consider now is: Can we do anything effective at this stage to remedy the damage that has been done by the surrender of this seal? I am afraid not. Possession is nine points of the law, and it would, in my view, be quite futile for us to prevail on the British authorites to restore the seal to us . . . As the result of the apparently thoughtless disposal what was, in fact, Irish state property, a golden opportunity of implementing, by a process of attrition, the former Executive Council's decision of the 21st May 1928 that the Order of the Knights of St Patrick should be allowed completely to disappear has been lost'.[4] Why Dr. Nolan should have pursued the matter of the Seal with such relentless intensity is puzzling, since the passage of 14 years must surely have been sufficient evidence that the Order was being allowed to lapse.

On 11 May 1949, Sir Hugh O'Neill (later Lord Rathcavan), Member of Parliament for Antrim, made a speech in the House of Commons during the debate on the Second Reading of the Ireland Bill, which gave recognition to Ireland's formal adoption of republican status, and her withdrawal from the Commonwealth. Beginning with a plea for the continued election of Irish Representative Peers to the House of Lords, he then went on to the Order: 'What is going to be the future of that great Order of Knighthood of St. Patrick which . . . has historic associations of the greatest importance? Is the Order of St. Patrick to go on, or is it not?'[5] He went on to argue for its transfer to Northern Ireland, which, in view of his close friendship with Sir Basil Brooke, the Prime Minister, was natural. Needless to add the government returned no answer, but there is evidence that the future of the Order was once more undergoing scrutiny. It seems that Brooke made a supreme and probably final effort to have the Order revived and transferred to Northern Ireland. Rumour had it in Northern Ireland some years ago that he himself ardently desired to be a K.P., and would have much preferred it to the Viscountcy he eventually received in 1952, although his family and colleagues deny that he had any personal interest in the Order. He was the last Prime Minister of Northern Ireland to take a serious interest in the Order. Lord O'Neill of the Maine (Prime Minister, 1963–69) remembers being in favour of the continuation of the Order before 1963, feeling that it could be made into a symbol of unity if leading Catholics of the Province could be persuaded to accept it. He raised the question of Irish peers being allowed to sit in the House of Lords with Jack Lynch (Prime Minister of Ireland, 1966–1973, 1977–1979), who seemed quite uninterested in the whole matter. Lord O'Neill was convinced that London would do nothing for the Irish peers without the consent of Dublin, and therefore they would do nothing for the

Patrick. 'I think we must now realise that London never had any intention of keeping the Patrick alive—*unless* Dublin itself was keen, and this was obviously never on'.[6]

Apparently in these twilight years, the Church of Ireland again laid a claim to the spiritual side of the Order. When plans were afoot for the extension of Saint Anne's Cathedral in Belfast, the Cathedral authorities offered informally to build a special chapel to house the Order, on the lines of the Thistle Chapel attached to Saint Giles Cathedral in Edinburgh—it the Order was revived. If the Order of Saint Patrick was discussed in Northern Ireland government circles at all after 1963, such discussion almost would certainly have ended after 1969 when the advent of the civil disturbances would have lowered priority of such matters.

The Order lingered on after 1949, forgotten by most people, and of insignificant size, yet its continued existence presented something of a problem at the Coronation of Queen Elizabeth II in 1953. The two elderly Heralds of the Order, Major Guillamore O'Grady, Dublin Herald, and Captain Richard Alexander Lyonal Keith, Cork Herald, had been appointed to their offices in 1908 and 1910 respectively at comparatively youthful ages, and 40 years later they were still alive. These surviving relics from the zenith of the Order's history presented a quandary for those charged with making preparations for the Coronation. At the Coronation of King George V in 1911, both Heralds presented claims to be present, which were allowed, though no duties were assigned, and at the Coronation of George VI in 1937 the procedure was repeated. But what was to happen in 1953? In 1937, Ireland was still a member of the Commonwealth, and an Ulster King of Arms still functioned in Dublin Castle, but the subsequent 15 years had brought dramatic changes. Ireland was now a republic outside the Commonwealth, and Ulster's office was no more. The presence of two Heralds named Dublin and Cork at the Coronation might cause offence to the Irish delegation and irritate Anglo-Irish relations on an otherwise happy and joyful occasion. The Secretary of the Central Chancery of the Orders of Knighthood and Garter King of Arms discussed the question. The name of Major O'Grady had, in fact, been omitted from the annual printed list of Knights and Officers of the Order for some years, probably due to his continued residence in Dublin. He died on 4 September 1952, at the age of seventy-three. Captain Keith, however, was still alive at the age of 68, and living happily in retirement at Newbury in Berkshire. After discussions between the Chancery and the College of Arms, Keith was approached and the tactful suggestion was made that he might care to submit his resignation from an office, which had been nothing more than a sinecure since 1922. Keith visited Norroy and Ulster at the College of Arms on 10 July 1952, and agreed to resign. A very handsome man and a tremendous socialite who adored parties, he was kind and thoughtful, enormously popular, and loved by all who met him. It was quite in keeping with his character that he should have resigned happily without fuss or objection.

By this time, the Order was little more than the shadow of a shade. The death of the Duke of Abercorn in 1953 reduced the number of Knights to four—the Dukes of Gloucester and Windsor, and the Earls of Arran and Shaftesbury. Although a Norroy and Ulster King still reigned in London, his titles of King of Arms, Registrar and Knight Attendant were empty of meaning. The Riband and Star of the Order were still occasionally seen in public in the 1960s, usually on the Duke of Gloucester. On a visit to Kenya in 1962, the Duke wore the insignia with the tropical uniform of the Royal Inniskilling Fusiliers, of which he was Colonel-in-Chief. When the colours of the Regiment were laid up a few years later in Saint Marcartin's Cathedral, Enniskillen, the Duke was again seen in the insignia of the Order. It was probably the last occasion on which the insignia of the Order was worn publicly in Ireland by a K.P. His death in June 1974 marked the end of an Order of which few people had heard.

Though strictly outside the scope of this history, it may be of interest to record briefly the various occasions on which the Irish government has given consideration to the establishment of a decoration to replace the Order of Saint Patrick. The first occasion was in the period 1929–30, towards the end of the British government's first serious attempt to revive the Patrick. No details are to hand concerning the name or structure of the proposed 'State decoration', but it was discussed by the Executive Council between December 1929 and July 1930. A preliminary draft had been prepared in the Department of External Affairs and modified by the Minister of Finance who then submitted it to a meeting of the Council on 10 December 1929. The plan was referred back to the Ministers of Finance and External Affairs and the Attorney-General for further discussion of the details. Eventually, in June 1930, they submitted a draft of the Letters Patent and Statutes. After preliminary consideration, the matter was discussed at an informal meeting of Ministers on 3 July. The Council decided that the scheme should go ahead, but not until unofficial negotiations had taken place with the British government, 'preferably verbally'. Why they should have felt such discussions to be necessary is not entirely clear since great efforts had been made to show the British government that the future of the Order of Saint Patrick was entirely within their jurisdiction. The then Minister of External Affairs undertook to bear the decision in mind for appropriate action at a suitable opportunity.

Apparently a suitable opportunity did not arise, and the defeat of the Cosgrave government at the General Election in March 1932 ended any possibility that it might be raised. The new Irish Premier, Eamonn de Valera was concerned with much weightier issues than a state decoration; such as the place of the Crown in the Irish Constitution, the presence of the Governor-General in Phoenix Park, the Oath of Allegiance, and payment of the Land Annuities. The creation of an Irish State Order was not high on his list of priorities, and the matter was not raised again until 1941.

On 23 August, Oscar Traynor, the Minister of Defence, submitted a new plan for an Irish Order to de Valera. The plan appears to have come almost entirely from his own imagination, combining a fascination for Irish antiquities, and an an admiration for the French Legion of Honour. He proposed the creation of an Order to be called 'The Order of the Lunulu', the name deriving from a crescent-shaped piece of gold dating from an early period of Irish history, 'since it represents a period when this country led the world in the use of gold as an ornament'. Traynor proposed that the Order should be divided into five classes or branches. Firstly, 'The Lunulu' limited to one recipient who in the opinion of the government had 'done most for Ireland'; secondly, 'Champions of the Lunulu', for distinguished or meritorious service to the State; thirdly, 'Commanders of the Lunulu' for the field of letters and learning; fourthly, 'Officers of the Lunulu' to be at 'the disposal of the Government'; and a fifth miscellaneous class called 'Members of the Lunulu'. The idea was a fanciful and romantic piece of nonsense thought up by someone with little experience in the field of orders and decorations, and was quickly discarded by de Valera.

It comes as something of a surprise to learn that the government of Sean Lemass (Taoiseach, 1959–1966) briefly toyed with the idea of setting up their own Order of St Patrick in 1963. In October 1962, a Mrs. Isabelle MacKenzie Lester of County Antrim wrote to Lemass suggesting that the Order should be revived and conferred on the President of Ireland, Eamonn de Valera. She felt it would be a very signal Irish honour conferred on a very celebrated personage in recognition of his life's work. She remembered being present in Saint Patrick's Hall at the beginning of the century at an investiture, and 'it was a most beautiful moving and colourful ceremony of which Irish men and women could be proud'.[7] Lemass courteously replied that though the Irish government had no honours or decorations of any kind at its disposal, the need for one was becoming more generally recognised, 'and some consideration has been given to its institution'.[8] Nothing resulted from this, until the matter was given a new impetus six months later with the impending visit of President John Kennedy of the United States. The Irish government realised too late that they had no honour at all to give the Irish-American President as a gesture of friendship and respect. The Department of the Taoiseach initially suggested that the President should be made an honorary citizen of Ireland, until it was pointed out that by Article 9 of the Constitution, loyalty to the State was expected from all citizens. This could hardly be expected of a foreign Head of State. Once more the question of the Order of Saint Patrick was raised. The Minister of External Affairs suggested that an Order of Saint Patrick should be set up as an award for foreigners, adding that he was aware of the existence of the 'dying British order',[9] but did not regard it as an inhibiting factor. Requesting the Irish Ambassador in Washington to ascertain the American practice regarding the acceptance of foreign Orders, he submitted his plans to the Taoiseach's Department.

Though undoubtedly well intentioned, the Minister clearly had little knowledge of Orders and Decorations, and we can only be thankful that his plans never came to fruition. The Order was to be divided into four classes: members of the Supreme Cross, members of the Grand Cross, members of the Cross, and members. Appointments to the Order were to be made by the President on the advice of the government, with the exception of the Supreme Cross to which appointments were only to be made after consultation with the Council of State. Recipients were to be persons who in the opinion of the government had 'done honour to the State', and who were 'citizens of States other than Ireland'.[10]

The reply from Washington indicated that the President was not allowed to accept foreign decorations, and the proposed Order was never implemented. Nor should it have been, for three reasons. Firstly, it was a stupid idea to try to put together an institution as intricate and important as an Order in such a short time, solely to meet one particular situation. The importance of this award, quite apart from the time and effort required to write a constitution and design and manufacture insignia, would have justified at least a year's work. Secondly, it was nonsensical to create an honour solely for award to foreigners. There are isolated examples of such honours, but an Order which is not highly coveted and highly prized at home is not really fit to give to foreigners as a token of that State's esteem and regard. Thirdly, why use the name of an existing Order which throughout its history was conferred on Irishmen or those intimately connected with Ireland? At the time of writing, Ireland still has no way of honouring its own citizens or foreigners other than the conferment of a degree by Trinity College. Should the matter be raised again, greater care and consideration might be given to the institution of an honour which, by its originality, will reflect the distinctive character of the Republic of Ireland.

How illustrious was the Order of Saint Patrick? On his appointment as a K.P. in November 1881, the distinguished Irish jurist, Lord O'Hagan, recorded his pride at being associated with an Order founded at the brightest period of the chequered history of Ireland. There had been 'no blot upon its escutcheon, no failure in its duty, and no declension of its untarnished fame'.[11] It had never been associated with any political faction, or with sectarian intolerance, and in its spirit and action it was a national Order.

We would not presume to say that Lord O'Hagan did not mean what he said, but we cannot help but feel that his delight at receiving the Order, probably coupled with a meagre knowledge of its beginnings, clouded his customary perspicacity. The Most Illustrious Order of Saint Patrick along with the Most Noble Order of the Garter, the Most Ancient and Most Noble of the Thistle and all their superlative companions was, in its origins at least, no more than a convenient and inexpensive way of saving the monarch from dispensing large amounts of cash as bribes. Despite Lord O'Hagan's claim that it stood above party strife, the Order remained very much a prerogative of the party in power.

Apart from a few distinguished exceptions, the politics of the new Knight were invariably those of the government of the day. In the period up to the dissolution of the Irish Parliament, party politics were to an extent irrelevant, since party majorities could vanish overnight on some issues. The most powerful and influential peers, whatever their politics, found the Order dangling in front of their noses to attract their support. While briefly Prime Minister in 1868, Benjamin Disraeli appointed two Conservative peers to the Order, the Earl of Erne and the Earl of Mayo. Again, in his second term of office from 1874 to 1880, he appointed a further three Conservative peers, the Duke of Manchester, the Marquess of Londonderry, and the Earl of Portarlington. In his first two years as Prime Minister, William Gladstone appointed a total of 15 peers to the Order. Excluding the Duke of Connaught, the Queen's second son, and Field Marshal Viscount Wolseley, who might reasonably be expected to stand above party politics, the remaining 13 were all Liberal peers. The long period of Conservative rule stretching with few interruptions from 1885 to 1905, under the Marquess of Salisbury and then Arthur Balfour, saw the appointment of 20 Conservative peers to the Order. The line was punctuated only by a solitary Liberal, the 9th Earl of Cavan, appointed during the brief Liberal administration of Lord Rosebery in 1894.

It would be a waste of effort to examine the careers of the 146 Knights in the hope of finding some deed or episode justifying their appointment to such a high Order. They were all wealthy land-owning peers and loyal party servants, and in Victorian England that was merit enough. The concept of meritocracy in the award of honours is a 20th-century phenomenon. But occasionally we can discern deserving merit behind appointments. There were the distinguished soldiers: Marquess Wellesley (1783); Viscount Gough (1857); Viscount Wolseley (1885); Earl Roberts (1897); Earl Kitchener of Khartoum (1911); and the 10th Earl of Cavan (1916). Slightly less well known were General the Earl of Cork (1835); Brigadier-General the Earl of Longford (1901), killed at Gallipoli in 1915; and Lieutenant-General Lord de Ros (1902). The Marquess of Dufferin and Ava (1864), diplomat and Viceroy of India; the lawyer, Lord O'Hagan (1882), who rose to be Lord Chancellor of Ireland; the Earl of Iveagh (1895), head of the famous Guinness brewing family; and Viscount Pirrie (1909), the shrewd and successful industrialist whose appointment caused so much offence to his fellow Knights.

Probably among the more famous and interesting Knights were the two astronomer Earls of Rosse; William, the third Earl (K.P., 1845), and Lawrence, the fourth Earl (K.P., 1890). The third Earl was one of the best known astronomers of his age. He began by constructing a telescope with a reflecting speculum in the grounds of his castle at Birr in Co. Offaly. He did everything himself as there were no telescopes like this to be bought, or, indeed, other astronomers to help him. He started with the aid of a carpenter, a blacksmith, and some unskilled labourers, whom he trained. He experimented with all kinds of alloys to see which would be best for the speculum, even soldering plates of fine metal to the back of brass, before finally selecting an alloy of copper and tin. Still not satisfied with the results of his three-foot telescope, he constructed one twice that size when his father died and he inherited the estate in 1841. The result was the famous Leviathan of Parsonstown, the greatest telescope on earth for over three-quarters of a century. It proved capable of gathering more light and seeing far further into space than any telescope had ever been able to do before. Lord Rosse saw objects more than ten million light years away in space, and discerned their spiral nature as galaxies. His castle became a place of pilgrimage for all interested in astronomy, because it was the only place on earth from which such distant galaxies could be seen.

On his death in 1867 he was succeeded by his eldest son, Lawrence, who had already learnt much from his father. The fourth Earl is most widely acclaimed for measuring the heat of the moon, designing and making an instrument on which a telescope could focus the lunar radiation. He made observations of Jupiter, measured the position of the satellites of Uranus, and confirmed the existence of the smaller ones of Mars. He counted the meteors which formed the shower ending of Beila's Comet and had his last assistant devote five years to drawing a map of the Milky Way. On his death in 1908, the astronomical work at Birr Castle came to a close, and the reflector of the famous Leviathan telescope was moved to the Science Museum in London The third Earl also deserves mention for his generosity towards the tenantry of his estate, a quality rare among 19th-century Irish landlords. He devoted all the revenue from his estates to relieve the distress caused by the appalling famine of 1846/7.

Another of the more philanthropic members of the Order was the 12th Earl of Meath (1905), who gave up a promising career in the Diplomatic Service in 1873, when he and his wife decided to devote themselves to the 'consideration of social problems and the relief of human suffering'. He founded the Hospital Saturday Fund Committee in 1874, and the Dublin Hospital Sunday movement, both to raise money for hospitals. In 1879 he founded the Young Men's Friendly Society which was later to develop into the Church of England Men's Society. He also founded the Metropolitan Public Gardens Association, and was the first Chairman of the Parks Committee of the London County Council. London owes the preservation of many of its open spaces, and the formation of parks, gardens and playgrounds covering thousands of acres to his energy and inspiration. After a long campaign, he succeeded in persuading the government to institute Empire Day, celebrated annually on 24 May, the birthday of Queen Victoria. Meath was something of a forbidding figure with his stern emphasis on discipline, service and citizenship—he was Chief Scout Commissioner for Ireland—but he had a dry humour, and an unquenchable enthusiasm and a practical knowledge of the world and its ways, which ensured that he always found friends and helpers for whatever scheme he embarked upon.

As achievement or lack of it was not a bar to admission to the Order, so neither was age. Of the 146 Knights, more than a third were aged 39 or under at the time of their appointment. Lord Mornington (later Lord Wellesley) was only 22 at the time of his investiture as one of the first K.P.s in 1783. Lord Ormonde was 28 at the time of his appointment in 1798. Lord Granard (1857) was only 24, as was the 5th Marquess of Waterford (1868). The tradition was continued with his son, the 6th Marquess, who was appointed in 1902 at the age of twenty-six. As late as 1916, Viscount Powerscourt was appointed at the age of thirty-six. The youngest of all Knights was the 2nd Marquess of Sligo, made a K.P. in March 1810, 10 months after his 21st birthday.

The practice of handing the Order out to successive heads of the same family or bearers of the same title followed the pattern of the Garter in England: the 2nd, 4th, 5th, and 6th Earls of Arran; the 1st, 4th, and 5th Earls of Carysfort; the 1st, 2nd, and 3rd Earls of Charlemont; the 3rd Earl, and the 1st and 2nd Marquesses of Ely; the 1st, 2nd, and 3rd Marquesses of Headfort; the 18th Earl and the 1st, 2nd, and 3rd Marquesses of Ormonde. The Beresford family was the most highly favoured of all: the 1st, 2nd, 3rd, 5th, and 6th Marquesses of Waterford were all appointed at comparatively youthful ages. The 4th Marquess would no doubt have been appointed had he lived long enough, and had the Order survived, the present Marquess might well enjoy the honour;

Whatever the quality of the earlier Knights, the calibre of the 20th-century appointments is reflected in the fact that nine K.P.s were elected either by the Privy Council or by their fellow peers to the Senate of the stillborn Legislature of Southern Ireland, envisaged by the Government of Ireland Act 1920. When the constitution of Southern Ireland was finalised in 1923, three Knights were nominated by William Cosgrave to serve as members of the Upper House (Seanad Eireann): the Earl of Dunraven (1923-6), the Earl of Mayo (1923-7), and the Earl of Granard (1923-34). Granard served as President of the Senate for several years and enjoyed the trust of both the Irish and British governments. He was eventually appointed to the Irish Council of State, a body of distinguished advisers to the President of Ireland.

After the effective loss of the Order of Saint Patrick in 1922, the interesting question arose of how to reward deserving Irish peers. The field was obviously much reduced since no British government could contemplate honouring peers living in the Irish Free State for fear of incensing the Irish government. But what of Irish peers living in Northern Ireland or in England? Anything below the three national Orders would hardly be adequate, and since the Patrick was now lost, the choice lay between the Garter and the Thistle. Of the two, the latter is emphatically Scottish in every aspect of its constitution, and excluding members of the Royal Family, only one non-Scotsman—the King of Norway—has ever been appointed a K.T. The Order of the Garter on the other hand has never been strictly an English Order. Its conferment has always been wider than the boundaries of England, and two of the earlier K.P.s, Earl Talbot and Marquess

Wellesley, resigned the Patrick on being appointed to the Garter. Irish peers, peers with Irish titles, or peers having some other connection with Ireland always seem to have been appointed to the Garter since 1922, as the following list shows:

Viscount Fitzalan of Derwent (last Lord Lieutenant and Grand Master) - - - - - -	K.G. 1925
Earl of Athlone (brother of Queen Mary) - -	K.G. 1928
Duke of Abercorn (K.P. 1922) - - - -	K.G. 1928
Viscount Alanbrooke - - - - - -	K.G. 1946
Viscount Alexander of Tunis - - - -	K.G. 1946
Viscount Montgomery of Alamein - - -	K.G. 1946
Earl of Iveagh - ' - - - - -	K.G. 1955
Lord Wakehurst (Governor of Northern Ireland, 1952–64) - - - - - - - -	K.G. 1962
Earl Alexander of Hillsborough - - - -	K.G. 1964
Viscount Brookeborough (Prime Minister of Northern Ireland, 1943–63) - - - - -	K.G. 1965
Earl of Longford - - - - - - -	K.G. 1971
Earl of Drogheda - - - - - - -	K.G. 1972

It seems unlikely that the Order of Saint Patrick will ever be revived now. Nor is there any reason why it should be. The few remaining Irish peers whose service to the Crown is such that they deserve a high honour can be quite happily accommodated in the ranks of the Knights of the Garter without the necessity of establishing a separate Order. Any attempt to revive the Order would almost certainly meet with the disapproval and even strong opposition of the government of the Irish Republic. In the present political climate, it is difficult to see what British government would press ahead with such an attempt in the face of such opposition.

Though few realised it at the time, the cataclysmic events of 1921/2 rendered the Order something of an anomaly. The civil servants and politicians of the 1920s failed to realise that the Order of Saint Patrick was, in essence, a small part of the whole Anglo-Irish establishment. The investitures were a social feature of the Viceregal Court as much as the Garter ceremonies were a feature of the English Court. The Viceroy in Dublin, with his Castle, his Court and his servants, and surrounded by his aristocracy, was in every respect a miniature replica of the King in London. His state entrance to the city at the beginning of his viceroyalty and his solemn investiture with the Grand Master's insignia by the Lords Justices, paralleled the Coronation. His equally solemn state exit at the end of his viceroyalty, along streets lined with troops, accompanied by the Commander-in-Chief of Ireland, resembled the departure of a monarch. It is against this background that the Order of Saint Patrick needs to be set, for a full understanding of its role. It then becomes very clear that when the whole paraphernalia of English rule in Ireland vanished overnight in 1922, the Order was left in a strangely isolated position. The supporting cast had disappeared, and for more than 20 years it languished in the wings while various groups and individuals floundered around trying to find a role it could usefully play. Had the British government seized the initiative and transferred the Order to Belfast almost as soon as partition had been accomplished, it *might* have survived. It would have been unwarrantably large for the few peers living in Northern Ireland, and such a change of the whole basis of the Order might have reduced its value in the eyes of possible recipients. A far better case could be made out for the erection of an entirely new Order for the people of Northern Ireland.

The departure of this great Irish Order will inevitably evoke some feelings of loss, if only for the fact that its attractive sky blue robes and insignia have disappeared from the public eye for good, but we should remember that the main reason for the existence of the Order of Saint Patrick departed with the British administration in 1922. Were it to be revived now, it could, at best, only be a pale shadow of its former glory, and there is something desperately pathetic about attempts to revive or preserve things which have long since lost all meaning. The Most Illustrious Order of Saint Patrick was the product of a particular period in Irish history. It was created because it was needed, and while the need continued, so did the Order, serving a purpose and playing a role. Since both purpose and role have ceased to exist, so, too, has the Order.

Chapter Nine

THE ROBES AND INSIGNIA–I

SOME DISCUSSION, the majority of it unrecorded, must have been given to the design and manufacture of the robes and insignia of the new Order in the early weeks of 1783, and there appear to have been two guiding principles. Firstly, the Order was to be distinctively Irish as befitted a newly independent Kingdom of Ireland. Secondly, it was to reflect the continuing bond between England and Ireland.

From the very scanty evidence available, it would seem that the insignia were designed by Joseph Edmondson, Mowbray Herald Extraordinary, whom Temple had invited to Dublin to superintend the arrangements relating to the Installation. His surviving papers include sketches of Ulster's Sceptre and the Usher's Rod. The basic elements of the design—the shamrock, the harp, and the so-called Cross of Saint Patrick—were borrowed from the insignia of the Friendly Brothers of Saint Patrick, a quasi-Masonic society founded in 1650 with the intention of preventing duelling. The Grand Master apparently wore a Collar similar in appearance to that designed for the Knights of Saint Patrick.

With the exception of the insignia, the colour of the robes is the most instantly recognisable feature of any Order. The colours of the three existing Orders, dark blue for the Garter, green for the Thistle, and scarlet for the Bath, left very little choice for the Patrick. Temple recorded that the colour orange was initially proposed for the Riband and Robes, in honour of William of Orange and 'the sense which this kingdom enjoys of the benefits she received from the glorious revolution, and from that great prince whose name is so deservedly dear to them'.[1] But the colour was rejected partly on the grounds that it was the colour of the riband worn by the Baronets of Nova Scotia, and partly to avoid placing the Order on any sectarian footing by giving it a colour so indissolubly wedded to Irish Protestantism. Temple records that there was a generally expressed wish to put an end to every appearance which could constitute a party distinction. To begin the new Order by clothing the Knights in such an aggressively Protestant colour would hardly have augured well for its future. No Catholic Knights were, in fact, appointed before the Earl of Fingall in 1821, but the point was important. The colour sky blue was eventually settled upon, being the colour of the field of the arms of Ireland. Evidently there was further discussion in London, for Temple wrote to his brother on 27 January urging that the colour should not be altered.

The Mantle was to be of sky-blue satin, lined with white silk with a symbolic hood of the same colours and materials attached to the right shoulder. It was fastened by a cordon of blue silk and gold with two blue silk and gold tassels at each end. The cordon was a cumbersome, yet very impressive, piece of workmanship. At 410cm. it was far longer than was actually necessary to fasten the Mantle, and needed to be looped into a rather large knot to prevent the tassels from trailing along the ground. It consisted of metal and sky-blue silk thread tightly interwoven, ending in two enormous Georgian-style tassels.

Temple was anxious from the beginning to use the occasion of the installation as a demonstration of Irish manufacturing skills, guessing how popular such a move would be with the people of Dublin in providing them with work. The *Dublin Evening Post* reported that 2–3,000 yards of satin were used in the manufacture of the costumes of the Knights and Esquires, 'the produce of several looms . . . which incessantly worked day and night for these six weeks past to complete in time the extensive commission'.[2]

The original material was prepared by the Castle draper, a Mr. Magan of High Street. Apparently it was originally intended that the robes should be of velvet, but it was found impossible to procure the necessary quantity by 17 March. Satin was adopted instead, 'and occasioned no small growling among the mercers that a woollen draper should presume to employ Irish artists on silk looms'.[3] The Mantles were made up by Mr. Ray, a tailor, of 27 Stafford Street, who was forced to place an advertisement in the *Dublin Evening Post* on 4 March addressed to the new Knights: 'Unless they forward their measures to him immediately to have their robes made, they will unavoidably be disappointed, as the time until the 17th inst. is so very short, it will not admit of any delay'.[4] Evidently the response was not overwhelming since the advertisement was repeated as late as 13 March.

Successive Viceroys followed Temple's pattern. Before the Installation of 1819, Lord Talbot (Viceroy, 1817-1821) gave Sir William Betham strict instructions to ensure that the occasion was as beneficial as possible to the manufacturers of Dublin. Despite the injunction contained in the original Statutes that the Mantles should be of Irish manufacture, they were for the first part of the 19th century invariably made of French satin. It was not until the Viceroyalty of the Earl of Carlisle (1855-8 and 1859-64) that the use of Irish material was introduced. The practice was continued by the revised statutes of 1905 which directed that the Mantle was to be made of satin or silk 'wrought in Ireland'. An embroidered form of the Star was attached to the left side of the Mantle. At some stage during the 19th century the embroidered Stars were replaced with heavy metal Stars. Why and when the change took place remains something of a mystery. The earliest example known to the author was made by Robinson and Steele of Dublin for the 3rd Earl of Kilmorey in 1890, and contemporary photographs would seem to indicate that all subsequent Mantle Stars were of metal, though Lord Castletown (K.P. 1907) seems to have worn an embroidered

Star. The Stars were crude enlargements of the much smaller Breast Star, measuring approximately 245mm. square. They were generally made of a base metal, possibly pewter, and the obverse was then coated with copper and silvered. Though their lifetime was longer than that of their embroidered predecessors, they were unwieldy and clumsy objects, and their sheer weight must have caused a certain amount of discomfort to the wearer, quite apart from damaging the fabric of the Mantle over the course of time.

The only other items of dress specified by the 1783 Statutes were white leather shoes with knots of crimson riband and a white satin hat. The Hat was lined with blue, turned up at the front and had an embroidered star fixed to it. It also had a band of crimson satin embroidered with the design of the Collar, and was surmounted by three falls of ostrich feathers coloured red, white and blue. This spectacular and gaudy item of headgear was apparently too much even for George IV. In August 1821, he commanded that the Hat should be made of black velvet without the band, otherwise remaining unchanged. The Installation of 1821 appears to have been the last occasion on which these incredible things were worn. Contemporary engravings of the Installation of 1868 show the Knights bareheaded, and it seems unlikely that they were ever worn outside Installations in the Cathedral with the exception of the Installation banquet of 1783. To have worn them for investitures in Saint Patrick's Hall or the Viceregal Lodge would have lent the whole ceremony the air of a comic opera.

Beneath the Mantle was a garment described as the Surcoat. Like the Mantle it was of sky-blue satin and lined with white silk. Though there is no mention of it in the Statutes, it was certainly worn by the Knights at the First Installation in 1783. Basically a coat for everyday wear, but in the materials and colours of the Order, it was worn by uninstalled Knights on their way to the Cathedral, who were then robed with the Mantle during the course of the ceremony.

The basic dress or Under Habit of each Knight is not prescribed in the 1783 Statutes and it is doubtful if one was worn before the Fifth Installation of 1821, or at any subsequent date. King George IV commanded the Knights Companions to wear a Doublet and Trunk Hose *à la Henri Quatre,* made with white satin trimmed with silver plate lace, and Vandyke fringe. They also wore white stockings with crimson knee rosettes. In place of the shoes of white leather with knots of crimson riband, the King substituted boots of white kid leather, turned up with sky blue, with red heels and a bow of crimson riband on the instep, attached to the spur leather, and gilt spurs. The Sword Belt, which was originally of crimson satin, was changed to crimson velvet. Surprisingly, this preposterous costume, more suited to a Regency dandy than a Knight, was still retained in the 1905 Statutes. It seems incomprehensible that the Edwardian revision of the Statutes should have authorised the wearing of Hats, Surcoats and Under Habits more than 80 years after they were last worn.

Until 1833 when the ceremony was dispensed with, each Knight was required to appoint three Esquires to attend him at Installations. There being no provision for Esquires in the Garter, this arrangement appears to have been copied from the Order of the Bath. Temple wrote that it would contribute much to the splendour of the Order, and 'it is particularly recommended by the noblemen as a thing which will be highly acceptable to them'.[5] The Ordinances of 28 February 1783 purport to relate to the Habit of the Esquires, but they are not described, nor are they mentioned in any subsequent Statute. The dress eventually devised for them consisted of a white satin Surcoat lined with blue silk, with an embroidered shield on the left breast depicting a red Cross of Saint Patrick on a silver background. Their Under Habit was a vest with sleeves, of blue satin, trimmed with white silk lace; breeches of blue satin, slashed with white and edged with red; white silk stockings; white knee and shoe rosettes; blue satin shoes; a lace ruff and ruffles, and a blue satin bonnet; together with a Knight's sword, in a sheath of crimson velvet. The impracticability of this costume as a defence against inclement weather was recorded in his memoirs by Lord Frederic Hamilton, one of the Esquires present at the 1868 Installation.

The Mantles of the Officers worn before the changes of 1833 were, with two exceptions, almost identical to those worn by the Knights. The anomalous position of the Grand Master becomes apparent almost immediately. As Grand Master, he was authorised to wear the robes and Collar, and the Badge sur-mounted by a crown from his neck, but he was not entitled to wear the Riband or Badge of a Knight Companion. The inconsistency of a Grand Master presiding over an Order of which he was not himself a member has no parallel in any other Order. His Mantle was the same as that of the Sovereign 'save only those altera-tions which befit Our dignity'.[6] The Sovereign's Mantle unfortunately no longer survives, nor is there any description of it, but we can safely assume that it was identical to a Knight's Mantle, probably with the addition of a long flowing train. At the Installation of 1821, four pages were needed to carry the train of the King's Mantle. The Mantles of the Prelate and the Chancellor were, again, identical to Knight's Mantles. In May 1833 a number of additional Statutes directed that the Officers should cease to wear the Star of the Order on their Mantles, replacing it with the Badge of the Order, a red Cross of Saint Patrick on a silver field, surrounded by the Motto and Date of the Order, QUIS SEPARABIT, MDCCLXXXIII, and a wreath of shamrocks. The Mantle of the Registrar was originally the same as that worn by the Chancellor and the Prelate, except that it was shorter. The same change from Star to Badge was made in May 1833. The Mantles of the Secretary and the Genealogist were the same length as that of the Registrar, but when the Stars were removed in 1833, they were replaced by a plain silver shield charged with a red Cross of Saint Patrick, without the Motto, Date or wreath of shamrocks.

A striking departure from normal practice occurs with the Mantles of the two lowest Officers, the Usher of the Black Rod, and the Ulster King of Arms. Instead of the familiar sky blue, the Mantles of the Usher and the King of Arms were directed by the Statutes to be made of crimson satin, and shorter than those of the Secretary and Genealogist. Before the removal of the Star from the left side in May 1833 and its replacement by the shield and cross, the two Officers must have presented an appearance similar to the Knights of the Bath.

When functioning as Ulster King of Arms, rather than as King of Arms of the Order of Saint Patrick, the holder of the office wore a tabard of velvet and cloth of gold, and a black velvet cap embroidered with a crowned harp badge. The two Heralds wore tabards of silk, with black velvet caps, and the four Pursuivants wore tabards of damask. When the Office of Registrar was amalgamated with Ulster King of Arms in 1890, Ulster continued to use the crimson mantle of the King of Arms, rather than the longer sky-blue mantle of the Registrar.

The desire to make the Order a reflection of the link between England and Ireland and at the same time do nothing to lessen its distinctive Irishness can clearly be seen in the design of the insignia. Collars, Stars and Badges are awash with harps and shamrocks on one hand, and roses and crowns on the other. The Collar consists of 27 pieces in all, seven roses and six harps placed alternately, and joined together with 14 gold knots—symbolically tying England and Ireland together. The leaves of each rose were enamelled alternately red within white and white within red—a curious echo of the Wars of the Roses—and in the late Georgian examples, surrounded by a ring of shamrocks. The central portion of the Collar from which the Badge was suspended, consisted of an imperial crown above a harp, emphasising the central role of the Crown in Ireland.

Little is known about the appearance of the original Collars. One slighting reference refers to their inferior construction, and there is one Collar surviving in official custody, of such poor workmanship, that it may well be an 18th-century example. It bears a remarkable resemblance to the one worn in a portrait by the 1st Marquess of Waterford, one of the first 15 Knights. The original Collars were made by a Mr. Clements of Parliament Street, Dublin. He appears to have had less than six weeks notice to make the Collars and Badges, being charged with the responsibility on or about 7 February. The *Dublin Evening Post* records that he went to London on that day to prepare the Collars and Badges, 'which were found impracticable to procure here in proper time'.[7] The *Post* also reported that the Collars were worth £200 each, and the Badges a further £100. There seems no reason to doubt this since, in an article on 22 February, the newspaper reported that each Knight had been required to deposit 500 guineas with the Usher to ensure that 'no risque whatever may be incurred by any of the tradesmen employed in furnishing the robes, jewels, etc.'[8] The Collars and Badges were completed in the remarkably short period of four weeks, and sent across to Dublin on 9 March. They were exhibited a few days later at Mr. Clement's house, shortly before the Installation.

In 1804, Viscount Somerton (Archbishop of Dublin and Chancellor of the Order, 1801-1809) decided to lay claim to a perquisite similar to that enjoyed by the Chancellor of the Order of the Garter—claiming as his own the Collars of deceased Knights. He talked to Sir Chichester Fortescue, who asked the

College of Arms in London for its opinion on the subject. The reply was returned by Francis Townsend, Windsor Herald, that the Collars of deceased Knights of the Garter had always been considered the perquisite of the Chancellor, and that he could find nothing in the Statutes of the Order of Saint Patrick preventing the Chancellor of that Order from enjoying the same privilege. Somerton communicated his request to the Earl of Hardwicke (Grand Master, 1801-1806). Hardwicke was apparently reluctant to deal with such a difficult and possibly expensive subject, since the Archbishop had received no reply by January 1806. By that time, the Duke of Leinster had died, and his Collar was returned direct to the Grand Master by the Duke's family. The Archbishop was annoyed at this move. He had submitted a claim backed by precedent and authoritative support to which the Grand Master had not bothered to reply. Hardwicke appears to have been the kind of person who ignores problems in the fervent hope that they will go away; not so the Archbishop. He called to see Hardwicke on 10 January, and the Grand Master, feeling himself cornered, admitted the Archbishop's claim and agreed to forward the Duke of Leinster's Collar.

Two and a half months later, the Archbishop had still not received the Collar, and he called on the Grand Master again. Hardwicke expressed surprise that the Archbishop had not received the Collar, informing him that he had issued instructions to a Mr. Marsden, in whose custody it reposed, to pass it to the Chancellor. Pursuing the matter with the relentless intensity of a bloodhound, the Archbishop then called on Mr. Marsden, who denied receiving any such orders from Lord Hardwicke! The Grand Master was clearly saying one thing and doing something else. He was not really prepared to admit the Archbishop's claim, but neither was he prepared to face the latter and say so, fearing a scene. Had he the courage to give a decisive 'no' to the Archbishop's claim in November 1804, the matter might have been easily and swiftly disposed of, instead of drifting on for 15 months. Hardwicke's continued evasiveness and inactivity served only to convince the Archbishop that his claim was more justified than, in fact, it was. Seven vacancies had occurred during the time of Archbishop Fowler as Chancellor (1783-1801), but no claim was made and the Collars were duly delivered to the new Knights. Considering that no similar privilege was enjoyed by the Chancellor of the Order of the Thistle, or by any Officer of the Order of the Bath, the Archbishop was on very shaky ground in basing his claim solely on the practice of the Order of the Garter. In his final letter to the Archbishop, Hardwicke explained what had worried him from the beginning. There was no fund available from which the expense of providing new Collars could be defrayed. The sum allotted for the Civil Establishment in Ireland was strictly appropriated, and contained no miscellaneous head of accounts for incidental charges such as the provision of new Collars for Knights of Saint Patrick. Therefore he felt that he could not sanction the Archbishop's claim and decided to refer the whole issue to the King. After further delay, a compromise was reached whereby the Chancellor was assigned the duty of reclaiming the Collars and Badges of deceased Knights, returning them to the Grand Master, and receiving a fee of £100 for every set so returned.

How far this provision operated is not very clear since the story of the return, storage and supply of insignia at the beginning of the 19th century is one of inefficiency and chaos. Sir Chichester Fortescue, Ulster King of Arms from 1788 to 1820, took very little care of the insignia. Until Sir William Betham took charge of the Order in the last years of Fortescue's reign, the story of insignia is one of misplaced Collars and Badges, and odd items turning up in offices all over Dublin Castle—anywhere, it seems, except the Chancery of the Order in the Bermingham Tower. Lord Carysfort, who was made a K.P. in 1784, did not receive a Collar until May 1806. The Collar of the Marquess of Waterford (K.P., 1783, died in 1800) was never apparently returned, and the fact was not noticed until six years later, during the negotiations between Hardwicke and Somerton. The Archbishop also told Hardwicke that the Duke of Portland had given him a Patrick Collar, though he did not know by whom it had been worn and how it had come into the Duke's possession. When the Marquess of Ely died in 1806, his Collar was delivered to the Earl of Carysfort, and the Badge was kept until the investiture of his successor, the Marquess of Headfort. But four years later, Lord Headfort was forced to write to the Home Secretary complaining that he had still not received any insignia, and, at the Installation of 1809, he had been the only Knight not to be invested with a Collar. It seems that some of the insignia were kept at Saint Patrick's Cathedral, since Betham wrote to the Dean in September 1814 asking him to return all Collars and Badges in his possession, together with the names of the Knights by whom they were worn. Before the Installation of 1819, Betham wrote to the Grand Master saying that he had an old Collar and Badge in his possession, but could not say by which deceased Knight it had formerly been worn. 'It was delivered to me by the late Mr. Taylor of the Chief Secretary's Office in whose possession it had been for some years, and he had forgotten from whom he had received it'.[9]

Like the Collar, the Badge of the Order was officially provided by the Crown, but beyond that deceptively simple statement we need to tread very carefully when considering the history and development of Patrick Badges. Nothing is known of the earliest examples, other than that they were round. The design consisted of the so-called Cross of Saint Patrick, a saltire gules, charged with a green shamrock bearing three crowns, one on each leaf, all mounted on a white enamel ground surrounded by the motto 'QUIS SEPARABIT MDCCLXXXIII' in gold letters on a gold ground. The linking of the red saltire with Saint Patrick is something of a mystery, since it had nothing whatever to do with him. The harp and the shamrock are certainly closely associated with Patrick, the latter as the emblem of his trinitarian faith. But the cross, the symbol of martyrdom, could be thought of as singularly inappropriate for one who died peacefully in his bed. The red saltire was traditionally the badge of the Fitzgerald family, and is still described by them as the 'Geraldine Cross'. The description 'Cross of Saint Patrick' was used in the 1783 Statutes, and the usage was confirmed when the Cross was incorporated into the Union flag in 1801. It is possible that since so many members of the family held high offices of state in Ireland up to the early 16th century, the use of their arms in such official contexts as the sealing of documents might have given the Cross the status of a national emblem over a period of time. It should also be remembered that the powerful and influential head of the family, the Duke of Leinster, was one of the founder Knights of the Order.

But there are indications that the red saltire was regarded as a national emblem much earlier than the late 18th century. The arms of Trinity College, Dublin, which were in use as early as 1612 show two flags flying from the turrets of the castle which forms the main part of the charge. One bears the Cross of Saint George, and the other, the red saltire, doubtless representing Ireland. Irish soldiers stationed in England in 1628 wore a cross of red ribbon on Saint Patrick's Day. A contemporary picture map of the siege of Duncannon Fort, Co. Wexford, in 1645 shows the attacking force marching under a saltire, and there are many other examples that indicate the widespread use of the red saltire as a national emblem in pre-18th century days.

By 1825 new oval Badges were being made with the centres open or pierced, and after 1832 the motto was rendered in gold on a ground of sky-blue enamel. The 1783 Statutes directed that the Badge should be removed from the Collar and worn from the Riband, when the Collar was not worn. We may infer from this that the Knights were supplied with one detachable Collar Badge. This is supported by the receipts signed by each new Knight from 1821 to 1845 which mention one Collar and one Badge appendant. The receipt signed by Earl O'Neill on 12 February 1814 mentions one Collar and two Badges, indicating that he may have been supplied with a separate Riband Badge. There are other recorded instances, but they are rare, and the custom had certainly lapsed by the end of the century. The Collar Badge was to be removed and worn on a Riband which each Knight had to provide at his own expense. The Riband itself was of sky-blue silk, four inches in width and was originally worn over the right shoulder, the bow and Badge resting on the left hip. On 19 July 1927, King George V commanded that the Knights of Saint Patrick should in future wear the Riband over the left shoulder, in line with the Knights of the Garter and the Thistle.

The official Badge presented something of a problem for the Knights of Saint Patrick. They were usually very large and very heavy. The oval Collar Badges measured as much as 65mm. by 80mm. and sometimes more. While they might look magnificent suspended from the Collar, they were awkward and uncomfortable things to wear from a riband at the left hip. This situation led to the manufacturing of a large number of small privately commissioned badges during the first half of the 19th century, sometimes enamelled, but more often in plain gold. Prior to 1830 they were generally round, and the earliest extant example bears a London hallmark of 1809. The differences between the original round Badges, the privately manufactured plain gold Badges, and the post-1825 oval Badges seems to have led to the erroneous belief in certain quarters that the Order of Saint Patrick had separate Collar and Riband Badges on the lines of the George and Lesser George of the Garter. This is not so; there was only one Badge of the Order, and the changes in its style between the late 18th and mid 19th centuries should not be taken to imply anything more.

The 1783 Statutes directed the Knights to wear on the left side of their outer garment, the Badge 'encircled within Rays in form of a Star of silver'.[10] This is the only mention in the Statutes of what for many people is the most often seen and most familiar item of insignia—the Star. The Knights of Saint Patrick were probably worse off in this area than the Knights of any other Order. They were not officially provided with a Star until as late as 1916, long after the Knights of all the other Orders. As a result of this policy, there are a large number of Stars in existence, varying in style and quality from the cheap and tawdry to a few magnificent jewelled pieces. Those Stars differing in design generally date from the first half of the 19th century. After about 1880 they were generally of a standard design—with a few exceptions—and the majority were made by West and Son, the Dublin jewellers.

The Statutes prescribe that the rays of the Star should be of silver, consisting of eight points, four greater and four lesser. This is the only stipulation about the Patrick Star, apart from placing the Badge at the centre, and the absence of any precise description gave full reign to the imagination and craftsmanship of London and Dublin jewellers. Even the regulations regarding the lengths of points were ignored in many cases. The rays of the Star are faceted in the majority of surviving pieces, though there are a number of Stars with fluted rays, particularly examples from the first half of the 19th century.

There are no surviving 18th-century Stars. In common with the other Orders, they would almost certainly have been embroidered. The wearing of Stars worked in silver and enamel became fashionable only after 1800, and many were manufactured by jewellers in London and Dublin. The earliest known example of a metal Patrick Star is that worn by the 2nd Earl of Arran (K.P., 1783, died 1809) which has the unique feature of fretwork gold lettering for the motto and date. The Star of the Duke of Kent (K.P., 1783, died 1820) (slightly later, about 1805-1810) has a tiny ring at the extremity of each of the eight points indicating that it was intended to be sewn to a coat. A few examples of jewelled Stars are known, and at least six still survive, mostly in private hands. The first recorded example is one made for the Earl of Mornington, later Marquess Wellesley (K.P., 1783, resigned 1810). Wellesley was Governor-General of Bengal in 1799 at the time of the subjugation of the rebel state of Mysore under Tippoo Sultan, and the army in gratitude for his leadership 'caused a star and badge of the Order of St Patrick to be prepared, in which as many of the jewels as could be found suitable were taken from the Treasury of Tippoo'.[11] After his resignation from the Order in 1810 to accept the Order of the Garter, he would not have been able to wear the Star again. He was in some financial difficulties in the last years of his life, and it may have been sold to pay his creditors, and even broken up. However, the following intriguing article appeared in *The Times* on 31 March 1885: 'There have been three Irishmen—namely, Lord Wellesley, Lord Mayo, and Lord Dufferin, who have been Governors-General of India and also Knights of Saint Patrick. When Lord Mayo went to India the Star of the Order worn by Lord Wellesley was lent to him by Mr. Alfred Montgomery, and he used it during the period of his Viceroyalty. After his death Mr. Montgomery presented the Star to Lady Mayo, and when Lord Dufferin went to India, she lent it to him and he now wears it'.[12] It is not known whether the Star referred to is the jewelled one made for Lord Wellesley, or whether it still exists.

The jewelled Star of the 6th Earl of Milltown (K.P., 1889) is a magnificent example of a jewelled Knight's Star, and is as near a replica as we are ever likely to get of the famous jewelled Star of the Grand Master. The rays, motto, date, field and crowns are composed wholly of diamonds, the shamrock of emeralds and the cross of four large rubies. Curiously for a jewel on a silver base, backed with a sheet of nine carat gold, it does not bear a hallmark. It was made by Garrard and Co., using the highest quality gems, for the 6th Earl, who was appointed a K.P. in September 1889. After enjoying the honour for little more than four months, he died in February 1890, and the Star was presented to the National Gallery of Ireland by his widow in 1902. There are several diamond Stars of the Order in existence, generally made for Knights whose wealth or popularity was such that they or their friends could afford to have such costly pieces produced. None of them were conscious replicas or imitations of the Grand Master's Star. Examples of Stars set with paste stones are occasionally found, but they give little credit either to their manufacturer or to the Order.

The anomalous position of the Grand Master was never satisfactorily resolved during the active period of the Order's existence, and nowhere is this more obvious than in his insignia. By the original Statutes, the Grand Master was permitted to wear the Mantle and Collar, and the Grand Master's Badge. This was a small Badge worn at the neck surmounted by a harp of gold and an enamelled Imperial Crown set with small stones. As he was not a member of the Order, it is questionable whether the Grand Master should ever have been allowed to wear the Mantle and Collar. He was not permitted to wear the Badge of a Knight Companion, the Star, or the Riband. But according to Sir William Betham, this injunction was ignored by all the Grand Masters in the period up to 1839, who regularly wore the Star on their coat. When a Lord Lieutenant resigned, he ceased to be Grand Master and to wear the insignia of that Office, but King William IV added to the confusion by permitting ex-Grand Masters to wear a replica of the Grand Master's Badge for the remainder of their lives. Since the office of Lord Lieutenant was a political appointment, and the holder changed with the government of the day, there was a fairly rapid turn over of

Grand Masters. It was quite a common situation to find three or four living ex-Grand Masters at any particular time. When the Earl of Aberdeen assumed office in 1905, seven of his predecessors were still alive, making a total of eight individuals entitled to wear the insignia of the Grand Master, though only one of them actually held the Office. It would be of interest to know whether all eight of them were ever present at the same function wearing their insignia.

This inconsistency was carried further by the King who subsequently authorised former holders of the Office to wear the Star as well. According to the earliest regulations, the Star could not be worn by any Knight, even though he may have been invested with the Riband and the Badge, until he had been installed or dispensed from Installation. The Star is described in the Statutes as the 'Ensign' of the Order, and it is very much a sign. Apart from the colour of a Riband, the Star is the most instantly recognisable sign of membership of the Order. To allow it to be worn by several persons who had never been appointed Knights of the Order was strikingly incongruous.

By far the most famous pieces of insignia worn by the Grand Master were the Diamond Star, the Diamond Badge, and the Gold Badge, which have collectively gone down in history as the Irish Crown Jewels. Believed to have been fashioned from some diamonds once the property of Queen Charlotte, the pieces were presented to the Order in 1831 by William IV to be worn by the Grand Master on formal occasions. They were made under the auspices of the London firm of Rundell, Bridge and Rundell, on Ludgate Hill. The rays of the Star were composed of Brazilian diamonds with a ruby cross, a shamrock of emeralds and three diamond crowns at the centre; the motto and date were picked out in rose diamonds on a blue enamel field. The Diamond Badge was of similar spendour, its shamrock of emeralds on a ruby cross being surrounded again by a blue enamel band bearing the motto and date in rose diamonds. The whole Badge was enclosed by an outer circle of large Brazilian diamonds, surmounted by a harp and loop, all formed of diamonds. Both these items were intended for evening functions. The Gold Badge, which is still in official custody is a well-made example of a Grand Master's Badge, of gold and enamel set with a few rubies and emeralds. The Diamond insignia were unfortunately stolen from Dublin Castle in 1907 in mysterious circumstances, as recorded in Chapter Five. The loss of these beautiful pieces took place in an age before photography was a widespread as it is today, and we only have drawings to indicate the glittering appearance of the originals. The Milltown Star bears the closest resemblance to what the Grand Master's Diamond Star must have looked like. Valued at £30,000 in 1899, the present value (1981) of the pieces would be approximately £500.000.

The Officers' Badges were with slight modifications and two exceptions, variants of the Kinghts' Badge. The Badge of the Prelate, like the Office itself, is not mentioned in the original Statutes, nor is its design authorised in any amending Statute, Warrant, or Ordinance. The Badge is a circular one, typical of those issued to Knights until about 1825, surmounted by an archiepiscopal mitre with its lappets trailing down the edges of the Badge. It was worn at the neck suspended from a sky-blue riband. After the death of Archbishop Marcus Beresford, the last Prelate, in 1885, the Badge remained in the possession of the Beresford family until 1971, when it was purchased by the Ulster Museum in Belfast. Made of 18 carat gold, it bears the Dublin hallmark for 1819 and was made by Clarke and West.

The Badge of the Chancellor was of embossed gold, of roughly square form representing a purse, with a circular Badge on the front without motto or date. It was worn at the neck with a sky-blue riband. The Badge of the Registrar was also of embossed gold, appropriately in the shape of a book, with the same circular device on the front as that of the Chancellor. After the death of the last clerical Registrar in 1890 and the amalgamation of the Office with Ulster King of Arms, the Badge was kept at Saint Patrick's Cathedral until 1895, when it was handed over to Ulster. The Badge of the Secretary is of a slightly oval form, consisting of a cross and shamrock on a white enamel background surrounded by a wreath of shamrocks on gold. In his *History of the Orders of Knighthood of the British Empire*, Nicolas gives an illustration of the Secretary's Badge surmounted by a Crown. This is not directed by the Statutes either of 1783 or of 1905, and there is no crown on the present surviving Badge. The Badge of the Genealogist was identical to that of the Secretary and the above comments and descriptions apply.

The Badges of the Usher and the King of Arms differ widely from those of the other Officers. The Usher's Badge is circular in shape and overlaid with sky-blue enamel. It has a gold harp in the centre and is encircled with the motto and date. The Usher's Rod is a rather unremarkable slender wooden rod some three feet in length, with silver gilt caps at each end. The upper end is topped with a ball surmounted by a lion sejant bearing a shield with the inscription 'VR'. The Badge of the King of Arms was designed to reflect his duel role as Ulster King of Arms and King of Arms of the Order of Saint Patrick. The obverse bears the Cross of Saint Patrick on a white background impaled with a gold harp on a dark blue background, encircled with the motto and date. The reverse contains the arms of the Office of Ulster, and escutcheon, or, charged with a cross gules, and on a chief of the second, a Lion of England between a harp and portcullis, all of the first, on a ground of green enamel, surrounded by a gold border with shamrocks. Alone of all the Officers, Ulster wore his Badge from a gold chain of three strands rather than a sky-blue riband. When functioning as Ulster rather than as King of Arms of the Order, he wore a Collar of SS from the centre of which hung a harp. He also carried a silver gilt sceptre, the top of which was square in form bearing on two faces the Royal Arms and the Cross of Saint Patrick, and on the other two, the Badge of the Order. As with the English and Scottish Kings of Arms, Ulster possessed a crown which was worn only at coronations. There was nothing to distinguish it from the crowns of the other Kings.

The Heralds and Pursuivants wore a Badge containing the Cross of Saint Patrick on a white background surrounded by the motto and date. The two Heralds wore Collars of SS and Athlone Pursuivant carried a small rod about 12 inches in length. It had silver caps at each end, one bearing a crown and the other a harp.

Unlike the other Orders of Knighthood, there is no description of the Seal in the foundation Warrant; and the Statutes merely refer to 'a Common Seal of the Arms of the Order'. Nicolas describes the Seal as the Cross of Saint Patrick on a field argent surcharged with a Shamrock, and inscribed 'THE SEAL OF THE MOST ILLUSTRIOUS ORDER OF SAINT PATRICK'. However, the Seal as last used is much more elaborate. Set in a heavy iron stand, it bears the Royal Arms and the Badge of the Order, and is surrounded by the motto in Latin: 'SIGILLUM ILLUSTRISSIMI ORDINIS DE SANCTO PATRICIO'.

Chapter Ten

THE ROBES AND INSIGNIA—II

WHEN WILLIAM BETHAM took over the management of the daily affairs of the Order from the ailing Chichester Fortescue sometime before 1819, he adopted a more conscientious approach to the custody and care of insignia than his predecessor. During his reign, the insignia were kept in an iron chest in the Office of Arms in the Castle. This was situated in the Bermingham Tower during the 19th century, and transferred to the Bedford Tower in 1903.

In readiness for the Installation, he ordered a new set of robes, including a sword and a badge for the Grand Master; three new Collars; new robes for the Prelate and the Registrar; new badges for the Prelate and the Chancellor; three dresses and swords for the Grand Master's pages; and shoes, swords and ruffs for the Officers. At least three further Collars were ordered for the Installation of 1821, and additional Collars were ordered throughout the 19th century as required. The last one was made by West and Son in 1919.

The privilege of claiming the Collars of deceased Knights, for which Archbishop Viscount Somerton had fought so persistently, 15 years earlier, was allowed to lapse with the appointment of William Magee as Archbishop of Dublin in 1822. Magee objected to receiving a fee on such an occasion, conceiving it to be inconsistent with his dignity as an Archbishop, and the grant was rescinded by Warrant on 17 May 1833. However, the claim surfaced again in December 1844, not from the Archbishop of Dublin, but from the Dean of Saint Patrick's Cathedral! The Very Reverend and Honourable Henry Pakenham was appointed Dean in 1843 inheriting a Cathedral that was in a serious state of decay. He saw the restoration of the Cathedral as his main task, but was seriously hampered by a lack of money. Understandably, he was anxious to get hold of every penny he could lay his hands on, and at some point he discovered the £100 fee formerly payable to the Archbishops of Dublin. Seeing the chance of obtaining a fairly frequent if irregular source of income, the Dean wrote to no less a person than Sir Robert Peel, the Prime Minister, claiming the fee, and happily blackening Archbishop Magee's name in the process. His argument ran something like this. The fee was of right given to the Archbishop of Dublin, not solely to Archbishop Magee who, though he may not have wished to receive it himself, had no right to surrender it for his successors. Archbishop Whateley, who had succeeded Magee in 1831, had not been informed of the termination of the fee in 1833. Furthermore,

Magee's son and executor insisted that his father had received the fee, and 'It must be remembered that Archbishop Magee was greatly impaired in his faculties before his death'.[1] Archbishop Whateley had considered the ruinous state of the Cathedral and was willing to surrender his claims to the Dean. The reaction in London was predictable. 'To repair a Protestant Cathedral by such means, when the wealth of the Irish Church is remembered, would be degradation in the extreme and no one but a Dean could contemplate such an arrangement'.[2]

From their intricate and delicate work, the late Georgian Collars are easily the finest examples. They were the first Collars to have been made since the originals in 1783, and every effort was made to remedy any defects. The crude and clumsy appearance of the 18th-century insignia was replaced by a light and graceful appearance. The knots joining the roses and harps together, for example, resemble pieces of silk cord which have been carefully looped with all the appropriate curves and bends, and tied together with a faithful reproduction of an intricate knot. Exactly what we might expect to see in a Regency drawing room. The knots on the original Collars resemble lengths of cable bent into shape and held there by two semi-circular pieces representing a knot from which depend four overweight tassels. The roses of the Georgian Collars are encircled by rings of shamrocks which are not specified in the Statutes, nor do they appear on earlier, or the majority of later examples. As might be expected, the Victorian Collars show a tendency to look heavy. The knots resemble the gilded versions of the ropes and tassels that were used to loop back velvet curtains in Victorian sitting rooms. The number of tassels on each knot was reduced from four to two during the reign of William IV.

There is little information concerning the cost of insignia. The *Dublin Evening Post* reported that the original Collars and Badges cost £300 each, which may be a slight overstatement. Garrard and Co., the Crown Jewellers in London, produced a gold and enamel badge in 1869 for £34, and a Star for £16 10s. 0d. When the decision was made in 1916 to provide all future Knights with a Star at the Treasury's expense, the Fee required of each Knight was raised from £50 to £65 to cover the cost. The Star was by far the least expensive item of the insignia to produce, and as late as 1939 the estimated cost of manufacture was still put at only £16 10s. 0d. Why the decision was made to provide each Knight with a Star as well as a Collar and Badge is not clear. The Knights of Saint Patrick were certainly at a disadvantage in having to procure their own Stars; Knights of all the other Orders having been officially provided with them since about 1858. The situation, however, is far from clear, and there appears to have been a certain amount of confusion as to which Stars were returnable and which were not. Of the eight Knights appointed between 1916 and 1922 inclusive, the Stars of four were not returned, and there are examples of Stars of Knights appointed before 1916 being returned and accepted with the other insignia.

The next figures we have are all for 20th-century pieces. The Treasury paid £262 10s. 0d. for a Collar and Badge in 1902, a figure which probably remained fairly constant throughout the 19th century. In 1911 West and Sons estimated the cost of a Collar and Badge at £252 10s. 0d., and a London firm estimated £213. The last occasion on which the Treasury purchased insignia for the Order was in 1919 when £245 was paid for a Collar alone. The last official estimate for producing a Collar and Badge was made by West's on 7 June 1938:

		£
The Collar in 14 carat gold..		324
The Badge in 14 carat gold..		50
Total		£375
The Collar in 18 carat gold..		375
The Badge in 18 carat gold..		60
Total		£435

The estimate was occasioned by the death of Lord Castletown, K.P., in May 1937. Lord Castletown was a celebrated character in his time. The only son of the 1st Lord Castletown, illegitimate son and heir of the last Earl of Upper Ossory, he was an ardent Irish nationalist, believed in fairies, and changed his politics as frequently as other people change their minds. While M.P. for Portarlington (1880–1883) he was the only member of the House to sit as a Liberal Conservative. He was nominated a Knight of Saint Patrick during his tenure of the office of Chancellor of the Royal University of Ireland in 1907, but the King ordered his investiture to be postponed until after the repercussions of the Crown Jewels affair had died down. His wife had died some ten years earlier, there was no heir to the title, and the residuary legatee, Colonel Geoffrey Fitzpatrick, died little more than a year later. In the resulting confusion, the staff at both Lord Castletown's homes were unable to trace his insignia for more than two years. The matter came to the notice of the Treasury in 1938 when the cost of a replacement Collar was being considered. Sir Nevile Wilkinson reported that there was no need to purchase an immediate replacement. In addition to the Sovereign's Collar, and that kept with the Crown Jewels at the Tower of London, each of the remaining 11 Knights possessed one, and there were 12 spare Collars at the Central Chancery of the Orders of Knighthood. The Chancery also possessed 15 Badges and five Stars. He felt that there was little need to buy a new Collar and the present stock was probably ample for all time. The sum of £250 was a sufficient amount to claim from the executors of the estate, being slightly more than the original cost. In response, the Treasury displayed its famous capacity for suspicion and Scrooge-like meanness. For all they knew Lord Castletown might well have sold his Collar, in response to an offer to purchase gold, and therefore why should his executors be allowed to pay anything less than the full market price? In any case, it was likely that a prudent receipient of an honour of this kind would have his insignia insured and revalued from time to time for that purpose. If the full replacement cost was charged to the executors, they could reclaim it from the insurance company. Wilkinson was being 'unnecessarily kind'[3] in selecting a figure as low as £250.

The matter drifted on until March 1939 when a box containing Lord Castletown's Badge and Star was discovered at his home, Grantstown Manor, though the Collar was still missing. Though the Star, for which Lord Castletown had paid £16 10s. 0d. in 1907, was the personal property of his family, the Treasury briefly considered the possibility of retaining it as part of the sum owed to them, though its low value made such a course hardly worth while. The Collar was eventually discovered at Lord Castletown's other home, Doneraile Court, in August 1939, prompting a rather cross remark from the Treasury: 'It would have saved us all a lot of trouble if the Collar had been treated with the care which its value warranted, but we can at least be grateful that we have not had the unpleasant duty of extracting full compensation from the heirs of the Estate'.[4]

Despite officially shunning attempts to revive the Order of Saint Patrick since 1928, the Irish government has shown some concern to preserve and restore what remaining remnants of the Order it still possessed. When the Provisional government took over Dublin Castle from the British authorities in 1922, they decided to maintain the State apartments exactly as they were at the time of the takeover, including Saint Patrick's Hall. The Hall had not been used for any investitures since 1911 and it had functioned as a hospital during the War, but the Banners, Helmets, Swords and Hatchments of the Knights were still fixed to the walls. The Provisional government could have been forgiven if they had decided to tear down these symbols of despised British rule, and burn them. The courageous Mr. Sadleir, running the Office of Arms virtually single handed while Sir Nevile Wilkinson resided at his home in London, informed the government that the Banners were the property of the Order and could not be removed without the authority of Ulster King of Arms. With a civil war and other important matters to attend to, the government dropped the matter, and the Banners remained in position, slowly disintegrating, for the next 40 years. By the beginning of 1962 they were in a sorry state. Of a full complement of 22, plus the Royal Standard, only nine Banners were still hanging, the remainder having fallen or been taken down. After a visit to the Hall by representatives of the Department of the Taoiseach and the Commissioners of Public Works in January 1962, it was decided to restore the existing Banners and replace the missing Banners with replicas. Since the decision of 1928 that the Order was a purely Irish Order and everything connected with it was a matter for the Irish government, there was no question that the Banners were State property. With the aid of the Genealogical Office, replicas of the missing banners were carefully produced and erected, in the following order:

Viscount Powerscourt	Earl of Mayo
Earl of Meath	Earl of Shaftesbury
Earl of Desart	Earl of Granard
Viscount Pirrie	Lord Oranmore and Browne
Earl of Enniskillen	Royal Standard
Earl of Listowel	Earl of Ypres
Duke of Abercorn	Lord Monteagle of Brandon
Earl of Donoughmore	Earl of Arran
Lord Castletown	Earl of Bandon
Earl of Dunraven	Earl of Iveagh
Earl of Midleton	Earl of Cavan

(main entrance)

With the exception of two rather unsightly and unnecessary interpreters' boxes which were recently added to the galleries, the Hall still retains its graceful and elegant 18th-century beauty. The casual visitor might be forgiven for thinking that the Hall has been laid out ready for an investiture the next day. The Banners, Helmets, Swords and Hatchments of the Knights existing in 1922 are still in position, and above the gallery two figures support a representation of the Star of the Order. The wall of the gallery itself is painted a fetching shade of sky blue. The lines of gilt chairs along the walls seem ready to receive members of the Viceregal household and the wives and friends of the Knights. All that we miss are the Grand Master and his Knights. With only slight changes the Irish government has shown great care to preserve the Hall as they found it, and for that we can be thankful. Some years ago, the 9th Earl of Granard presented his late father's Star of the Order to the government for permanent display in the Hall. As a relic of one who tried unsuccessfully to preserve the Order in the 1920s, it is a fitting tribute and a suitable resting place.

Less than a mile from Dublin Castle stands the Cathedral of Saint Patrick, spiritual home of the Order for the first 88 years of its life. On the disestablishment of the Church of Ireland in 1871, the Cathedral ceased to play any role in the life of the Order, but by special wish of the Queen, the Banners then hanging remained in position. More than 110 years later, they still hang there, in the following order:

North Side, west to east	*South Side, west to east*
Duke of Connaught	The Sovereign
Duke of Connaught	Duke of Cambridge
Lord Farnham	Marquess of Drogheda
Earl of Roden	Earl of Arran
Marquess of Headfort	Marquess of Londonderry
Earl of Cork	Marquess Conyngham
Lord Lurgan	Marquess of Dufferin

Earl of Dunraven	Marquess of Donegall
Earl of Howth	Earl of Charlemont
Earl of Gosford	Earl of Carysfort
Earl of Mayo	Earl of Dartrey
Marquess of Waterford	Marquess of Clanricarde
Earl of Granard	Earl of Erne

The fact that there are two Banners for the Duke of Connaught and none for the Prince of Wales is something of a mystery. The Prince was installed in April 1868, three years before the Church was disestablished, and his Banner would certainly have been affixed. Furthermore, hardly any of the Banners are hanging over their matching Hatchment plates—though before being too critical, we should be grateful that they are still hanging at all. There appears to be only one possible explanation for this state of confusion. In 1942 a fire broke out in the choir of the Cathedral, and while there was mercifully little flame, there was dense smoke. Some of the Banners were seriously damaged and had to be removed, and a number of the Hatchments were defaced. This came to the notice of Sir John Maffey, the United Kingdom Representative in Dublin, who expressed his concern and offered to have the damaged Royal Standards replaced. It is probably at this stage that the mistake was made. While new standards for the Sovereign and the Duke of Cambridge were received, a second Connaught Banner was sent, instead of a new one for the Prince of Wales. Incidentally, the Prince, later Edward VII, had died in 1910, but the Duke of Connaught, who had been made a Knight of Saint Patrick as far back as 1869, was still alive at the age of ninety. The two Connaught Banners are basically the same, but one is obviously much older than the other. The labelling is the same (in the centre a cross gules and on each of the others a fleur-de-lys azure), but on the older Banner is the inescutcheon representing the arms of Saxony. The newer Banner, received in 1942, omits the inescutcheon. The retention of the arms of Saxony would have been rendered anomalous by the loss of independence of that state. By the end of the First World War, Saxony, along with all the other German states, had been consigned to oblivion.

The symbolic Swords and Helmets of each Knight are still fixed to the canopy of each stall below the Banners, and the Hatchment plates fastened to the backs of the stalls provide a colourful heraldic record of the Knights appointed between 1783 and 1871. The Banners themselves require little maintenance, being made of a substance which needs no more than the occasional dusting by the Cathedral Verger. In spite of all the vicissitudes in Anglo-Irish relations during the last 100 years, there is something faintly nostalgic about the fact that in this one small corner of Dublin, the commands of Queen Victoria are still faithfully obeyed.

Although more than 115 years have passed by since the Knights last walked through the Cathedral in their Mantles, the visitor to the Cathedral can still see the initially startling sight of a procession of figures clad in sky blue. By the early 1970s, the black cassocks worn by the Cathedral Choir were badly worn and in need of replacement. The Dean, Dr. Victor Griffin, imaginatively decided to replace them with sky-blue cassocks to commemorate the link with the Order. The Dean and Canons themselves wear a thin band of sky-blue material just below their clerical collars, and the symbolic Helmets above each stall are covered with sky-blue lambrequins. The procession of the Choir is a strange evocation of the old Installation ceremonies and with a little imagination it is possible to visualise the solemn processions of the Knights of Saint Patrick to their stalls.

For those who cannot make the journey to Dublin to see the temporal and spiritual homes of the Order, there are two other surviving relics closer to hand than many may have realised. On 1 April 1900, the Regiment of the Irish Guards was formed by command of Her Majesty Queen Victoria to commemorate the bravery of the Irish troops who fought in the Boer War. The first recruit enlisted on 21 April, and many more Irishmen already serving in Regiments of the Brigade of Guards and Regiments of the Line took the opportunity of transferring. The Star of the Order was taken as the Cap Badge and it remains so to this day. The Star is also the Badge of the Irish Guards Association, and attractive miniature Stars can be seen gracing the wives of members of the association.

Very occasionally one finds replicas of the insignia or even the insignia themselves worn as decorative jewellery, and three instances are known to the author. Since the Order is no longer conferred and there is nobody alive, with the exception of the Sovereign, entitled to wear the insignia, the practice of wearing the insignia by unauthorised persons, though slightly dubious, is difficult to discourage. The number of individuals who recall the Order as a high honour conferred by the Crown is steadily diminishing year by year, and the insignia arouses more curiosity than recognition. Furthermore, its use as jewellery is merely an extension of the wearing of sky-blue dresses, a custom much in evidence at the Royal Installation of 1821. Florence, Viscountess Massereene and Ferrard (d. 1929), wife of the 11th Viscount and daughter-in-law of the 10th Viscount, K.P., had a replica of the Star, minus the rays, made in jewels for use as a brooch. Wearing it one night at a ball, she attracted the attention of King Edward VII, who expressed his surprise that ladies were now eligible for admission to the Order of Saint Patrick. The Viscountess pointed to the fact that the brooch was not an exact copy of the Star, and the King was appeased!

The other relic is to be found, rather surprisingly, in a familiar and endearing comic opera. On 25 November 1882, the *Savoy* theatre in London witnessed the opening night of a new two-act opera by William Gilbert and Arthur Sullivan. It was entitled *Iolanthe,* or *The Peer and the Peri,* and the rather superficial plot disguises a humorous and witty piece of satire on the peerage and the House of Lords. After 100 years, the opera is still a firm favourite among devotees of the famous partnership. The supporting cast consists in part of a chorus of 16 peers who wear coronets differing according to their rank. But instead of the traditional scarlet parliamentary robes, the peers make their spectacular entrance attired in the Mantles and Collars of the four senior Orders of Knight-hood: the Garter, the Thistle, the Patrick, and the Bath. The D'Oyly Carte Opera Company, set up to continue performing the operas in the manner faithful to the wishes of author and composer, adhered strictly to the costume directions of the original production. The events of 1922 which ended the useful existence of the Order made no difference to the stage Knights who continued to be received with great applause by audiences, until the sad demise of the Company in the spring of 1982. *Iolanthe,* however, remains a very popular production with the many amateur Gilbert and Sullivan societies, so it seems that the Knights of the Most Illustrious Order of Saint Patrick will continue to exist in the world of make-believe for many years to come.

*   *   *   *   *   *   *

EPILOGUE—PATRICK'S FAREWELL

In the summer of 1981, seven years after the death of the last Knight of Saint Patrick, the possibility was raised of marking the bicentenary of the foundation of the Order in March 1983. It was felt, in certain quarters, to be appropriate that the occasion should be used to commemorate something which, for all its short-comings, had been the national honour of Ireland for nearly 140 years. It was also felt that the 146 Knights of the Order should be remembered, and thanks given to God for their life and work.

The matter was discussed at a number of meetings during the winter of 1982/3 and the decision was taken to hold a Service of Thanksgiving in Saint Patrick's Cathedral on Sunday, 13 March 1983, at 3.15 p.m., followed by a Reception in the Deanery. Invitations were issued to as many descendants of Knights of the Order as could be traced, together with representatives of a number of related societies and organisations, and a congregation of more than 500 people, headed by the Lord Mayor of Dublin, gathered on 13 March.

The Service began with an anthem specially composed by the Cathedral organist, a setting of the full biblical phrase from which the motto of the Order had been extracted, *'Quis separabit nos a caritate dei quae est in Christo Jesu Domino Nostro*—Who shall separate us from the love of God which is in Christ Jesus Our Lord?' The Service was conducted by the Dean, the Very Rev. Dr. Victor Griffin, seven of whose predecessors had held the office of Registrar of the Order, from 1783 to 1890. The first lesson was read by the Earl of Rosse, a descendant of two Knights of Saint Patrick, and, through the ill-health of the Earl of Iveagh, the second lesson was read by Bishop George Simms, former Archbishop of Armagh, whose predecessors had held the office of Prelate of the Order from 1783 to 1885. After the singing of the anthem, Parry's setting of Psalm 122—'I was glad when they said unto me, we will go into the house of the Lord', an address was delivered by the author, and the Service concluded with the singing of the Te Deum—preserving a tradition from the Installation services begun 200 years earlier.

NOTES

ABBREVIATIONS USED IN THE NOTES

1. Repositories of sources cited in the notes

B.L.	British Library, London
C.C.	Central Chancery of the Order of Knighthood
P.R.O.	Public Record Office
P.R.O.N.I	Public Record Office of Northern Ireland
RA	Royal Archives
S.P.O.D.C.	State Paper Office, Dublin Castle

2. Abbreviations of titles of sources cited more than once in the notes

Note.—On the occasion of the first citation of each source, the title is given in full; thereafter as given below

B.N.L.	*Belfast News Letter*
B.L. Add. MS.	B.L. Additional Manuscript Collection, held in the Department of Western Manuscripts, B.L.
C.P.	Cokayne, G. E. (ed.), *The Complete Peerage* (1910–1964)
C.S.O.R.P.	Registered Papers of the Chief Secretary's Office, held in S.P.O.D.C.
D.E.P.	*Dublin Evening Post*
D.O.	Dominions Office Papers, held in P.R.O.
I.T.	*Irish Times*
H.M.C.	Historical Manuscripts Commission volumes
H.M.C. C.	Charlemont MSS., listed in H.M.C.
H.M.C. F.	Fortescue, MSS., listed in H.M.C.
H.M.C. R.	Rutland MSS., held in H.M.C.
H.O.	Home Office Papers, held in P.R.O.
R.O.S.P.	Register of the Order of St Patrick, held in C.C.
S.P.C.C.M. (1)	St Patrick's Cathedral Chapter Minutes, 1764–1792
S.P.C.C.M. (2)	St Patrick's Cathedral Chapter Minutes, 1793–1819

Chapter One

1. Central Chancery of the Orders of Knighthood: Register of the Order of St Patrick, Vol. I: Royal Warrant of 5 February 1783.
2. P.R.O.N.I., T3429/1/9, Buckinghamshire to Hotham Thompson, 9 April 1777.
3. P.R.O., Calendar of Home Office Papers, No. 531.
4. Cockayne, G. E. (ed.), *The Complete Peerage* (series publication, 1910–64), Vol. VII, p. 576: entry for 'Leinster', quoting letter from Rutland to Sydney, 8 May 1784.
5. P.R.O., H.O. 100/3, Temple to Townshend, 16 November 1782.
6. B.L. Add. MS., 40, 177, f.134, Temple to Townshend, November 1782.
7. B.L. Add. MS. 58, 874, f. 20, Temple to Grenville, 21 December 1782.
8. B.L. Add. MS. 58, 874, f. 23, Temple to Grenville, 25 December 1782.
9. Historical Manuscripts Commission, Fortescue MSS., Vol. I, p. 177. Temple to Grenville, 2 January 1783.
10. B.L. Add. MS. 40, 177, Temple to Townshend, 17 January 1783.

11. H.M.C. F., p. 199, Temple to Grenville, 1 March 1783.
12. P.R.O., H.O. 100/8, Temple to Townshend, 13 January 1783.
13. H.M.C. F., p. 190, Temple to Grenville, 9 February 1783.
14. P.R.O. H.O. 100/8, Temple to Townshend, 13 January 1783.
15. (anonymous), *The Order of Saint Patrick: An Ode* (1783), Stanza XIV.
16. H.M.C. Charlemont MSS., Vol. I, p. 156.
17. H.M.C. C., Vol. I, pp. 152 ff.
18. H.M.C. F., p. 184, Temple to Grenville, 22 January 1783.
19. H.M.C. F., p. 189, Temple to Grenville, 5 February 1783.
20. H.M.C. F., p. 190, Temple to Grenville, 9 February 1783.
21. *Dublin Evening Post*, 25 January 1783.
22. *D.E.P.*, 15 March 1783.

Chapter Two

1. C.C.: R.O.S.P.: Statutes of the Most Illustrious Order of St Patrick, 1783, article 2.
2. H.M.C. F., p. 201, Temple to Grenville, 7 March 1783.
3. H.M.C. Rutland MSS., Vol. 3, p. 78, Rutland to Temple, 8 March 1784.
4. H.M.C. F., p. 183, Temple to Grenville, 17 January 1783.
5. H.M.C. F., p. 190, Temple to Grenville, 9 February 1783.
6. B.L. Add. MS. 40, 856, f. 78, Clanricarde to Temple, 15 February 1783.
7. P.R.O., H.O. 100/8, Temple to Sydney, 2 April 1783.
8. *London Gazette*, 11 March 1783.
9. *D.E.P.*, 21 January 1783.
10. St Patrick's Cathedral Chapter Minutes, 1764–1792; 8 February 1783.
11. S.P.C.C.M. (1), 22 February 1783.
12. S.P.C.C.M. (1), 4 March 1783.
13. *D.E.P.*, 18 March 1783.
14. B.L. Add MS. 58, 874, f. 41, Temple to Grenville, 15 January 1783.
15. Temple to Charlemont, 6 January 1783, quoted in Hardy F., *Memoirs of the Political and Private Life of J. Caulfield, Earl of Charlemont* (2 vols., 2nd edn. 1812), Vol. II, p. 67.
16. H.M.C. F., p. 197, Temple to Grenville, 20 February 1783.
17. B.L. Add. MS. 58, 874, f. 80, Temple to Grenville, 20 March 1783.
18. H.M.C. F., p. 190, Temple to Grenville, 9 February 1783.

Chapter Three

1. P.R.O., H.O. 100/12, Northington to North, 23 December 1783.
2. Sydney to the King, 17 January 1784, quoted in Aspinall, A., *The Correspondence of George III* (5 vols., 1962), Vol. I, p. 25.
3. H.M.C. R., Mornington to Rutland, 17 April 1787.
4. Cornwallis to Ross, 20 May 1799, quoted *Correspondence of Charles, 1st Marquis Cornwallis* (edited by Charles Ross, 1859); Vol. III, p. 100.
5. St Patrick's Cathedral Chapter Minutes, 1793–1819, 29 July 1800.
6. *Saunder's News Letter and Daily Advertiser*, 12 August 1800.
7. *D.E.P.*, 4 July 1809.
8. S.P.C.C.M. (2), 4 August 1809.
9. *Irish Times*, 29 August 1821.
10. An unpublished article by Mrs. P. B. Phair, based on the letter books of Sir William Betham and used here with her permission (no pagination).

11. *Ibid.*
12. *I.T.*, 29 August 1821.
13. *Ibid.*
14. *Ibid.*
15. *D.E.P.*, 18 August 1821.
16. Phair article.
17. *Ibid.*
18. Public Record Office of Northern Ireland, D619/28G, p. 267/142, Grey to Anglesey, 23 March 1833.
19. *The Times*, 19 September, 1845.

Chapter Four

1.   Cited, Blake, R., *Disraeli* (1966), pp. 178–9.
2.   P.R.O.N.I., T.2541, V.R. 85/59, Abercorn to Mayo, 4 March 1868.
3.   P.R.O.N.I., T.2541, V.R. 85/63, Abercorn to Mayo, 6 March 1868.
4.   Disraeli to the Queen, 6 March 1868; Benson, A. C., Esher, Viscount, and Buckle, G. E. (eds.), *Letters to Queen Victoria* (1926), Vol. I, pp. 512–3.
5.   The Queen to General Grey, from *ibid.*, 7 March 1868, pp. 513–4.
6.   The Queen to the Prince of Wales, from *ibid.*, 9 March 1868, pp. 514–5.
7.   *The Clerical Journal*, 16 April 1868.
8.   *The Daily Telegraph*, 20 April 1868.
9.   *The Morning Star*, 20 April 1868.
10. Hamilton, Lord Frederic, *The Days Before Yesterday* (1920), pp. 91–2.
11. Royal Archives, D27/83, Spencer to Gladstone, 1 July 1871.
12. State Paper Office, Dublin Castle, Registered Papers of the Chief Secretary's Office, 8317; Burke to Mulhall, 5 March 1891.
13. *Times*, 4 August 1871.
14. S.P.O.D.C., C.S.O.R.P. 11178, Vicars to Balfour, 12 July 1890.
15. *Ibid.*, C.S.O.R.P. 8317, Vicars to Zetland, 17 March 1891.
16. *Ibid.*, Vicars to Ridgway, 26 March 1891.
17. P.R.O., H.O. 45/9860 B. 12823, Cadogan to Home Secretary, 28 April 1899.

Chapter Five

1.   *Statutes of the Order of St Patrick, 1905* (printed book, published September 1905; no indication on title page of author, publisher or place of publication), article 23.
2.   RA X13/4, Knollys to Aberdeen, 26 August 1907.
3.   B.L. Add. MS. 46, 065, ff. 66–75, November 1907.
4.   *Ibid.*
5.   *Ibid.*
6.   *Ibid.*, f. 82, Gladstone to Birrell, 13 January 1908.
7.   'Circumstances of the Loss of the Regalia of the Order of St Patrick', Command No. 3936, Report of the Viceregal Commission, article 23; 23 January 1908.
8.   Bamford, F., and Bankes, V., *Vicious Circle* (1965), p. 187;
9.   *Ibid.*, p. 189.
10. *Ibid.*, p. 205.
11. S.P.O.D.C., S.3926, 1 June 1927.

12.   Lee, Sir Sidney, *King Edward VII: A Biography* (two vols., 1925-7), Vol. II, p. 452.
13.   Wilkinson, Sir Nevile Rodwell, *To All and Singular* (1922), p. 174.

Chapter Six

1.   RA GV, 0537/54, Wimborne to Stamfordham, 14 May 1915.
2.   *Ibid.*, Stamfordham to Wimborne, 15 May 1915.
3.   *Ibid.*
4.   *Times*, 6 December 1922.
5.   P.R.O., C.O. 739/21, Sturgis to Anderson, 5 May 1923.
6.   P.R.O., D.O. 35/14, Martin-Jones to Rae, 12 February 1926.
7.   *Ibid.*, 35/35, Anderson to Whiskard, 1 March 1927.
8.   *Ibid.*
9.   *Ibid.*, Granard to Stamfordham, 18 March 1927.
10.   S.P.O.D.C., S.3926, Memorandum by Cosgrave, 23 March 1927.
11.   *Belfast News Letter*, 9 June 1927.
12.   P.R.O., D.O., 35/35, Statutes of . . . Order of St Patrick, article 28 (1927).
13.   *Ibid.*, 35/61, aide-memoire for the use of Lord Granard . . ., 5 March 1928.
14.   S.P.O.D.C., S.3926, Costello to Cosgrave, 18 May 1928.
15.   P.R.O., D.O., 117/108, Memorandum by Cosgrave, 21 May 1928.
16.   *Ibid.*, Cosgrave to Granard, 21 May 1928.
17.   *Ibid.*, Joynson-Hicks to Baldwin, 19 June 1928.
18.   P.R.O., D.O. 117/108 Amery to Baldwin, 23 July 1928.
19.   S.P.O.D.C., S.3926, Passfield to McGilligan, 19 August 1929.
20.   *Ibid.*, Memorandum by Irish Minister of Finance, 19 October 1929.
21.   *Ibid.*, McGilligan to Passfield, 29 January 1930.
22.   D.O. 117/108, Memorandum to No. 10, 2 September 1930.

Chapter Seven

1.   *B.N.L.*, 30 June 1934.
2.   *Ibid.*, 18 March 1936.
3.   *Irish Independent*, 18 March 1936.
4.   S.P.O.D.C., S.3926, Memorandum, 31 December 1936.
5.   *Ibid.*, Walshe to McDunphy, 4 November 1938.
6.   P.R.O., D.O., 35/1132/H.616, Garner to Hardinge, 17 December 1941.
7.   S.P.O.D.C., S. 3926, Walshe to Moynihan, 16 January 1942.
8.   P.R.O., D.O., 35/1132/H.616, Sadleir to Garter, 15 February 1943.
9.   MacLysaght, E. *Changing Times: Ireland since 1898* (1978), pp. 182-3.
10.   P.R.O., D.O., 130/37, Sadleir to Markbreiter, 3 July 1943.
11.   *Ibid.*, Memorandum by Sir Charles Dixon, 28 April 1943.

Chapter Eight

1.   P.R.O., H.O., 45/20289, Rowan to Peterson, 15 July 1946.
2.   S.P.O.D.C., S.5708, Memorandum, 7 May 1948.

3.   *Ibid.*
4.   *Ibid.*, Memorandum, 26 May 1948.
5.   Hansard Col., 1877, 11 May 1949.
6.   Letter to the author from Lord O'Neill of the Maine, 30 March 1981.
7.   S.P.O.D.C., S.5708, Lester to Lemass, 15 October 1962.
8.   *Ibid.*, Lemass to Lester, 17 October 1962.
9.   *Ibid.*, McCann to the Department of the Taoiseach, 9 April 1963.
10. *Ibid.*, 'Draft heads of a Bill to establish an Honour to be known as the Order of St Patrick' (typed sheet, no indication of authorship).
11. *Times*, 18 January 1882.

Chapter Nine

1.   P.R.O., H.O., 100/8, Temple to Townshend, 13 January 1783.
2.   *D.E.P.*, 18 March 1783.
3.   *Ibid.*, 22 February 1783.
4.   *Ibid.*, 4 March 1783.
5.   P.R.O., H.O. 100/8, Temple to Townshend, 13 January 1783.
6.   'Ordinances touching the Badges, Devices and Habits of Our Knights Companions of our Most Illustrious Order of St Patrick; the Habits of their Esquires, and the Badges and Habits of the Officers of the said Order', 28 February 1783. C.C.: R.O.S.P., Vol. I.
7.   *D.E.P.*, 8 February 1783.
8.   *Ibid.*, 22 February 1783.
9.   Genealogical Office MS. 312, p. 13, 1819.
10. 'Ordinances touching the Badges . . .'; C.C.: R.O.S.P., Vol. I.
11. H.M.C. F., Vol. VI, Floyd to Harris, 9 November 1799.
12. *Times*, 31 March 1885.

Chapter Ten

1.   B.L. Add. MS. 40,555, ff. 61-7, Pakenham to Peel, 4 December 1844.
2.   *Ibid.*
3.   P.R.O., T.160, 997 F/1391/3, Knox to Sydney-Turner, 25 July 1938.
4.   *Ibid.*, Flett to Wilkinson, 15 August 1939.

BIBLIOGRAPHY

I.—MANUSCRIPT SOURCES

(1)   Central Chancery of the Orders of Knighthood
Register of the Order of Saint Patrick (2 vols.).

(2)   British Library: Department of Manuscripts (B.M. Add. MSS.).
B.M. Add. MSS. 58,874, f. 20, f. 23, f. 41, f. 80; 40,177, f. 134; 40,856, f. 78; 46,065, ff. 66–75, f. 82; 40,555, ff. 61–7; 14,410, f. 10; 38,716, f. 140; 6,283, f. 29.

(3)   Historical Manuscripts Commission (H.M.C.).
Charlemont MSS.; Fortescue MSS.; Rutland MSS.

(4)   Public Record Office (P.R.O.).
Cal. H.O. Papers, No. 531—Home Office; H.O. 100/3—Home Office; H.O. 100/8; H.O. 100/12; H.O. 45/9860 B.12823; C.O. 739/21—Colonial Office; D.O. 35/14—Dominions Office; D.O. 35/35; D.O. 35/61; D.O. 117/108; D.O. 35/1132/H.616; D.O. 130/37; H.O. 45/20289; T.160 997 F/1391/3—Treasury.

(5)   Public Record Office of Northern Ireland (P.R.O.N.I.).
T.3429/1/9; D.619/28G; T.2541 V.R. 85/59.

(6)   Royal Archives (R.A.).
(1) D.27/83; (2) X.13/14; Geo. V 0537/54; Geo. V 0537/56.

(7)   Saint Patrick's Cathedral, Dublin (S.P.C.C.M.).
Chapter Minutes: Volumes 1764–1792 and 1793–1819.

(8)   State Paper Office, Dublin Castle. (S.P.O.D.C.)
C.S.O.R.P. 8317, 11178; S.3926; S.5708.

(9)   Genealogical Office, Dublin Castle (G.O. MS.).
150–153, Miscellaneous warrants; 308, Receipts for insignia; 310, Illustrations of insignia; 312, Installation papers, 1819; 315, Press cuttings, 1868; 316, Declarations and admonitions; 317, Miscellaneous warrants; 320, Investiture invitations 1902; 335, Investiture ceremonial; 344, Certificates of noblesse.

113

II.—NEWSPAPERS

Belfast News Letter; Clerical Journal; Daily Telegraph; Dublin Evening Post; Irish Independent; Irish Times; Morning Star; Saunder's News Letter and Daily Advertiser; The Times

III.—SECONDARY SOURCES

Aberdeen, John Campbell, 1st Marquess of, and Ishbel, Marchioness of: *'We Twa'* (1925, 2 vols); *More Cracks with 'We Twa'* (1929).

Allen, Gregory, 'The Great Jewel Mystery', *Garda Review* (August 1976).

Aspinall, Arthur, *The Correspondence of George III* (1962ff, five vols.).

Bamford, Francis, and Bankes, Viola, *Vicious Circle: The Case of the Missing Irish Crown Jewels* (1965).

Benson, A. C., Esher, Viscount, and Buckle, G. E., *Letters of Queen Victoria* (2nd series, 1926).

Birrell, Augustine, *Things Past Redress* (1937).

Blake, R., *Disraeli* (1966).

Bond, M. and Beamish, D., *The Gentleman Usher of the Black Rod* (H.M.S.O., 1976).

Brynn, Edward, *Crown and Castle* (1978).

Fingall, Elizabeth, Countess of, *Seventy Years Young* (1937).

Frankland, Noble, *Prince Henry, Duke of Gloucester* (1979).

Freer, Stephen, 'Arms and the Flag: St Patrick's Cross', *The Coat of Arms* (Spring 1977).

Gilbert, Sir John Thomas, *History of the Viceroys of Ireland* (1865).

Gilmartin, John, 'Vincent Waldré's Ceiling Paintings in Dublin Castle', *Apollo* (January 1972).

Hardy, Francis, *Memoirs of the Political and Private Life of J. Caulfield, Earl of Charlemont* (2nd edn., London 1812, 2 vols.).

Hayes-McCoy, G. A., *A History of Irish Flags* (1979).

Jackson, Victor, *St Patrick's Cathedral, Dublin* (1976).

Johnston, Edith, *Great Britain and Ireland: A Study in Political Administration* (1963).

Lecky, W. E. H., *History of Ireland in the Eighteenth Century* (1913).

Lee, Sir Sidney, *King Edward VII: A Biography* (1925-7, 2 vols.).

Lyons, F. S. L., *Ireland since the famine* (1973).

McDowell, R., *Irish Public Opinion, 1750–1800* (1944); *The Irish Administration, 1801–1914* (1964).

MacLysaght, Edward, *Changing Times—Ireland since 1898* (1978).

Malloch, R. J., 'The Missing Regalia of the Grand Master of the Order of Saint Patrick', *Orders and Medals* (Autumn 1977).

Meath, Reginald, 12th Earl of, *Memoirs of the Nineteenth Century* (1923).

Nicholas, Sir Nicholas Harris, *History of the Orders of Knighthood of the British Empire* (1842, 4 vols.).

O'Brien, Richard Barry, *Dublin Castle and the Irish People* (1909).

Perrin, Robert, *Jewels* (1977).

Risk, James Charles, 'The Insignia of the Order of Saint Patrick', *Orders and Medals* (Winter 1976).

Rosse, William Brendan, 7th Earl of, *Birr Castle* (1982).

Wilkinson, Sir Nevile Rodwell, *To All and Singular* (1922).

Wynne, Michael, 'A Replica Crown Jewel', *Apollo* (February 1982).

APPENDIX ONE

Grand Masters of the Most Illustrious Order of Saint Patrick

1. George Nugent-Temple-Grenville, 3rd Earl Temple (later 1st Marquess of Buckingham) [1783]
   Born: 18 June 1753
   Invested: 11 March 1783
   Died: 11 February 1813

2. Robert Henley, 2nd Earl of Northington [1783-1784]
   Born: 3 January 1747
   Invested: 3 June 1783
   Died: 5 July 1786

3. Charles Manners, 4th Duke of Rutland [1784-1787]
   Born: 15 March 1754
   Invested: 24 February 1784
   Died: 24 October 1787

4. George Nugent-Temple-Grenville, 1st Marquess of Buckingham [1787-1790]
   Born and died: (as for 1)
   Invested: 16 December 1787

5. John Fane, 10th Earl of Westmorland [1790-1795]
   Born: 1 June 1759
   Invested: 5 January 1790
   Died: 15 December 1841

6. William Fitzwilliam, 2nd Earl Fitzwilliam [1795]
   Born: 30 May 1748
   Invested: 4 January 1795
   Died: 8 February 1833

7. John Jeffreys Pratt, 2nd Earl Camden [1795-1798]
   Born: 11 February 1759
   Invested: 31 March 1795
   Died: 8 October 1840

8. Charles Cornwallis, 1st Marquess Cornwallis [1798-1801]
   Born: 31 December 1738
   Invested: 20 June 1798
   Died: 5 October 1805

9. Philip Yorke, 3rd Earl of Hardwicke [1801-1806]
   Born: 31 May 1757
   Invested: 25 May 1301
   Died: 18 November 1834

10. John Russell, 9th Duke of Bedford [1806-1807]
    Born: 6 July 1766
    Invested: 28 March 1806
    Died: 20 October 1839

11. Charles Lennox, 4th Duke of Richmond [1807-1813]
    Born: 9 December 1764
    Invested: 19 April 1807
    Died: 28 August 1819

12. Charles Whitworth, 1st Earl Whitworth [1813-1817]
    Born: 29 May 1752
    Invested: 26 August 1813
    Died: 13 May 1825

13. Charles Chetwynd Chetwynd-Talbot, 2nd Earl Talbot [1817-1821]
    Born: 25 April 1777
    Invested: 9 October 1817
    Died: 13 January 1849

14. Richard Wellesley, 1st Marquess Wellesley [1821-1828]
    Born: 20 June 1760
    Invested: 29 December 1821
    Died: 26 September 1842

15. Henry William Paget, 1st Marquess of Anglesey [1828-1829]
    Born: 17 May 1768
    Invested: 1 March 1828
    Died: 29 April 1854

16. Hugh Percy, 5th Duke of Northumberland [1829-1830]
    Born: 20 April 1795
    Invested: 6 March 1829
    Died: 11 February 1847

17. Henry William Paget, 1st Marquess of
    Anglesey [1830–1833]
    Born and died: (as for 15)
    Invested: 23 December 1830

18. Richard Wellesley, Marquess Wellesley
    [1833–1835]
    Born and died: (as for 14)
    Invested: 26 September 1833

19. Thomas Hamilton, 9th Earl of Haddington
    [1835]
    Born: 21 June 1780
    Invested: 6 January 1835
    Died: 1 December 1858

20. Constantine Henry Phipps, 2nd Earl of Mul-
    grave (later 1st Marquess of Nor-
    manby [1835–1839]
    Born: 15 May 1797
    Invested: 11 May 1835
    Died: 28 July 1863

21. Hugh Fortescue, 2nd Earl Fortescue
    [1839–1841]
    Born: 13 February 1783
    Invested: 3 April 1839
    Died: 14 September 1861

22. Thomas Philip de Grey, 2nd Earl de Grey
    [1841–1844]
    Born: 8 December 1781
    Invested: 15 September 1841
    Died: 14 November 1859

23. William A'Court, 1st Lord Heytesbury
    [1844–1846]
    Born: 11 July 1779
    Invested: 26 July 1844
    Died: 31 May 1860

24. John William Ponsonby, 4th Earl of Bess-
    borough [1846–1847]
    Born: 31 August 1781
    Invested: 11 July 1846
    Died: 16 May 1847

25. George William Frederick Villiers, 8th Earl
    of Clarendon [1847–1852]
    Born: 26 January 1800
    Invested: 26 May 1847
    Died: 27 June 1870

26. Archibald William Montgomerie, 13th Earl
    of Eglington [1852–1853]
    Born: 29 September 1812
    Invested: 10 March 1852
    Died: 4 October 1861

27. Edward Granville Eliot, 3rd Earl of St
    Germans [1853–1855]
    Born: 29 August 1798
    Invested: 6 January 1853
    Died: 7 October 1877

28. George William Frederick Howard, 10th
    Earl of Carlisle [1855–1858]
    Born: 18 April 1802
    Invested: 13 March 1855
    Died: 5 December 1864

29. Archibald William Montgomerie, 13th Earl
    of Eglington [1858–1859]
    Born and died: (as for 26)
    Invested: 12 March 1858

30. George William Frederick Howard, 10th
    Earl of Carlisle [1859–1864]
    Born and died: (as for 28)
    Invested: 18 June 1859

31. John Wodehouse, 3rd Lord Wodehouse
    (later 1st Earl of Kimberley)
    [1864–1866]
    Born: 7 November 1826
    Invested: 8 November 1864
    Died: 8 April 1902

32. James Hamilton, 2nd Marquess of Aber-
    corn (later 1st Duke of Abercorn)
    [1866–1868]
    Born: 21 January 1811
    Invested: 20 July 1866
    Died: 31 October 1885

33. John Poyntz Spencer, 5th Earl Spencer
    [1868–1874]
    Born: 27 October 1835
    Invested: 23 December 1868
    Died: 13 August 1910

34. James Hamilton, 1st Duke of Abercorn
    [1874–1876]
    Born and died: (as for 32)
    Invested: 2 March 1874

35. John Winston Spencer-Churchill, 7th Duke
    of Marlborough [1876–1880]
    Born: 2 June 1822
    Invested: 12 December 1876
    Died: 5 July 1883

36. Francis Thomas de Grey Cowper, 7th Earl
    Cowper [1880–1882]
    Born: 11 June 1834
    Invested: 5 May 1880
    Died: 19 July 1905

37. John Poyntz Spencer, 5th Earl Spencer
   [1882-1885]
   Born and died: (as for 33)
   Invested: 6 May 1882

38. Henry Howard Molyneux Herbert, 9th Earl
   of Carnarvon [1885-1886]
   Born: 24 June 1831
   Invested: 30 June 1885
   Died: 28 June 1890

39. John Campbell Hamilton-Gordon, 7th Earl
   of Aberdeen (later 1st Marquess of
   Aberdeen and Temair) [1886]
   Born: 3 August 1847
   Invested: 10 February 1886
   Died: 7 March 1934

40. Charles Stewart Vane-Tempest-Stewart, 6th
   Marquess of Londonderry
   [1886-1889]
   Born: 16 July 1852
   Invested: 5 August 1886
   Died: 8 February 1915

41. Lawrence Dundas, 3rd Earl of Zetland
   (later 1st Marquess of Zetland)
   [1889-1892]
   Born: 16 August 1844
   Invested: 5 October 1889
   Died: 11 March 1929

42. Robert Offley Ashburton Milnes, 2nd Lord
   Houghton (later 1st Marquess of
   Crewe) [1892-1895]
   Born: 12 January 1858
   Invested: 22 August 1892
   Died: 20 June 1945

43. George Henry Cadogan, 6th Earl Cadogan
   [1895-1902]
   Born: 12 May 1840
   Invested: 8 July 1895
   Died: 6 March 1915

44. William Humble Ward, 2nd Earl of Dudley
   [1902-1905]
   Born: 25 May 1867
   Invested: 16 August 1902
   Died: 29 June 1932

45. John Campbell Hamilton-Gordon, 7th Earl
   of Aberdeen (later 1st Marquess of
   Aberdeen and Temair)
   [1905-1915]
   Born and died: (as for 39)
   Invested: 14 December 1905

46. Ivor Churchill Guest, 1st Lord Wimborne
   (later 1st Viscount Wimborne)
   [1915-1918]
   Born: 16 January 1873
   Invested: 18 February 1915
   Died: 14 June 1939

47. John French, 1st Viscount French of Ypres
   (later 1st Earl of Ypres) [1918-1921]
   Born: 28 September 1852
   Invested: 11 May 1918
   Died: 22 May 1925

*48. Edmund Bernard Fitzalan-Howard, 1st
   Viscount Fitzalan of Derwent
   [1921-1922]
   Born: 1 June 1855
   Invested: 2 May 1921
   Died: 18 May 1947

*There were a total of 40 Grand Masters. Eight held the office twice.

APPENDIX TWO

Chronological List of the Knights of St Patrick

1. H.R.H. Prince Edward, Duke of Kent
   Born: 27 November 1767
   Nominated: 5 February 1783
   Invested: 16 March 1783 (invested in
   Dublin by proxy—11 March)
   Installed: 17 March 1783 (installed by
   proxy)
   Died: 23 January 1820

2. William Fitzgerald, 2nd Duke of Leinster
   Born: 13 March 1749
   Nominated: 5 February 1783
   Invested: 11 March 1783
   Installed: 17 March 1783
   Died: 4 October 1804

3. Henry de Burgh, 12th Earl of Clanricarde
   (later Marquess of Clanricarde)
   Born: 8 January 1743
   Nominated: 5 February 1783
   Invested: 11 March 1783
   Installed: 17 March 1783
   Died: 8 December 1797

4. Thomas Nugent, 6th Earl of Westmeath
   Born: ? (baptised 18 April 1714)
   Nominated: 5 February 1783
   Invested: 11 March 1783
   Installed: 17 March 1783
   Died: 6 September 1790

5. Murrough O'Brien, 5th Earl of Inchiquin
   (later 1st Marquess of Thomond)
   Born: 1726
   Nominated: 5 February 1783
   Invested: 11 March 1783
   Installed: 17th March 1783
   Died: 10 February 1808

6. Charles Moore, 6th Earl of Drogheda (later
   1st Marquess of Drogheda)
   Born: 29 June 1730
   Nominated 5 February 1783
   Invested: 11 March 1783
   Installed: 17 March 1783
   Died: 22 December 1821

7. George de la Poer Beresford, 2nd Earl of
   Tyrone (later 1st Marquess of Water-
   ford)
   Born: 8 January 1735
   Nominated: 5 February 1783
   Invested: 11 March 1783
   Installed: 17 March 1783
   Died: 3 December 1800

8. Richard Boyle, 2nd Earl of Shannon
   Born: 30 January 1737
   Nominated: 5 February 1783
   Invested: 11 March 1783
   Installed: 17 March 1783
   Died: 20 May 1807

9. James Hamilton, 2nd Earl of Clanbrassil
   Born: 23 August 1730
   Nominated: 5 February 1783
   Invested: 11 March 1783
   Installed: 17 March 1783
   Died: 6 February 1798

10. Richard Wellesley, 2nd Earl of Mornington
    (later 1st Marquess Wellesley)
    Born: 20 June 1760
    Nominated: 5 February 1783
    Invested: 11 March 1783
    Installed: 17 March 1783
    Resigned: 3rd March 1810 (on being
    appointed a Knight of the Garter)
    Died: 26 September 1842

11. Arthur Gore, 2nd Earl of Arran
    Born: 25 July 1734
    Nominated: 8 March 1783
    Invested: ?
    Installed: 17 March 1783
    Died: 8 October 1809

12. James Stopford, 2nd Earl of Courtown
    Born: 28 May 1731
    Nominated: 5 February 1783
    Invested: 11 March 1783
    Installed: 17 March 1783
    Died: 30 March 1810

13. James Caulfield, 1st Earl of Charlemont
    Born: 18 August 1728
    Nominated; 5 February 1783
    Invested: 11 March 1783
    Installed: 17 March 1783
    Died: 4 August 1799

14. Thomas Taylour, 1st Earl of Bective
    Born: 20 October 1724
    Nominated: 5 February 1783
    Invested: 11 March 1783
    Installed: 17 March 1783
    Died: 14 February 1795

15. Henry Loftus, 3rd Earl of Ely
    Born: 18 November 1709
    Nominated: 5 February 1783
    Invested: (The Earl of Ely died abroad
        before being invested on installed)
    Installed: (as above)
    Died: 8 May 1783

16. Joshua Proby, 2nd Baron Carysfort (later
        1st Earl of Carysfort)
    Born: 12 August 1751
    Elected: 5 February 1784 (in place of
        No. 15)
    Invested: 5 February 1784
    Installed: 11 August 1800 (by proxy)
    Died: 7 April 1828

17. Charles Loftus, 4th Earl of Ely (later 1st
        Marquess of Ely)
    Born: 23 January 1738
    Elected: 12 December 1794 (in place of
        No. 4)
    Invested: 12 December 1794
    Installed: 11 August 1800
    Died: 22 March 1806

18. William Fortescue, 1st Earl of Clermont
    Born: 5 August 1722
    Elected: 30 March 1795 (in place of
        No. 14)
    Invested: (date unknown, but probably
        soon after election)
    Installed: 11 August 1800
    Died: 30 September 1806

19. Walter Butler, 18th Earl of Ormonde
        (later 1st Marquess of Ormonde)
    Born: 5 February 1770
    Elected: 19 March 1798 (in place of
        No. 3)
    Invested: 19 March 1798
    Installed: 11 August 1800
    Died: 10 August 1820

20. Charles Dillon, 12th Viscount Dillon
    Born: 6 November 1745
    Elected: 19 March 1798 (in place of
        No. 9)
    Invested: 19 March 1798
    Installed: 11 August 1800
    Died: 9 November 1813

21. John Browne, 3rd Earl of Altamont (later
        1st Marquess of Sligo)
    Born: 11 June 1756
    Elected: 5 August 1800 (in place of
        No. 13)
    Invested: 5 August 1800
    Installed: 11 August 1800
    Died: 2 January 1809

22. Henry Conyngham, 3rd Baron (afterwards
        1st Marquess) Conyngham
    Born: 26 December 1766
    Elected: 22 January 1801 (in place of
        No. 7)
    Invested: 22 January 1801
    Installed: 29 June 1809
    Died: 28 December 1832

23. Henry de la Poer Beresford, 2nd Marquess
        of Waterford
    Born: 23 May 1772
    Elected: 14 March 1806 (in place of
        No. 2)
    Invested: 14 March 1806
    Installed: 29 June 1809
    Died: 16 July 1826

24. Thomas Taylour, 1st Marquess of Head-
        fort
    Born: 18 November 1757
    Elected: 15 May 1806 (in place of
        No. 17)
    Invested: June 1806
    Installed: 29 June 1809
    Died: 23 October 1829

25. Robert Jocelyn, 2nd Earl of Roden
    Born: 26 October 1756
    Elected: 13 November 1806 (in place of
        No. 18)
    Invested: 13 November 1806
    Installed: 29 June 1809
    Died: 29 June 1820

26. John Loftus, 2nd Marquess of Ely
    Born: 15 February 1770
    Elected: 3 November 1807 (in place of
        No. 8)

(26) John Loftus—*cont.*
Invested: 3 November 1807
Installed: 29 June 1809
Died: 23 September 1845

27. Henry Boyle, 3rd Earl of Shannon
Born: 8 August 1771
Elected: 5 April 1808 (in place of No. 5)
Invested: 5 April 1808
Installed: 29 June 1809
Died: 22 April 1842

28. Charles O'Neill, 1st Earl O'Neill
Born: 22 January 1779
Elected: 13 February 1809 (in place of No. 21)
Invested: 13 February 1809
Installed: 29 June 1809
Died: 25 March 1841

29. William O'Brien, 2nd Marquess of Thomond
Born: about 1765
Elected: 11 November 1809 (in place of No. 11)
Invested: 11 November 1809
Installed: 27 May 1819
Died: 21 August 1846

30. Howe Brown, 2nd Marquess of Sligo
Born: 18 May 1788
Elected: 24 March 1810 (in place of No. 10)
Invested: 11 June 1811 (invested at Malta by dispensation)
Installed: 27 May 1819
Died: 26 January 1845

31. John Cole, 2nd Earl of Enniskillen
Born: 23 March 1768
Elected: 27 April 1810 (in place of No. 12)
Invested: 27 April 1810
Installed: 27 May 1819
Died: 31 March 1840

32. Thomas Pakenham, 2nd Earl of Longford
Born: 14 May 1774
Elected: 17 December 1813 (in place of No. 20)
Invested: 17 December 1813
Installed: 27 May 1819
Died: 24 May 1835

33. H.R.H. Prince Ernest Augustus, 1st Duke of Cumberland and Teviotdale, King of Hanover

(33) H.R.H. Prince Ernest Augustus—*cont.*
Born: 5 June 1771
Elected: ? (in place of No. 1)
Invested: 20 August 1821 (by proxy)
Installed: 28 August 1821 (by proxy)
Died: 18 November 1851

34. George Chichester, 2nd Marquess of Donegal
Born: 13 August 1769
Elected: ? (in place of No. 25)
Invested: 20 August 1821
Installed: 28 August 1821
Died: 5 October 1844

35. Du Pre Alexander, 2nd Earl of Caledon
Born: 14 December 1777
Elected: ? (in place of No. 19)
Invested: 20 August 1821
Installed: 28 August 1821
Died: 8 April 1839

36. Charles Chetwynd-Talbot, 2nd Earl Talbot
Born: 25 April 1777
Nominated a Knight Extraordinary: 19 July 1821
Invested: 20 August 1821
Installed: 28 August 1821
Became a Knight in Ordinary: 22 December 1821 (in place of No. 6)
Resigned: 11 October 1844 (on being made a K.G.).
Died: 13 January 1849

37. James Butler, 19th Earl of Ormonde (later 1st Marquess of Ormonde)
Born: 15 July 1777
Nominated a Knight Extraordinary: 19 July 1821
Invested: 20 August 1821
Installed: 28 August 1821
Became a Knight in Ordinary: 16 July 1826 (in place of No. 23)
Died: 18 May 1838

38. John Brabazon, 10th Earl of Meath
Born: 9 April 1772
Nominated a Knight Extraordinary: 19 July 1821
Invested: 20 August 1821
Installed: 28 August 1821
Became a Knight in Ordinary: 7 April 1828 (in place of No. 16)
Died: 15 March 1851

39. Arthur Plunkett, 8th Earl of Fingall
Born: 9 September 1759
Nominated a Knight Extraordinary: 19 July 1821

(39) Arthur Plunkett—*cont.*
Invested: 20 August 1821
Installed: 28 August 1821
Became a Knight in Ordinary: 23 October 1829 (in place of No. 24)
Died: 30 July 1836

40. James Stopford, 3rd Earl of Courtown
Born: 15 August 1765
Nominated a Knight Extraordinary: 19 July 1821
Invested: 20 August 1821
Installed: 28 August 1821
Became a Knight in Ordinary: 28 December 1832 (in place of No. 22)
Died: 15 June 1835

41. Robert Jocelyn, 3rd Earl of Roden
Born: 27 October 1788
Nominated a Knight Extraordinary: 19 July 1821
Invested: 20 August 1821
Installed: 28 August 1821
Became a Knight in Ordinary: 24 January 1833 (by Statute)
Died: 20 March 1870

42. Arthur Hill, 3rd Marquess of Downshire
Born: 8 October 1788
Nominated a Knight Extraordinary: 8 September 1831
Invested: 24 November 1831
Became a Knight in Ordinary: 24 January 1833 (by Statute)
Installed: 30 January 1833 (by dispensation)
Died: 12 April 1845

43. Ulick de Burgh, 1st Marquess of Clanricarde
Born: 20 December 1802
Nominated a Knight Extraordinary: 8 September 1831
Invested: 19 October 1831
Installed: 30 January 1833 (by dispensation)
Became a Knight in Ordinary: 24 January 1833 (by Statute)
Died: 10 April 1874

44. Francis Caulfield, 2nd Earl of Charlemont
Born: 3 January 1775
Nominated a Knight Extraordinary: 8 September 1831
Invested: 19 October 1831
Installed: 30 January 1833 (by dispensation)
Became a Knight in Ordinary: 24

(44) Francis Caulfield—*cont.*
January 1833 (by Statute)
Died: 26 December 1863

45. Francis Matthews, 2nd Earl of Llandaff
Born: 2 or 20 January 1768
Nominated a Knight Extraordinary; 8 September 1831
Invested: 24 November 1831
Installed: 30 January 1833 (by dispensation)
Became a Knight in Ordinary: 24 January 1833 (by Statute)
Died: 12 March 1833

46. Francis Conyngham, 2nd Marquess Conyngham
Born: 11 June 1797
Nominated: 27 March 1833 (by the increase of the Order under the Statute of 24 January 1833)
Invested: 27 March 1833
Installed: 3 April 1833 (by dispensation)
Died: 17 July 1876

47. Nathaniel Clements, 2nd Earl of Leitrim
Born: 9 May 1768
Elected: 8 April 1834 (by the increase of the Order under the Statute of 24 January 1833)
Invested: 8 April 1834
Installed: 31 May 1834 (by dispensation)
Died: 31 December 1854

48. John Hely-Hutchinson, 3rd Earl of Donoughmore
Born: 1787
Elected: 8 April 1834 (in place of No. 45)
Invested: 8 April 1834
Installed: 31 May 1834 (by dispensation)
Died: 14 September 1851

49. Edmund Boyle, 8th Earl of Cork
Born: 21 October 1767
Nominated: 22 July 1835 (in place of No. 32)
Invested: 22nd July 1835 (by dispensation)
Installed: 22 July 1835 (by dispensation)
Died: 30 June 1856

50. Thomas St Lawrence, 3rd Earl of Howth
Born: 16 August 1803
Nominated: 22 July 1835 (in place of No. 40)

(50) Thomas St Lawrence—*cont.*
    Invested: 22 July 1835 (by dispensation)
    Installed: 22 July 1835 (by dispensation)
    Died: 4 February 1874

51. Thomas Southwell, 3rd Viscount Southwell
    Born: 25 February 1777
    Elected: ? (in place of No. 39)
    Invested: 12 September 1837
    Installed: 20 September 1837 (by dispensation)
    Died: 29 February 1860

52. Thomas Taylour, 2nd Marquess of Headfort
    Born: 4 May 1787
    Elected: 15 April 1839 (in place of No. 37)
    Invested: 15 April 1839
    Installed: 18 April 1839 (by dispensation)
    Died: 6 December 1870

53. William Hare, 2nd Earl of Listowel
    Born: 22 September 1801
    Elected: 29 April 1839 (in place of No. 35)
    Invested: 29 April 1839
    Installed: 7 May 1839 (by dispensation)
    Died: 3 February 1856

54. Joseph Leeson, 4th Earl of Milltown
    Born: 11 February 1799
    Elected: ? (in place of No. 31)
    Invested: 13 March 1841
    Installed: 21 March 1841 (by dispensation)
    Died: 31 January 1866

55. Philip Gore, 4th Earl of Arran
    Born: 23 November 1801
    Elected: 6 May 1841 (in place of No. 28)
    Invested: 6 May 1841
    Installed: 19 July 1841 (by dispensation)
    Died: 25 June 1884

56. H.R.H. The Prince Consort
    Born: 26 August 1819
    Declared: 20 January 1842 (an extra Knight)
    Invested: 20 January 1842 (by dispensation)
    Installed: 20 January 1842 (by dispensation)
    Died: 14 December 1861

57. William Howard, 4th Earl of Wicklow
    Born: 13 February 1788
    Invested: 15 June 1842 (in place of No. 27)
    Installed; 5 November 1842 (by dispensation)
    Died: 22 March 1869

58. William Parsons, 3rd Earl of Rosse
    Born: 17 June 1800
    Invested: 4 January 1845 (in place of No. 34)
    Installed: 9 January 1845 (by dispensation)
    Died: 31 October 1867

59. Henry de la Poer Beresford, 3rd Marquess of Waterford
    Born: 26 April 1811
    Invested: 4 January 1845 (in place of No. 36)
    Installed: 9 January 1845 (by dispensation)
    Died: 29 March 1859

60. John Fitzgibbon, 2nd Earl of Clare
    Born: 10 June 1792
    Appointed: 17 September 1845
    Invested: 20 September 1845 (in place of No. 30)
    Installed: 20 September 1845 (by dispensation)
    Died: 18 August 1851

61. John Butler, 2nd Marquess of Ormonde
    Born: 24 August 1808
    Appointed: 17 September 1845
    Invested: 20 September 1845 (in place of No. 42)
    Installed: 20 September 1845 (by dispensation)
    Died: 25 September 1854

62. Henry Maxwell, 7th Baron Farnham
    Born: 9 August 1799
    Invested: 14 November 1845 (in place of No. 26)
    Installed: 14 November 1845 (by dispensation)
    Died: 20 August 1868

63. Arthur Plunkett, 9th Earl of Fingall
    Born: 29 March 1791
    Invested: 21 October 1846 (in place of No. 29)
    Installed: 21 October 1846 (by dispensation)
    Died: 21 April 1869

64. John Foster-Skeffington, 10th Viscount Massereene and 3rd Viscount Ferrard
Born: 30 November 1812
Invested: 3 July 1851 (in place of No. 38)
Installed: 3 July 1851
Died: 28 April 1863

65. H.R.H. Prince George, 2nd Duke of Cambridge
Born: 26 March 1819
Invested: 17 November 1851 (in place of No. 60)
Installed: 17 November 1851 (by dispensation)
Died: 17 March 1904

66. Robert Carew, 1st Baron of Carew
Born: 9 March 1787
Invested: 18 November 1851 (in place of No. 48)
Installed: 18 November 1851 (by dispensation)
Died: 2 June 1856

67. Richard Dawson, 3rd Baron Cremorne (later 1st Earl of Dartrey)
Born: 7 September 1817
Invested: 22 February 1855 (in place of No. 61)
Installed: 21 April 1855 (by dispensation)
Died: 11 May 1897

68. Archibald Acheson, 3rd Earl of Gosford
Born: 20 August 1806
Invested: 22 February 1855 (in place of No. 47)
Installed: 21 April 1855 (by dispensation)
Died: 22 June 1864

69. Frederick Stewart, 4th Marquess of Londonderry
Born: 7 July 1805
Invested: 28 August 1856 (in place of No. 53
Installed: 23 December 1856 (by dispensation
Died: 25 November 1872

70. George Forbes, 7th Earl of Granard
Born: 5 August 1833
Invested: 30 January 1857 (in place of No. 66)
Installed: 10 March 1857
Died: 25 August 1889

71. Hugh Gough, 1st Viscount Gough
Born: 3 November 1779
Invested: 20 January 1857 (in place of No. 49)
Installed: 10 March 1857 (by dispensation)
Died: 2 March 1869

72. George Chichester, 3rd Marquess of Donegal
Born: 10 February 1797
Invested: (not invested, but permitted to wear the insignia by warrant of the Grand Master, January 28, 1857) (in place of No. 33)
Installed: 10 March 1857 (by dispensation)
Died: 20 October 1883

73. Arthur Hill, 4th Marquess of Downshire
Born: 6 August 1812
Invested: 24 May 1859 (in place of No. 59)
Installed: 2 July 1859 (by dispensation)
Died: 6 August 1868

74. Richard Boyle, 9th Earl of Cork
Born: 19 April 1829
Invested: 13 June 1860 (in place of No. 51)
Installed: 20 June 1860 (by dispensation)
Died: 22 June 1904

75. Frederick Hamilton-Blackwood, Baron Dufferin and Claneboyne (later 1st Marquess of Dufferin and Ava)
Born: 21 June 1826
Invested; 28 January 1864 (in place of No. 64)
Installed: 11 February 1864 (by dispensation)
Died: 12 February 1902

76. Charles Brownlow, 2nd Baron Lurgan
Born: 10 April 1831
Invested: 31 March 1864 (in place of No. 44)
Installed: 12 April 1864 (by dispensation)
Died: 16 January 1882

77. James Caulfield, 3rd Earl of Charlemont
Born: 6 October 1820
Invested: 28 December 1865 (in place of No. 68)
Installed: 26 February 1866 (by dispensation)
Died: 12 January 1892

78. Edwin Wyndham-Quin, 3rd Earl of Dunraven
    and Mount Earl
    Born: 19 May 1812
    Invested: 13 March 1866 (in place of
    No. 54)
    Installed: 31 March 1866 (by dispensa-
    tion)
    Died: 6 October 1871

79. Henry Moore, 3rd Marquess of Drogheda
    Born: 14 August 1825
    Invested: 7 February 1868 (in place of
    No. 58)
    Installed: 20 February 1868 (by dis-
    pensation)
    Died: 29 June 1892

80. H.R.H. The Prince of Wales (later King
    Edward VII)
    Born: 9 November 1841
    Invested: 18 March 1868
    Installed: 18 April 1868
    Became Sovereign of the Order: 22
    January 1901
    Died: 6 May 1910

81. John de la Poer Beresford, 5th Marquess of
    Waterford
    Born: 21 May 1844
    Invested: 17 November 1868 (in place of
    No. 73)
    Installed: 16 January 1869 (by dispen-
    sation)
    Died: 23 October 1895

82. John Crichton, 3rd Earl of Erne
    Born: 30 July 1802
    Invested: 17 November 1868 (in place
    of No. 62)
    Installed: 16 January 1869 (by dispen-
    sation)
    Died: 3 October 1885

83. Richard Bourke, 6th Earl of Mayo
    Born: 21 February 1822
    Created a Knight Extraordinary: 11
    November 1868
    Invested: (at Calcutta) 18 January 1869
    Became a Knight in Ordinary: 2 March
    1869 (in place of No. 71)
    Installed: 12 April 1869 (by dispensa-
    tion)
    Died: 8 February 1872

84. H.R.H. Prince Arthur, 1st Duke of Con-
    naught and Strathearn
    Born: 1 May 1850

(84) H.R.H. Prince Arthur—cont.
    Invested: 30 March 1869
    Installed: 1 May 1869 (by dispensa-
    tion)
    Died: 16 January 1942

85. Granville Proby, 4th Earl of Carysfort
    Born: 18 January 1836
    Invested: 2 June 1869 (in place of
    No. 57)
    Died: 18 May 1872

86. Archibald Acheson, 4th Earl of Gosford
    Born: 19 August 1841
    Invested: 2 June 1869 (in place of
    No. 63)
    Died: 11 April 1922

87. Mervyn Wingfield, 7th Viscount Powers-
    court
    Born: 13 October 1836
    Invested: 2 August 1871 (in place of
    No. 41)
    Died: 5 June 1904

88. Thomas Southwell, 4th Viscount South-
    well
    Born: 6 April 1836
    Invested: 2 August 1871 (in place of
    No. 52)
    Died: 26 April 1878

89. Robert Carew, 2nd Baron Carew
    Born: 28 January 1818
    Invested: 29 February 1872 (in place of
    No. 78)
    Died: 8 September 1881

90. Valentine Browne, 4th Earl of Kenmare
    Born: 16 May 1825
    Invested: 3 June 1872 (in place of No.83)
    Died: 9 February 1905

91. William Hare, 3rd Earl of Listowel
    Born: 29 May 1833
    Invested: 20 February 1873 (in place of
    No. 69)
    Died: 5 June 1924

92. William Proby, 5th Earl of Carysfort
    Born: 18 January 1836
    Invested: 31 August 1874 (in place of
    No. 50)
    Died: 4 September 1909

93. George Vane-Tempest, 5th Marquess of
    Londonderry

(93) George Vane-Tempest—*cont.*
    Born: 26 April 1821
    Nominated: 23 April 1874 (in place of
        No. 43)
    Invested: 31 August 1874
    Died: 5 November 1884

94. Windham Wyndham-Quin, 4th Earl of Dun-
        raven and Mount Earl
    Born: 12 February 1841
    Nominated: 7 August 1872 (in place of
        No. 85)
    Invested: 13 May 1876
    Died: 14 June 1926

95. William Montague, 7th Duke of Manchester
    Born: 15 October 1823
    Invested: 3 March 1877 (in place of No.
        46)
    Died: 21 March 1890

96. Henry Dawson-Damer, 3rd Earl of Portar-
        lington
    Born: 5 September 1822
    Invested: 8 February 1879 (in place of
        No. 88)
    Died: 1 March 1889

97. H.R.H. Prince Alfred, 1st Duke of Edin-
        burgh
    Born: 6 August 1844
    Invested: 14 May 1880
    Died: 30 July 1900

98. Thomas O'Hagan, 1st Baron O'Hagan
    Born: 29 May 1812
    Invested: 17 January 1882 (in place of
        No. 89)
    Died: 1 February 1885

99. Chichester Parkinson-Fortescue, Baron
        Carlingford (2nd Baron Cler-
        mont)
    Born: 18 January 1823
    Nominated: 9 February 1882 (in place
        of No. 76)
    Invested: 11 April 1882
    Died: 30 January 1898

100. William St. Lawrence, 4th Earl of Howth
    Born: 25 June 1827
    Invested: 8 May 1884 (in place of No.
        72)
    Died: 9 March 1909

101. Luke White, 2nd Baron Annaly
    Born: 26 April 1829

(101) Luke White—*cont.*
    Nominated: 1 January 1885 (in place of
        No. 55)
    Invested: 9 February 1885
    Died: 17 March 1888

102. Thomas Rice, 2nd Baron Monteagle of
        Brandon
    Born: 31 May 1849
    Nominated: 1 January 1885 (in place of
        No. 93)
    Invested: 9 February 1885
    Died: 24 December 1926

103. Garnet Wolseley, Viscount Wolseley
    Born: 4 June 1833
    Invested: 28 November 1885 (in place of
        No. 98)
    Died: 25 March 1913

104. Thomas Taylour, 3rd Marquess of Headfort
    Born: 1 November 1822
    Invested: 28 November 1885 (in place of
        No. 82)
    Died: 22 July 1894

105. H.R.H. Prince Albert, Duke of Clarence
        and Avondale
    Born: 8 January 1864
    Invested: 28 June 1887
    Died: 14 January 1892

106. James Butler, 3rd Marquess of Ormonde
    Born: 5 October 1844
    Invested: 26 April 1888 (in place of No.
        101)
    Died: 26 October 1919

107. John Crichton, 4th Earl of Erne
    Born: 16 October 1839
    Invested: 4 April 1889 (in place of No.
        96)
    Died: 2 December 1914

108. Edward Leeson, 6th Earl of Milltown
    Born: 9 October 1835
    Nominated: 26 September 1889 (in
        place of No. 70)
    Invested: 7 February 1890
    Died: 30 May 1890

109. Francis Needham, 3rd Earl of Kilmorey
    Born: 2 August 1842
    Nominated: 22 April 1890 (in place of
        No. 95)
    Invested: 24 May 1890
    Died: 28 July 1915

110. Lawrence Parsons, 4th Earl of Rosse
Born: 17 November 1840
Nominated: 7 July 1890 (in place of No. 108)
Invested: 29 August 1890
Died: 29 August 1908

111. H.S.H. Prince Edward of Saxe-Weimar
Born: 11 October 1823
Nominated: 30 September 1890
Invested: 24 November 1890 (at Windsor); 18 December 1890 (at Dublin)
Died: 16 November 1902

112. William Perry, 3rd Earl of Limerick
Born: 17th January 1840
Nominated: 8 February 1892 (in place of No. 77)
Invested: 18 March 1892
Died: 8 August 1896

113. Edward O'Brien, 14th Baron Inchiquin
Born: 14 May 1839
Invested: 5 August 1892 (in place of No. 79)
Died: 8 April 1900

114. Frederick Lambart, 9th Earl of Cavan
Born: 21 October 1839
Nominated: 25 September 1894 (in place of No. 104)
Invested: 3 November 1894
Died: 14 July 1900

115. Edward Guinness, 1st Baron Iveagh (later 1st Earl of Iveagh)
Born: 10 November 1847
Nominated: 27 November 1895 (in place of No. 81)
Invested: 25 February 1896
Died: 7 October 1927

116. James Alexander, 4th Earl of Caledon
Born: 11 July 1846
Nominated: 14 November 1896 (in place of No. 112)
Invested: 11 February 1897
Died: 27 April 1898

117. H.R.H. Prince George, Duke of York (later King George V)
Born: 3 June 1865
Nominated: 6 July 1897
Invested: 20 August 1897
Became Sovereign of the Order: 6 May 1910
Died: 20 January 1936

118. Frederick Roberts, 1st Baron Roberts (later 1st Earl)
Born: 30 September 1832
Nominated: 4 June 1897 (in place of No. 67)
Invested: 20 August 1897
Died: 14 November 1914

119. Arthur Gore, 5th Earl of Arran
Born: 6 January 1839
Nominated: 9 March 1898 (in place of No. 99)
Invested: 15 March 1898
Died: 14 March 1901

120. George Bingham, 4th Earl of Lucan
Born: 8 May 1830
Nominated: 8 May 1898 (in place of No. 116)
Invested: 2 March 1899
Died: 5 June 1914

121. James Bernard, 4th Earl of Bandon
Born: 12 September 1850
Nominated: 24 April 1900 (in place of No. 113)
Invested: 29 August 1900
Died: 18 May 1924

122. Luke Dillon, 4th Baron Clonbrock
Born: 16 March 1834
Nominated: 2 August 1900 (in place of No. 114)
Invested: 29 August 1900
Died: 12 May 1917

123. Thomas Pakenham, 5th Earl of Longford
Born: 19 October 1864
Nominated: 15 May 1901 (in place of No. 119)
Invested: 10 June 1901
Died: 21 August 1915

124. Henry de la Poer Beresford, 6th Marquess of Waterford
Born: 28 April 1875
Invested: 15 March 1902 (in place of No. 75)
Died: 1 December 1911

125. Lowry Cole, 4th Earl of Enniskillen
Born: 21 December 1845
Invested: 11 August 1902
Became a Knight in Ordinary: 17 March 1904 (in place of No. 65)
Died: 28 April 1924

APPENDICES

126. Dudley Fitzgerald-de-Ros, 23rd Baron de Ros
Born: 11 March 1825
Invested: 11 August 1902
Became a Knight in Ordinary: 5 June 1904 (in place of No. 87)
Died: 29 April 1907

127. Dermot Bourke, 7th Earl of Mayo
Born: 2 July 1851
Invested: 3 February 1905 (in place of No. 74)
Died: 31 December 1927

128. Reginald Brabazon, 12th Earl of Meath
Born: 31 July 1841
Invested: 13 April 1905 (in place of No. 90)
Died: 11 October 1929

129. Bernard Fitzpatrick, 2nd Baron Castletown
Born: 29 July 1849
Invested: 29 February 1908 (in place of No. 126)
Died: 29 May 1937

130. William James, 1st Viscount Pirrie
Born: 31 May 1847
Invested: 4 February 1909 (in place of No. 110)
Died: 6 June 1924

131. Bernard Forbes, 8th Earl of Granard
Born: 17 September 1874
Invested: 21 May 1909 (in place of No. 100).
Died: 10 September 1948

132. Arthur Gore, 6th Earl of Arran
Born: 14 September 1868
Invested: 13 December 1909 (in place of No. 92)
Died: 19 December 1958

133. Horatio Kitchener, 1st Earl Kitchener of Khartoum
Born: 24 June 1850
Appointed: 19 June 1911
Invested: 10 July 1911
Died: 5 June 1916

134. Anthony Ashley-Cooper, 9th Earl of Shaftesbury
Born: 31 August 1869
Nominated: 19 June 1911
Invested: 10 July 1911
Died: 25 March 1961

135. Edward Ponsonby, 8th Earl of Bessborough
Born: 1 March 1851
Invested: 28 May 1915
Died: 1 December 1920

136. Richard Hely-Hutchinson, 6th Earl of Donoughmore
Born: 21 March 1875
Invested: 18 April 1916
Died: 19 October 1948

137. Mervyn Wingfield, 8th Viscount Powerscourt
Born: 16 July 1880
Invested: 18 April 1916
Died: 21 March 1947

138. William Brodrick, 1st Earl of Midleton
Born: 14 December 1856
Invested: 18 April 1916
Died: 13 February 1942

139. Frederick Lambart, 10th Earl of Cavan
Born: 16 October 1865
Invested: 18 November 1916
Died: 28 August 1946

140. John French, 1st Viscount French (later 1st Earl of Ypres)
Born: 28 September 1852
Appointed: 4 June 1917
Invested: 6 June 1917
Died: 22 May 1925

141. Geoffrey Browne, 3rd Baron Oranmore and Browne
Born: 6 January 1861
Appointed: 3 June 1918
Invested: 22 June 1918
Died: 30 June 1927

142. Hamilton Cuffe, 5th Earl of Desart
Born: 30 August 1848
Invested: 18 December 1919
Died: 4 November 1934

143. James Hamilton, 2nd Duke of Abercorn
Born: 30 November 1869
Appointed: ?
Invested: 21 December 1922
Died: 12 September 1953

144. H.R.H. The Prince of Wales (later King Edward VIII and Duke of Windsor)
Born: 23 June 1894
Appointed: 3 June 1927
Invested: 3 June 1927

(144) H.R.H. The Prince of Wales—*cont.*
Sovereign: 20 January to 10 December 1936
Died: 28 May 1972

145. H.R.H. Prince Henry, Duke of Gloucester
Born: 31 March 1900
Appointed: 29 June 1934
Invested: ? (the Insignia were sent to Buckingham Palace on 30 June 1934)
Died: 10 June 1974

146. H.R.H. Prince George, Duke of York (later King George VI)
Born: 14 December 1895
Appointed: 17 March 1936
Invested: ? (the Insignia were sent to Buckingham Palace on 17 March 1936)
Sovereign: from 10 December 1936
Died: 6 February 1952

Alphabetical Index of Knights of the Order of Saint Patrick

APPENDIX THREE

The Officers of the Order
I. Prelates

Archbishops of Armagh (1783-1885)

The Most Reverend Richard Robinson (later 1st
Lord Rokeby [1783-1794]
Born: *c.* 1708*
Nominated: 11 March 1783
Invested: 21 May 1783
Died: 11 October 1794

The Most Reverend William Newcome [1795-1800]
Born: 10 April 1729
Invested: 29 January 1795
Died: 11 January 1800

The Most Reverend and Honourable William
Stewart [1800-1822]
Born: ?

Hon. William Stewart—*cont.*
Invested: 16 December 1800
Died: 6 May 1822

The Most Reverend Lord John George Beresford
[1822-1862]
Born: 22 November 1773
Invested: 27 July 1822
Died: 18 July 1862

The Most Reverend Marcus Gervais Beresford
[1862-1885]
Born: 14 February 1801
Invested: 4 November 1862
Died: 26 December 1885

The Office of Prelate was abolished in 1885 on the death of Archbishop Beresford, in accordance
with the Royal Warrant of 1871.

*The date of Lord Rokeby's birth is uncertain. *See* the article in *The Complete Peerage.*

II. Chancellors

A. Archbishops of Dublin (1783-1884) [1886]

The Most Reverend Robert Fowler [1783-1801]
Born: 1726 ?
Nominated: 5 February 1783
Invested: 11 March 1783
Died: 10 October 1801

The Most Reverend Charles Agar, Viscount Somer-
ton (Earl of Normanton from 1806)
[1801-1809]
Born: 22 December 1736
Invested: 15 December 1801
Died: 14 July 1809

The Most Reverend Euseby Cleaver [1809-1819]
Born: 1746
Invested: 17 October 1809
Died: 10 December 1819

The Most Reverend Lord John George Beresford
[1820-1822]

Lord John George Beresford—*cont.*
Born: 22 November 1773
Invested: 16 May 1820
Died: 18 July 1862

The Most Reverend William Magee [1822-1831]
Born: 18 March 1766
Invested: 29 July 1822
Died: 18 August 1831

The Most Reverend Richard Whateley
[1831-1863]
Born: 1 February 1787
Invested: 24 November 1831
Died: 8 October 1863

The Most Reverend Richard Chevenix Trench
[1863-1886]
Born: 9 September 1807
Invested: 28 June 1864
Died: 27 March 1886

B. Chief Secretaries of Ireland (1886–1922)

The Right Honourable Sir Michael Hicks-Beach
(later 1st Earl St Aldwyn)
[1886–1887]
Born: 23 October 1837
Invested: 7 January 1887
Died: 30 April 1916

The Right Honourable Arthur James Balfour (later
1st Earl of Balfour) [1887–1891]
Born: 25 July 1848
Invested: 18 March 1887
Died: 19 March 1930

The Right Honourable William Lawies Jackson
(later 1st Lord Allerton)
[1891–1892]
Born: 16 February 1840
Invested: ?
Died: 4 April 1917

The Right Honourable Walter Hume Long (later
1st Viscount Long of Wraxall)
[1905]
Born: 13 July 1854
Invested: 14 April 1905
Died: 26 September 1924

The Right Honourable James Bryce (later 1st
Viscount Bryce) [1905–1907)
Born; 10 May 1838
Invested: (never invested, but sworn
14 December 1905)
Died: 22 January 1922

The Right Honourable Augustine Birrell
[1907–1916]
Born: 19 January 1850
Invested: 29 January 1907
Died: 20 November 1933

The Right Honourable Henry Edward Duke
(later 1st Lord Merrivale)
[1916–1918]
Born: 5 November 1855

The Right Honourable John Morley (later 1st
Viscount Morley of Blackburn)
[1892–1895]
Born: 24 December 1848
Invested: 10 September 1892
Died: 23 September 1923

The Right Honourable Gerald William Balfour
(later 2nd Earl of Balfour)
[1895–1900]
Born: 9 April 1853
Invested: 16 July 1895
Died: 14 January 1945

The Right Honourable George Wyndham
[1900–1905]
Born: 19 August 1863
Invested: 24 November 1900
Died: 8 June 1913

Hon. Henry Edward Duke—cont.
Invested: 11 August 1916
Died: 20 May 1939

The Right Honourable Edward Shortt
[1918–1919]
Born: 10 March 1862
Invested: 11 May 1918
Died: 10 November 1935

The Right Honourable Ian Macpherson (later 1st
Lord Strathcarron) [1919–1920]
Born: 14 May 1880
Invested: 2 June 1919
Died: 14 August 1937

The Right Honourable Sir Hamar Greenwood
(later 1st Viscount Greenwood)
[1920–1922]
Born: 7 February 1870
Invested: 19 June 1920
Died: 10 September 1948

(Office vacant since 1922)

III. Registrars

A.—Deans of the Cathedral Church of Saint Patrick, Dublin (1783–1890)

The Very Reverend William Craddock [1783-1793]
    Born: ?
    Invested: 11 March 1783
    Died: 1 September 1793

The Very Reverend James Verschoyle [1793-1810]
    Born: 1750
    Invested: 18 March 1798
    Died: 13 April 1834

The Very Reverend John Keating [1810-1817]
    Born: 18 May 1769
    Invested: 19 March 1798
    Died: 6 May 1817

The Very Reverend and Honourable Richard
    Ponsonby [1817-1828]
    Born: 1772
    Invested: 13 July 1818
    Died: 27 October 1853

The Very Reverend Henry Richard Dawson
    [1828-1840]
    Born: ?
    Invested: 24 March 1828
    Died: 24 October 1840

(Vacant 1840-1842)

The Very Reverend Robert Daly [1842-1843]
    Born: 8 June 1783
    Invested: (never invested)
    Died: 16 February 1872

The Very Reverend and Honourable Henry
    Pakenham [1843-1863]
    Born: 24 August 1787
    Invested: 1843
    Died: 25 December 1863

The Very Reverend John West
    [1864-1890]
    Born: 1806
    Invested: 31 March 1864
    Died: 5 July 1890

B. Ulster Kings of Arms (1890–1943)

C. Norroy and Ulster Kings of Arms since 1943

IV. Kings of Arms

A. Ulster Kings of Arms (1783-1943)

Sir William Hawkins [1783-1787]
  Born: 16 March 1730
  Appointed: 5 February 1783
  Invested: 11 March 1783
  Died: 27 March 1787

Gerald Fortescue [1787]
  Born: 15 November 1751
  Appointed: ?
  Invested: 9 April 1787
  Died: 27 October 1787

Rear-Admiral Sir Chichester Fortescue
  [1788-1820]
  Born: 7 June 1750
  Appointed: 31 January 1788
  Invested: 21 February 1788
  Died: 22 March 1820

Sir William Betham [1820-1853]
  Born: 22 May 1779
  Appointed: 18 April 1820
  Invested: 25 April 1820
  Died: 26 October 1853

Sir Bernard Burke [1853-1892]
  Born: 5 January 1814
  Appointed: 18 November 1853
  Invested: ?
  Died: 12 December 1892

Sir Arthur Vicars [1893-1908]
  Born: 27 July 1864
  Appointed: 23 February 1893
  Invested: 7 March 1893
  Removed: 30 January 1908
  Died: 14 April 1921

Sir Nevile Wilkinson [1908-1940]
  Born: 26 October 1869
  Appointed: 30 January 1980
  Invested: 4 February 1909
  Died: 22 December 1940

* * *

Thomas Ulick Sadleir (acting) [1940-1943]
  Born: 15 September 1882
  Died: 21 December 1957

B. Norroy and Ulster Kings of Arms (1943-   )

Sir Algar Howard [1943-1944]
  Born: 7 August 1880
  Appointed: 5 April 1943
  Died: 14 February 1970

Sir Gerald Woods Woolaston [1944-1957]
  Born: 2 June 1874
  Appointed: 2 June 1944
  Died: 4 March 1957

Aubrey John Toppin [1957-1966]
  Born: 1881
  Appointed: 20 July 1957
  Died: 7 March 1969

Richard Preston Graham-Vivian [1966-1971]
  Born: 10 August 1896
  Appointed: 10 November 1966
  Died: 30 September 1979

Walter John George Verco [1971-1980]
  Born: 18 January 1907
  Appointed: 8 September 1971

John Philip Brooke Brooke-Little [1980-   ]
  Born: 6 April 1927
  Appointed: 7 July 1980

C. *Deputy Ulster Kings of Arms*

Sir William Betham	1807–1820
Molyneaux Cecil John Betham	1839–1880
Sir Henry Farnham Burke	1889–1893
George Dames Burtchaell	1910–1911 and 1915–1921
Thomas Ulick Sadleir	1921–1943

V. Secretaries

George Frederick Nugent, Viscount Delvin (later
    Earl of Westmeath) [1783–1791]
    Born: 18 November 1760
    Appointed: 5 February 1783
    Invested: 11 March 1783
    Resigned: ?
    Died: 30 December 1814

(Vacant 1791–1793)

Sir Richard Bligh St George, Bt. [1793–1800]
    Born: 5 June 1765
    Appointed: ?
    Invested: 15 February 1793
    Resigned: ?
    Died: 29 December 1851

Sir Frederick John Falkiner, Bt. [1800–1815]
    Born: 1768
    Appointed: ?
    Invested: ?
    Died: 1815

(Vacant 1815–1828)

Major-General George John Forbes, Viscount
    Forbes [1828–1836]
    Born: 3 May 1785

Major-General George John Forbes—*cont.*
    Appointed: ?
    Invested: 28 March 1828
    Died: 13 November 1836

The Honourable Robert Boyle [1837–1853]
    Born: March 1809
    Appointed: ?
    Invested: 27 September 1837
    Resigned: 28 February 1853
    Died: 3 September 1854

Lowry Vesey Townley Balfour [1853–1878]
    Born: 1819
    Appointed: 18 April 1853
    Invested: 22 February 1855
    Died: 11 February 1878

Gustavus William Lambart [1878–1886]
    Born: 7 August 1814
    Appointed: 1 March 1878
    Invested: 8 February 1879
    Died: 1 November 1886

Sir Gustavus Francis William Lambart [1886–1926]
    Born: 25 March 1848
    Appointed: 3 December 1886
    Invested: 26 April 1887
    Died: 16 June 1926

(Office vacant since 1926)

VI. Genealogists

1. Charles Henry Coote (2nd Lord Castlecoote
    from 1 March 1802)
    [1783–1804]
    Born: 25 August 1754
    Appointed: 5 February 1783
    Invested: 11 March 1783
    Died: 22 January 1823

2. Sir Stewart Bruce [1804–1841]
    Born: ?

Sir Stewart Bruce—*cont.*
    Appointed:?
    Invested: 18 December 1804
    Died: 19 March 1841

3. Sir William Edward Leeson [1841–1885]
    Born: February 1801
    Appointed: ?
    Invested: 6 May 1841
    Died: 21 April 1885

(Office abolished in 1885 in accordance with the Royal Warrant of 1871)

(Office revived in 1889)

4. Sir Henry Farnham Burke [1889–1930]
    Born: 12 June 1859
    Appointed: 16 August 1889
    Invested: 7 February 1890
    Died: 21 August 1930

(Office vacant since 1930)

VII. Ushers of the Black Rod

1. John Freemantle [1783]
    Born: ?
    Appointed: 5 February 1783
    Invested: 11 March 1783
    Died: ?

2. Sir Willoughby Aston [1783–1784]
    Born: c. 1748
    Appointed: ?
    Invested: 13 October 1783
    Died: 22 March 1815

3. Col. Andrew Barnard [1784–1790]
    Born: ?
    Appointed: ?
    Invested: 26 February 1784
    Died: ?

4. The Honourable Henry Fane [1790–1796]
    Born: ?
    Appointed: ?
    Invested: 20 January 1790
    Died: ?

5. Nicholas Price [1796–1799]
    Born: ?
    Appointed: ?
    Invested: ?
    Died: ?

6. Thomas Lindsay [1799–1806]
    Born: ?
    Appointed: ?
    Invested: ?
    Died: ?

7. Sir Charles Hawley Vernon [1806–1835]
    Born: ?
    Appointed: ?
    Invested: 14 March 1806
    Died: 24 June 1835

8. Major the Hon. Sir Francis Charles Stanhope [1835–1838]
    Born: 29 September 1788
    Appointed: ?

Sir Francis Charles Stanhope—cont.
    Invested: 22 July 1835
    Removed: ?
    Died: 9 October 1862

9. Sir William Edward Leeson [1838–1841]
    Born: February 1801
    Appointed: 8 May 1838
    Invested: 15 April 1839
    Died: 21 April 1885

10. Lieutenant-Colonel Sir George Morris [1841–1858]
    Born: 1774
    Appointed: ?
    Invested: 6 May 1841
    Died: May 1858

11. Sir George Burdett L'Estrange [1858–1878]
    Born: 1796
    Appointed: 10 June 1858
    Invested: 24 May 1859
    Died: 5 February 1878

12. Colonel the Viscount Charlemont [1879–1913]
    Born: 20 March 1830
    Appointed: 1 February 1879
    Invested: 8 February 1879
    Died: 4 July 1913

13. Sir John Olphert [1915–1917]
    Born: 2 September 1844
    Appointed: 15 May 1915
    Invested: (never invested)
    Died: 11 March 1917

14. Sir Samuel Murray Power [1918–1933]
    Born: 29 September 1863
    Appointed: 29 October 1918
    Invested: ?
    Died: 17 March 1933

(Office vacant since 1933)

APPENDIX FOUR

Heralds and Pursuivants

I. Cork Heralds

William Bryan [1783–1796]
    Born: ?
    Appointed: 15 March 1783
    Died: ?

Solomon Delane [1796–1813]
    Born: ?
    Appointed: 11 January 1796
    Died: ?

Theobald Richard O'Flaherty [1813–1829]
    Born: ?
    Appointed: ?
    Died: 1829

Molyneaux Cecil John Betham [1829–1880]
    Born: 14 August 1813
    Appointed: 29 September 1829
    Died: 31 January 1880

(The Office of Cork Herald was abolished in 1880 in accordance with the Royal Warrant of 1871. It was revived in the revised Statutes of 1905)

Peirce Gun Mahony [1905–1910]
    Born: 30 March 1878
    Appointed: 25 September 1905
    Resigned: ?
    Died: 26 July 1914

Captain Richard Alexander Lyonal Keith
        [1910–1952]
    Born: 10 August 1883
    Appointed: 8 December 1910
    Removed: 24 July 1952
    Died: November 1955

(Vacant since 1952)

II. Dublin Heralds

Thomas Meredyth Winstanley [1783–1827]
    Born: ?
    Appointed; 15 March 1783
    Died: ?

James Rock [1827–1833]
    Born: ?
    Appointed: 31 March 1827
    Died: 18 May 1833

Captain Sheffield Philip Fiennes Betham
        [1834–1890]
    Born: 15 April 1817
    Appointed: ?
    Died: 2 July 1890

(The Office of Dublin Herald was abolished in 1890 in accordance with the Royal Warrant in 1871. It was revived in the revised Statutes of 1905)

Francis Richard Shackleton [1905–1907]
    Born: 19 September 1876
    Appointed: 25 September 1905
    Resigned: November 1907
    Died: 1941

Major Guillamore O'Grady [1908–1952]
    Born: 1879
    Appointed: 18 June 1908
    Invested: 4 February 1909
    Died: 4 September 1952

(Vacant since 1952)

III. Athlone Pursuivants

George Twisleton Ridsdale [1783–1807]
    Born: ?
    Appointed: 27 May 1783
    Died: ?

William Betham [1807–1820]
    Born: 22 May 1779
    Appointed: 7 November 1807
    Died: 26 October 1853

James Rock [1820–1827]
    Born: ?
    Appointed: 2 May 1820
    Died: 18 May 1833

Molyneaux Cecil John Betham [1827–1829]
    Born: 14 August 1813
    Appointed: 12 February 1827
    Died: 31 January 1880

William Crawford [1829-1865]
    Born: ?
    Appointed: 29 September 1829
    Died: ?

Captain Robert Smith [1865-1882]
    Born: 14 September 1792
    Appointed: 10 March 1865
    Died: 26 November 1882

Bernard Louis Burke [1883-1892]
    Born: 17 May 1861
    Appointed: 13 January 1883
    Died: 5 July 1892

John Edward Burke [1892-1899]
    Born: 19 March 1868
    Appointed: 27 July 1892
    Removed: 13 May 1899
    Died: 9 March 1909

Henry Claude Blake [1899-1907]
    Born: 5 December 1874
    Appointed: 13 May 1899
    Resigned: 7 February 1907
    Died: ? (after 1932)

Francis Bennett-Goldney [1907]
    Born: 1865
    Appointed: 14 February 1907
    Resigned: November 1907
    Died: 27 July 1918

George Dames Burtchaell
    [1908-1921]
    Born: 12 June 1853
    Appointed: 18 June 1908
    Invested: 4 February 1909
    Died: 18 August 1921

(Vacant since 1921)

IV. *Junior Pursuivants*

— Croker [1783-?]

— Minchin [1783-?]

Bryan Connor [1795-1813]

William Baker [1796-?]

Theobald Richard O'Flaherty [1803-1813]

P. Kennedy [1803-?]

John O'Flaherty [1813-1823]
    Appointed: 30 April 1813
    Removed: 1823 (having taken Holy Orders)

James Rock [1813-1820]

P. J. Mahony [1819-?]

Molyneaux Cecil John Betham [1820-1827]
    Born: 14 August 1813
    Died: 31 January 1880

Alfred Betham [1825-1841]
    Appointed: 14 June 1825
    Died: 1841

Sheffield Philip Fiennes Betham [1825-1834]
    Born: 15 April 1817
    Died: 2 July 1890

William Crawford [1827-1829]

William Heron [1829-? after 1837]
    Appointed: 29 September 1829

Joseph Cotton Walker [1830-?]

Joseph Baker ? [in 1837 ?]

William Skeys (afterwards Skey) [1839-1848]
    Appointed: 11 October 1839
    Removed: 1848

Robert Smith [1840-1865]
    Born: 14 September 1792
    Appointed: 14 June 1840
    Died: 26 November 1882

Francis Beetham [1841-?]
    Appointed: 22 June 1841

Charles Patrick MacDonnell [1850-1870]
    Died: 1870

Columbus Patrick Drake [1854-1889]
    Appointed: 28 January 1854
    Died: 1889

George Frith Barry [1865-1891]
    Appointed: 21 March 1865
    Died: 1891

V. *Cork Pursuivant*

Major Gerald Achilles Burgoyne [1924–1936]
Born: 1874
Died: March 1936

VI. *Deputy Athlone Pursuivants*

Joseph Nugent Lentaigne [1874–1882]
Born: ?
Appointed: 12 June 1874
Resigned: 1882
Died: ?

Bernard Louis Burke
[1882–1883]
Appointed: 11 February 1882

INDEX

Compiled by Ann Hudson

This index contains all the personal names and the more important places mentioned in the text and appendices

140